The Book of Uncommon Prayer

Liturgies and Prayers Exploring Inclusive
Language and Biblical Imagery of the
Feminine Divine and the Natural World

Annie Heppenstall

Augsburg Books

MINNEAPOLIS

THE BOOK OF UNCOMMON PRAYER
Liturgies and Prayers Exploring Inclusive Language and Biblical Imagery of
the Feminine Divine and the Natural World

© Copyright 2015 Annie Heppenstall.
Original edition published in English under the title THE BOOK OF
UNCOMMON PRAYER by Kevin Mayhew Ltd, Buxhall, England.

Cover image: © iStock 2020: Stained Glass/Pixelated Flower Frame stock photo by Bang
Cover design: Emily Drake

Print ISBN: 978-1-5064-6029-1

Contents

This book is dedicated to my mother, Gwen Heppenstall,
and to my sisters, Jane and Mary, and their families: Mike,
Ronan, Andrew, Michael, Mark and Nick, with love.

I am about to do a new thing;
now it springs forth, do you not perceive it?
I will make a way in the wilderness
and rivers in the desert.
The wild animals will honour me,
the jackals and the ostriches;
for I give water in the wilderness,
rivers in the desert,
to give drink to my chosen people,
the people whom I formed for myself
so that they might declare my praise.

Isaiah 43:19-21

About the author

Annie Heppenstall is a qualified teacher and has a degree in Theology and Religious Studies from Cambridge University. Trained in spiritual direction and counselling skills, she applies her experience and interests in writing, leading workshops and retreats and supporting others in different ways in their own spiritual journeys. Among other things, Annie is a professed Franciscan Tertiary, drawn to expressions of Earth Spirituality and expressions of the Feminine Divine. She lives in a richly multi-faith area of the Midlands with her husband and son.

For details of other books by Annie Heppenstall published by Kevin Mayhew, please refer to our website: www.kevinmayhew.com

Acknowledgements

As always, I want to thank my husband Ray Gaston, first, for his continuous support for my writing, for our shared interest in liturgy writing and delivery and, in particular, for coming up with the title for this book. I have had the privilege of working with a number of groups over the last ten years or so, in trying out different ideas for alternative liturgies, and this book has grown from the encouragement, participation and feedback of many people.

More recently, this has included an exploration into the enriching worlds of Earth Spirituality and of Jewish feminism, especially where it embraces 'earthy' spirituality, and I was delighted this summer to be invited to work with Rabbi Debbie Young-Somers on a shared liturgy of the moon, and offer some other Earth Spirituality workshops, for participants at the festival 'Limmud in the Woods', so thank you to Rabbi Debbie and the people of Limmud.

Thanks also to my internet community of friends of diverse faiths, cultures and spiritualities for sharing all kinds of thoughts on how prayer and ritual has meaning to them, especially those who responded to my questions, asking what people would like to have liturgies about.

Special thanks are also due to Carey Saleh and the Morton Bagot group and to Margaret and Richard Deimel for suggesting we take the 'Holy Ground' project on, some years back. Apart from the 'grain song', which was written for a Lammastide service, the liturgies in this book are not Morton Bagot liturgies, but they have certainly grown out of the fond memory of lovely candlelit evenings shared together in the tiny medieval church of Holy Trinity.

Last but not least, I want to thank Kevin Mayhew for suggesting that I write a book of 'unusual liturgies'. I have appreciated the opportunity to draw ideas together which have been important to me for so long; and thanks too to the team working together in producing this book, especially Virginia Rounding, for tidying up my liturgies: no mean feat!

Part 1
Introduction and Guidance

Introduction

The Book of Uncommon Prayer unearths some buried treasures of biblical imagery, especially feminine and natural, to explore the potential for relating to creation, God and one another in fresh and relevant ways, especially through liturgy and personal prayer. While it is important that traditions are respected and carried down through the generations, as the Church has done faithfully for centuries, there needs to be sufficient confidence and flexibility within the tradition to allow freedom of enquiry into how we can maintain relevance today. In that spirit of enquiry, this book is a contribution to the exploration of 'fresh expressions' in contemporary spirituality. There are exciting questions to ask in the process of exploring biblical imagery about God:

- What potential for creative personal spiritual development opens up?

- How can fresh expressions reinvigorate the tradition?

- What possibilities emerge for reconciliation with those who have been hurt by the over-assertion of an apparently masculine God?

- What meeting ground can be found with those who seek an earth-centred spirituality, including those of other faith traditions?

- In what ways can such material support outreach to the increasing numbers who have grown up without any particular faith root?

- How can such resources stir us up and challenge each of us to reflect on our own reservations, stumbling blocks, preferences and comfort zones?

A significant part of *The Book of Uncommon Prayer* is a 'Prayer Bank', a collection of material inspired by and rooted in biblical tradition. The prayers and ideas in this section can stand alone for insertion into existing liturgies and personal reflection, but can also be woven into new liturgical forms, according to the suggestions towards the end of the section. In particular, we can construct new forms of daily prayer, through drawing together prayers specific to holy hours, days and seasons.

The final part of the book draws on material in the Prayer Bank, through a variety of liturgies. These liturgies fall into loose groups, with focus on connectedness with the natural world, explorations of the feminine divine, women's issues and wider issues of daily life, and a more mystical approach to God, seeking the divine within ourselves.

This book builds on a firm foundation of theological debate, creativity and research over many decades, into gender and spirituality, women's place in the Church, the feminine divine, the movement towards inclusivity in language and the shift towards ecologically sensitive approaches to spirituality – in Christianity as well as in other faith paths. The groundwork has already been done, and is still going on, among more able theologians than myself, and for this reason I am not going to spend many pages defending or justifying the content of *The Book of Uncommon Prayer*. If you have the book in your hands, my hope is that you are at least aware of this movement in thinking, are interested in alternative liturgies which address these issues, and that you will find something of interest here. A section in the following pages addresses some questions that might arise.

Guidance on using
The Book of Uncommon Prayer

The following guidelines and comments are especially intended to encourage and empower those who might otherwise not be involved in the leading of worship, to facilitate small groups and offer support for those interested in exploring alternative language for God. It is hoped that the guidelines will also be of passing interest to more experienced worship leaders. If you read nothing else from this section, but aim to use the liturgies, please take note of just three points:

- I almost always write my liturgies for a group sitting in a circle with a visual focus – including a candle – in the centre.

- To enhance the liturgies in this book, choose songs and music that reflect your group's preferences. There are an increasing number of hymn writers now writing at least some of their songs in inclusive and even feminine language about God. [See Appendix for a list of recommended hymn writers and resources.]

- In the liturgies, normal type is for a single voice, **bold type** is for all to say together, and *italics* are for instructions.

Use of singing, music, silence and mood

Choice of music is very personal and also determined by resources and preferences within a group. In this book, I have often suggested *where* I think music would enhance the experience but have not usually said what kind of music. Personally, I often prefer simple songs and short repetitive chants such as those produced by Taizé, the international Christian spiritual community located in France, and some of the Iona Community's songs, which are contemplative and easy to learn.

If you want to sing in a small group, consider who is going to lead the songs, and whether people in the group are actually likely to join in. In church contexts, participants may be very familiar with songs and sing with gusto, even in harmony, but people who are not used to worship situations may not have sung much since primary school days and may need conditions to be just right before they can feel safe joining in. Singing unaccompanied can be very effective if people are confident in holding the tune, but expecting people to sing when they are not used to it can affect the mood of the whole event, causing self-consciousness, embarrassment and more, if nobody joins in, or joins in under duress.

Live music – guitars, pianos, drums, flutes and the like – can be wonderful and add special energy to a gathering, but be warned! Musicians are powerful, especially in small group venues, and need to be a balanced, subtle part of the shared experience. Drowning out voices or becoming the centre of attention detracts from worship. I once went, for example, to a small, meditative, candlelit liturgy, which was beautifully serene until a violinist who had neither rehearsed nor tuned their violin started to play. Much stifled laughter ensued, and I am sure I am not the only one for whom this is the abiding memory of the event! I know, to my shame, that I have caused the same distracting hilarity myself by poor piano playing, and have also, in my younger days, and playing instruments I have more competence in, rather egotistically seen invitations to play during worship as opportunities for 'look at me!'. In short, musical accompaniment in liturgy needs to be pleasantly and unobtrusively supportive of the main focus. A group of five to fifteen people do not need accompanying by an entire band. It is a completely different matter, of course, if inviting participants to bring and share musical contributions is a feature of the event, in which case any contribution is to be warmly celebrated.

I usually like to begin and end liturgies and other services with recordings of atmospheric music which can be phased in and out. Especially at the start, this can help people move into a different headspace ready for engagement at a deeper level. Personally, I am wary of hymns which might alienate some people and which lack inclusive language – I check words carefully before using anything, but of course, different subjects upset different people. Naturally, somebody else leading a liturgy I have written may choose entirely different songs and music and produce a very different – yet equally valid – feel to the whole experience.

To help you and your group make decisions about music, here are some questions to ask yourself:

- What mood do we want to evoke? Peaceful, friendly, warm, calm . . .

- How many people are likely to come, and how likely are they to enjoy singing?

- What kind of music are the people in this group familiar or comfortable with? Contemporary, classical, folk, multicultural . . .

- How can words and sounds in music reflect the content of the liturgy – especially through inclusive and feminine language?

- How does this impact on people with hearing difficulties?

- What is possible, given resources already available? What equipment do we need?

- What about movement and other forms of self-expression?

- Where can I find songs which use inclusive language?

The use of silence is equally important: a pause of a few seconds can help create an atmosphere of calm, and longer periods of silence can allow a deepening sense of spiritual encounter. The length of silences depends a little on what people are used to and it is helpful to tell people what to expect: 'We are going to sit in silence for five minutes now, until the bell rings.' Otherwise, there will be people sitting with their eyes shut, whose only thought is, 'When is this going to end?' I once led a meditative evening in which it seemed everyone was familiar with just dropping into periods of extended silence after readings, which is what we did, until about half way through, when somebody interrupted a silence by saying, 'Well, since nobody seems very willing to say anything, I think I need to break the ice . . .' They then gave their opinion on the Bible reading and everybody listened very politely. I could have anticipated this and prevented awkwardness by explaining the process in advance and checking everyone was happy with the idea.

Guided visualisation or imaginative contemplation

A Christian term for guided visualisation, or visual and imaginative contemplation, is 'Ignatian Contemplation'. This is a technique going back many centuries, used by Ignatius of Loyola among other contemplatives, to imagine oneself into a scenario in order to engage at a deeper level. Ignatius practised this while recovering from an injury sustained in war. Traditionally, scenarios are drawn from the Gospels and other biblical passages, and practitioners use their imagination to experience environments, people and even conversations with biblical figures. The Christian practice of imagining Jesus to be present and talking to him as a friend could be seen in this way. 'Guided visualisation' tends to be led by someone describing an inner journey or scenario for participants to follow, and uses the same principle of purposeful imagination, but may explore a situation that is based on the natural world or some other theme. It is increasingly used as a gentle way of helping people to get in touch with their own feelings, to understand themselves better and to build confidence.

Guided visualisation or imaginative contemplation in a spiritual context should never be presented in a way that manipulates or controls people's thoughts; participants should simply be guided into safe opportunities to form their own impressions.

While for many, visual contemplation is a valuable part of spiritual life, others, it has to be said, are wary of exploring their own unconscious – the realm of dreams, fantasy and visions. This needs to be fully respected, especially when there may be mental health issues. For some Christians, the unconscious mind is a grey area where 'unclean spirits' or unwanted influences might be lurking, or might find their way in. To accommodate this, suggest in your introduction that participants can make a short prayer of protection before they begin, or listen with their eyes open so they feel more in control of their thoughts. Some may find it reassuring to invite the presence of Jesus to be with them throughout the experience, but a more long-term solution is for people to explore concerns with a trusted spiritual director or companion or, in the case of a mental health concern, with a trained counsellor. It is also important for participants to trust their own instincts about what works for them.

To lead a guided visualisation:

- Give a short explanation of what the visualisation is going to involve, so that people do not feel they are being led into the unknown. Emphasise that we can always opt out by opening our eyes and thinking about something else and can begin with a silent prayer.

- Reassure those who do not feel they have a strong visual imagination, that they can connect with the words and notice their feelings and sensations, or memories that come up. It can help to think about how they might draw a picture or make a film of the scene you are describing.

- Use the relaxation exercise below, allowing at least five minutes for preliminary relaxation if at all possible.

- Read the visualisation clearly and gradually, with pauses, and an awareness of how long it will take people to follow what you say. Try to imagine how much you would be able to take in at a time, and how much time you would need.

- Allow silent pauses for people to concentrate, and resist the temptation to spoil the pauses by continuing to give more and more details. Trust that something is going on behind the closed eye lids!

- Do not tell people what to think – just describe the scene or the journey, rather like a travel guide, and allow freedom for personal interpretation.

- When you reach the end, bring people back to everyday reality gradually, by suggesting stretching, awareness of breathing and posture, opening eyes and sitting quietly for a few minutes before the next activity.

- Participants may want to talk about what they have experienced or process it in other ways such as through artwork, and there needs to be allowance for this – for example, by offering time afterwards over cups of tea to talk to each other, or by getting into supportive listening pairs. If you want to incorporate this sharing into the liturgy, allow plenty of time and be ready to restore a contemplative mood with some quiet time, afterwards.

- Avoid the temptation to psychoanalyse people unless you are qualified and they have asked for your opinion.

Relaxation exercise

Before meditation or guided visualisation, it helps to be relaxed, both physically and mentally. We often have more tensions in our bodies than we realise, so spending a few minutes guiding participants in body-awareness can help. Below is a version of the process. Use it for yourself or read it out with pauses, giving people time to respond to the instructions, and be sensitive to individual physical needs – if supporting a wheelchair user, for example, or someone who is bed-bound, adjust the words, and beware of giving over-prescriptive instructions on breathing, for the sake of those who are prone to asthma. If people want to explore body-awareness or breathing as a form of meditation in its own right, there are plenty of resources available on the internet, in books and meditation groups.

Relaxing:

Read with pauses for each activity

Sit upright in your chair and, if you wish, close your eyes.

Notice your back, and your overall posture. Notice how your head feels, sitting on your neck.

Notice your shoulders – roll them around and give them a little shrug, shake your arms and hands, flex your wrists, wiggle your fingers and let your upper body settle again, more loosely.

If there are still tensions and aches, gently move into a more comfortable posture.

Now let your attention go to the feeling of your lower body, pressing against the chair.

Again, notice where there are tensions, and move gently to ease your legs and ankles, wriggle your toes.

Place your feet down firmly, notice their contact with the floor.

Now notice your breathing.

Try to let your breath go down into your lungs, so that it expands your ribcage. Let your breathing be deep and unrushed.

As you breathe in, think 'wellbeing', and as you breathe out, think 'peace'.

Talking sticks and stones

Using an object such as a stick, shell or pebble to create an atmosphere of respectful listening is now a well-known practice in group work, so participants may already be familiar with the idea. In short, place the chosen object in the centre of the circle and invite people to pick it up if they have something they want to say. They can talk while holding the object, without being interrupted, and then replace it. It is worth reaching some agreements, such as time-limits, or speaking only once, especially in a large group. Be aware of mobility issues created by placing a talking object in the centre: if this means someone cannot access it freely, create a different system such as passing the object round the circle.

Leadership styles

Different leaders have different styles. For some, it is fine to explain things as they go along and keep up an everyday kind of banter, happy for people to interrupt with comments, laughter and questions. This can be very warm, friendly and relaxed but I have to say, this is not my style! I like to teach songs and explain what is going to happen beforehand so there is little need for stage directions, and then I like to build up a focus, asking for everyone to support the intention of the gathering and one another's spiritual journeying, and to save comments for afterwards. I begin with a few moments of silence, then aim for a special atmosphere where people can relax and go as deep as they like, in peace. I draw on my profession as a teacher to achieve this and it may be more controlled than some would wish – although most appreciate the opportunity for genuine peace. Feedback from participants can be helpful in striking a happy medium.

Creating 'Sacred Space'

Choosing a venue for a gathering can be a challenge in itself. How many are coming? Is it accessible to everyone? Are there suitable toilet and tea-making facilities? Many of the liturgies in this book are for outdoor use, especially if you can arrange seating and easy access for everybody. It may be appropriate to meet in a church or community building, but equally, if the meeting involves people who feel ambivalent about church or come from different spiritual backgrounds, it may be better to meet on neutral ground. Somebody's home might work. Having a cup of tea and a chat afterwards can contribute to the development of group dynamics – if outdoors, consider going to a local café or having a picnic afterwards. Bear in mind that some may not want to stay for social time afterwards; their departure need not be a criticism of the event. I, for one, often like to go and reflect quietly on what has touched me, and find that talking about spiritual experiences sometimes takes the wonder out of them for me; if you are concerned about someone, consider following up with a friendly but non-intrusive call later.

If indoors, consider layout and enhance the space in advance with colours, fabrics, natural artefacts, candles and so on. You can invite people to bring things on the theme, to add to the display, and give time for them to talk about why they have brought them. When possible, sit in a circle with a table or cloth in the centre and a focus object such as a candle, rather than in rows.

Preparing the space can be a preliminary group activity, especially if the point is to reclaim a neglected or unhappy place. If meeting outdoors, preparation might simply be to spend some time loving aspects of nature or doing something to care for the life of the place. Always leave a natural environment free of human traces: do not leave tea lights or incense burning and do not light candles on tree trunks, stones and the like, even in foil holders; the heat and wax can cause damage and kill micro-organisms. It may be safe to put a candle in a jam jar or lantern on a tile or brick or other heatproof surface, with care. Do not light fires unless you know for a fact that this is safe and acceptable.

If tempted to use candles outdoors because they look nice, take some time to think about what you want to communicate, and whether burning paraffin-based wax, a by-product of the petro-chemical industry, is the best way to demonstrate a genuine regard for the environment.

Special needs and emotional sensitivity

Individual needs vary greatly. Trying to make sure everyone has an equal opportunity to access an event is an important aim but can be challenging, especially when working in a voluntary capacity with limited resources. With all the good will in the world, we do not always get it right for everybody, especially when we do not know the participants, and this can cause difficult feelings for ourselves and any we inadvertently patronise, exclude or humiliate. Sensitive inquiry before an event may help, so can flexibility and common sense. At times, situations are only saved by the generosity of spirit, wisdom and creativity of participants. We all, myself included, sometimes misjudge situations, make wrong assumptions and cause embarrassment. This is not a reason to give up, but it is a reason to cultivate humble and genuine willingness to listen – openness to feedback from participants helps us to improve our practice.

Here are some things I have got wrong over the years – learning the hard way. In my defence, some of these incidents date back almost two decades but have stuck in my mind. Ask yourself what you would do differently:

- I set up a beautiful display for everyone to sit around and reflect on, at the top of some steps which meant that one person stayed at the bottom of the steps and listened from a distance.

- To save ink and paper, I printed service sheets out using a small font, for use at night in a candlelit room. A lot of us struggled to read the text.

- I used a venue with no toilet, which caused me discomfort, let alone everybody else.

- I asked people to go round a circle reading from a rather lengthy unprepared text, without giving a choice or 'pass' option. This caused embarrassment to a person who has dyslexia.

- I spoke softly because I wanted to create a peaceful atmosphere, but there was no hearing loop and one participant could not hear me at all.

- I said children were welcome but then created an atmosphere for deep and mature spiritual engagement in which I know I made a child and parent feel distinctly unwelcome.

- I used a building with no heating, in the winter, and expected people to sit without moving, for over 20 minutes.

- I created an interactive display on the floor, inviting people to kneel down to engage with it. This excluded several people.

- I presented a meditation on the 'fruits of the vine and work of human hands' but only provided alcoholic wine for sampling. A recovering alcoholic was present.

- I led a workshop which involved threading small beads on thin cord, for an elderly group, in which several were challenged by arthritis and eyesight issues. We all found this quite frustrating.

- In my inexperience, I spoke to someone who is non-sighted as though they were a child, rather than a competent adult with lifelong skills in engaging independently with the world, and spent the session wincing at their fair but scathing response.

The list goes on.

There is always scope for self-reflection, and as we prepare shared experiences, it is worth asking ourselves whether our material may actually be very difficult for somebody to engage in. Sometimes we cannot know the answer, but can take steps in the general direction of accessibility. Food is one area where we can apply basic principles, for example: avoid nuts, avoid anything that is not vegetarian (beware gelatine in sweets), make sure there are non-alcoholic options for drink, and consider gluten-free options for bread products.

Sometimes we face emotional rather than physical needs. The subjects we deal with, in exploring spirituality, are often emotive – birth, death, health, sexuality, identity, fears, hopes, loves, losses – tears or anger can come up without anybody expecting it. Gentleness, patience, kindness, a listening ear . . . in the end we respond from our innate humanity. If somebody becomes upset in the course of an event, be calmly supportive. It will often be another member of the group who steps in to offer some immediate support, allowing you to continue with the liturgy, in which case offer time to listen afterwards, or suggest someone who would be a good listener. Before you offer an event, ask yourself, 'Could anyone feel excluded by this?' Then spend some moments with the equal opportunities non-discrimination standard that most contemporary organisations – most of our work places – are committed to, regarding sexuality, gender, disability, age, economic status, religion, cultural group and so on, and ask yourself how your intention matches up.

Inclusivity, fresh expressions, alternative worship and 'mainstream' sensibilities

While some are crying out for material in this genre, others are not keen to engage with it at all and this is to be respected. Gentle challenge out of our comfort zones is often healthy, but it can be unwise to inflict potentially disturbing experiences on the unwary, the unwilling and those who treasure the tradition as it is and do not want or need it tampering with. I suggest introducing full liturgies to groups and individuals who are interested in exploring 'fresh expressions' or 'alternative' ways into spiritual thought, prayer and practice, rather than assuming that a regular Sunday church congregation will take it all on board. Otherwise, use extracts with discernment, patience and sensitivity, gauging response.

The Book of Uncommon Prayer aims to be as inclusive as possible, especially of people who have previously experienced exclusion from faith communities, deliberate or otherwise. If some readers and participants (rather ironically) feel excluded or offended by use of feminine language and themes, I would gently point out that this is something for prayerful reflection, as it mirrors the experience of women in church since the earliest days and indicates, perhaps, why so many today, given interesting new options, leave for the sake of spiritualities which fully embrace the feminine divine.[1] Some of the questions and answers below, and also the introduction to the Liturgies of the Feminine Divine, may be helpful in discussing this issue.

Some questions and answers

Below, I aim to anticipate some concerns which may come up, for people thinking of engaging with the prayers and liturgies in this book. Please feel free to refer only to relevant questions, or to come back to this as appropriate.

Is this just another attempt to evangelise me, when I'd rather go my own way?

No, this is not an attempt to persuade anyone to change beliefs, come to church or move away from their own spiritual path, and while the content may prompt you to reflect on how you relate to the divine it is non-coercive. It is a resource for exploration and spiritual accompaniment, which may prompt questions, open up new horizons, reawaken interest and invite sharing with others on a similar journey. The book draws on biblical texts and imagery, in a spirit of openness and respect: nobody has a monopoly on interpretation. Liturgical language is, traditionally, an interweaving of scripture, and liturgy is rather empty without it, but I hope my choice and interpretation of scripture offers fresh perspectives and a sense of freedom to explore deeply in

---

[1] This is explored in my earlier book, *Rejoice with Me* (Kevin Mayhew, 2103).

all directions. Personally, I feel that contemporary feminist/ womanist and/or earth spiritualities offer much that the Church needs to listen to and take on board if it wishes to be relevant today, so if anyone is being called to change, perhaps it is the Church itself!

Do I need to 'believe in' the Bible to use this book or to participate in these liturgies?

No! Each person that reads the Bible forms their own view. 'Believing in' can also mean different things to different people. As others have pointed out,[2] the English word 'belief' is of Anglo-Saxon etymology, and derives from the old word for love – be-loved. What we love deeply is what we 'believe' deep down in our hearts. The religious understanding of the word, as a mental acceptance of something as true, came much later.

There is no pressure in this book to take the Bible literally, accepting it word for word, and this is not my way of interpreting it. The Bible is a very complex collection of writings. However, if you feel most comfortable with a literal understanding, I hope the content of this book will still enrich your faith. There is also no pressure to take 'a Christian viewpoint', since there are many differing Christian viewpoints. In this book, I mainly avoid faith-based assertions about Jesus, to allow room for personal exploration, but he is often quoted and referred to, and if you have strong beliefs about him, I hope, again, that the content will enrich your faith and not diminish it. There is no pressure to follow any particular belief about 'God', although *The Book of Uncommon Prayer* does work with the prevalent biblical view that there is a benevolent Supreme Being, while proposing that

---

[2] Thanks to Emma Restall Orr for first pointing this out to me in her talks and writing: for example, *Living with Honour: A Pagan Ethics* (O Books, 2008) pp. 176-7. See also the online etymology dictionary, http://www.etymonline.com/index.php?allowed_in_frame=0&search= belief&searchmode=none

exclusively male language about this Supreme Being is inadequate. None of us know enough about God to be a real authority. Language about God is always flawed; if you prefer to think in terms of an underlying Spirit, avoiding anthropomorphisms completely, or a dispersal of spiritual presence or energy in all things, there is still biblical precedent, and again, I hope the content of the book enriches your faith. It is said, after all, that God fills heaven and earth (Jeremiah 23:23-24).

There are different approaches to living a life of 'faith'. Some want to start with the Bible (or another sacred text) as a source of authority, and see how life as they perceive it squares up with the text – as they read it. We each read texts in different ways, however, and find different elements which particularly resonate with us, depending on what is already in our hearts. Often, because sacred texts are ancient and complex, sometimes in unfamiliar languages, we rely on experts or supposed experts to guide our thinking. This guidance can be very helpful, but it can also become controlling; unless we too are experts, we risk losing our autonomy, yet for some, to follow in a simple way is all they want. This is a choice; it can be a way of peace, with a good shepherd. Beginning to ask questions stirs things up; the more we read and study, the more we are likely to realise not how right we are, but how much we do not understand, and in a sense this is the 'truth', beautifully expressed by the ancient Mesopotamian character Job, who began by challenging God, and after a humbling spiritual encounter of divine expansiveness, declared, '…I have uttered what I did not understand, things too wonderful for me, which I did not know' (Job 42:3b). There is a liturgy towards the very end of the book, in honour of Job's realisation.

Scriptural experts come in many shapes and sizes, from the truly wise and humble, to the dogmatic, defensive, arrogant and rigid, who wage war, metaphorical or otherwise, on any who dare to disagree. What a person gains from their sacred text is reflected in their whole demeanour. We can choose to get the best we are able to, out of a text. Our best, as human beings, may never be perfect, but if it is part of our wider struggle to grasp what humanity means, what life, death and the whole of existence are about, it will have an integrity but also a flexibility to it, allowing us still further room for maturation. So, we need to choose our guides with discernment. The ones who proclaim themselves as having unique understanding tend to be the ones to avoid; they are on an ego trip, however cleverly disguised. But then, the blundering and bewildered, the falsely self-abasing, are also to be avoided. It is difficult to decide who to trust, unless we have a clear sense of our own values, and this self-understanding shifts in time, as life shapes us. Someone who acted as a helpful teacher in our younger days will not necessarily be the person we need later on.

Not everybody starts with a sacred text. Others start by looking at life, their experience of the world, and go to the Bible or other inspirational texts to see if anything helps them navigate or interpret experience in a meaningful way. They may be more ready to read a variety of scriptures and sources of wisdom, searching for something that resonates with their experience, gradually building up a bank of definitive texts which speak to their own life experience. Choice may be an emotional response, or a rational one – sometimes words simply jump out of the page and arrest our attention, sinking deep and changing, comforting or challenging us in an unexpected way. A poem or the words of a song, anything in our environment, may suddenly speak to us in this way. This approach to scripture or holy word tends to be led not by the guidance of an expert beyond ourselves, but by our own intrinsic sense of what feels right in a given moment. It can be individualistic, lacking the rigour of a traditional spiritual faith path, but it can also be liberating, creative, boundary-pushing, and as spiritually deep as our own personality allows.

There are many today who identify as spiritual seekers, from a Christian or other background, whose journey is rather along these lines.

Increasingly, today, there are many people with an interest in 'spirituality' who have no background or particular interest in the sacred texts of recognised world religions. Just getting on with living, without reference to a sacred text, influenced by other people and formative experiences, by the natural world, the reality of immediate circumstances, and personal intuitions and gut feelings, is enough. A genuine spiritual seeker may develop a powerful personal ethic, a framework for decision-making and outlook, over which they have complete ownership. Relationship with scripture varies; it may be unfamiliar territory, something best left alone, or it may have been rejected because of 'toxic' experiences. While there are words in scripture which can support great peace of mind, there are also words which can hurt, or be used to hurt. Exposure to some expressions of faith can, after all, have a significantly damaging effect. Who wants to have their personal life controlled? Who wants values imposed on them by an authoritarian figure? Who wants to be coerced or frightened into adopting an outlook that they do not warm to or fully understand, by someone claiming superior knowledge? Who wants to surrender their autonomy? That people say 'no, thank you' to the heavy-handedness of some religious practitioners is causing the Church to search very deeply, even now, for different ways of being in the world. For many who wish to live outside of church influence, there is still a hunger for direction, for spiritual enrichment, for connection with the divine – but using different language: language that is relevant, language that is free of outmoded paternalism.

This book does draw on the Bible, as a rich resource. The Bible, on the whole, is a collection of works with different viewpoints – as in society. There is a prevalent view in biblical texts, that the world, the universe, exists because a transcendent deity wishes it to exist, who is partially self-revealed in the world, to those graced by discernment or a revelation. Most Christians would say that this divine self-revelation is fullest in the person of Jesus, in whom it is said that all the fullness of God was pleased to dwell (Colossians 1:19). Most of the liturgies in this book follow this predominant biblical perspective that there is a supreme being who can be experienced on earth and to whom creation is accountable but who also transcends earthly existence.

Not everybody with a spiritual outlook sees things this way. Some might say it is impossible to speak of or speculate on ideas of deity or a metaphysical 'beyond' of which we have no experience, so our lives, our outlooks, our spirituality, can only be about our experience of life on earth, informed by what we know of the past and human observations. This could be described as a form of agnosticism – not knowing – or as a more experiential, 'earth-centred' view. It is worth remembering Paul's advice in 1 Thessalonians 5:20-22 (part of a longer passage) that we need to make our own minds up about matters of faith: 'Do not despise the words of prophets, but test everything; hold fast to what is good; abstain from every form of evil.' That is, we can show respect and act with integrity, while retaining our critical faculties, and we can often respect others who reach different conclusions from our own.

On the subject of spiritual enquirers who are not necessarily committed to the same spiritual path as ourselves, we might reflect on Peter's words in the Acts of the Apostles, when he, a Jew, wrestles with the issue of Gentile (that is, non-Jewish) acceptability to God: 'Then Peter began to speak to them: "I truly understand that God shows no partiality, but in every nation anyone who fears him and does what is right is acceptable to him."' (Acts 10:34-35: I have left the masculine language about God alone since these are Peter's words.)

My hope is that this resource will be helpful to anyone exploring their own spiritual path, as they discern what makes sense for themselves, drawing from the ancient well of words in the Bible, but also from nature, which speaks to us with such immediacy.

What are ritual and liturgy and are they for me?

Ritual is a bit like a vehicle that can carry us from one place to another, or a bit like the journey itself. There does not need to be any great mystique about it. A liturgy is a corporate ritual, one provided for people to share together with a common purpose.

Ritual is often a comforting process which, if used frequently, becomes a routine that we can slip into without having to expend too much conscious energy – the decisions have already been made, we know what to do and say, the things we need are in place and there is a satisfying flow about the whole thing which frees us from the pressure to be making decisions and judgements all the time, so that we can focus on other things. It gives us a protected space and time, in which we can relax a little and open up to inspiration.

On workdays in our house, as an example, my husband and I have a morning ritual of making a cup of tea with a kettle in our room, rather than going down two flights of stairs to the kitchen. It simply means we can relax with a cup of tea in bed. This is preceded by a preparatory ritual the evening before, of taking a tea tray furnished with mugs, water and so on, up to the bedroom. Both rituals are worth it because, together, they help with the bigger task of starting the new day well.

Our tea-tray ritual is mundane, inspired by pleasant experiences of bed-and-breakfast establishments, but worthwhile as it increases quality time. It's not a particularly 'deep' ritual.

Deep rituals have a symbolic and often spiritual value, sometimes said to be the enactment of prayer. To deepen the ritual, words and actions become more purposeful. Sometimes, rituals help people to reach deep within or beyond themselves, to the transcendent. In my tea-making example, we could replace the words 'Here you are, dear' and 'Thank you', with something helping us to access the symbolic value of our act, which does after all exist below the surface.

Tea-giver: Receive this humble token of my love, and may God bless you today and always.

Response: Our lives are knitted together and there is no other who could bring me tea in bed; may God bless you today and always.

Both: Long may we be able to begin and end our days together and may we be able to afford tea and pay for electricity, now and always. Amen.

The tea is drunk. On the next occasion, the roles are reversed.

In an intentionally spiritual ritual, we follow procedures and use words which have been carefully chosen for their meaning, to express an intention or hope, to access a feeling of 'something other', to reach deeper and higher into and beyond ourselves than the everyday world often allows. Although some will always prefer free prayer and feel uneasy with the repetition of printed words, familiar ritual can be helpful, especially when we are going through stressful and uncertain times when we feel we have little control over our lives. Ritual can help us reconnect with what matters most to us.

The word 'liturgy' is mainly associated with religious ritual today, but comes from an Ancient (pagan) Greek civic institution.

In this world, religious devotion seeped into much more of life than it tends to today, so a civic event would not be entirely secular. Wealthy and influential members of a community would be expected to provide events for ordinary people to take part in – for example, the honouring of a deity or commemoration of a significant day. This was a public ritual paid for and administered on behalf of the people – *laos*, hence 'laity'. Events became quite competitive and could be expensive for the benefactor. The role of a religious leader or team of leaders today is still to provide opportunities for people to gather and take part in meaningful rituals – liturgies. A liturgy, then, tends to be an organised group event with a particular focus.

A pivotal ritual – a liturgy – of Christianity is the celebration of the Eucharist. It draws much of its symbolism from the enactment of a shared meal, and owes a debt to older symbolic meals of Judaism (which have continued to evolve separately from Christian ritual). A number of emerging spiritualities today also explore ritualised meal-sharing in different ways, some inspired by the Eucharist. As with my morning tea tray, preparation is required before a Eucharist can be celebrated, and the preparation is a spiritual activity in itself – there is an intention about everything. It is worth investing time to prepare carefully because participants will experience something quite profound, something beyond eating a morsel of bread and drinking a sip of wine. The experience is enhanced if all runs smoothly and participants can focus on the meaning rather than it being a surface-level encounter full of distractions.

The Eucharist brings up the issue of leadership. In many denominations the Eucharist is presided over only by individuals who have been trained and ordained in some sense for this role and have recognised authority within a community. In others, the equality of believers is emphasised so that anyone, or a wider group, is free to bless, break and distribute bread and wine. There is a place for both. In making use of liturgies in this book, please make adjustments according to the preference of your group.

Other liturgies for which a good deal of preparation is required are weddings, christenings and funerals. While the Church has a traditional hold on such rites of passage, and clergy are trained in pastoral care, in today's diverse culture there is more freedom to choose a ministry and rite that suits personal preference. Increasingly, those for whom the ritual is intended have a part in planning the content of the words and actions themselves, to make it personally meaningful. The call for creative liturgies and rituals is increasing. In using the prayers and liturgies in this book, there may be circumstances where changes to the text will help to make them more directly appropriate – please follow your heart.

Liturgy can be approached in different ways. One approach is to use the same liturgy each time people gather, with the same structure, prayers, songs and rituals, so that regular participants know the words well, even off by heart, and notice if anything is missed out or changed. The liturgy in such a case will have little variation – mainly the variation of scripture readings using a framework, the lectionary, and a set prayer for the day, week or season. When we learn words by heart, they penetrate deeply and become part of us in some way, and such a liturgy may have a meditative, calming, timeless quality about it for those who attend regularly, yet be considered extremely boring by others. It may seem that the liturgy is bigger than the individuals who come; it rolls on unchanging and people step into it, are held by it. If one does not feel 'held' by the liturgy, one might instead feel alienated and undervalued as an individual.

At the other end of the spectrum, gatherings take place in which leaders or leadership teams are creating a new experience for every occasion. There may be some things which follow a familiar pattern, such as the general order: a welcome, a song, a prayer, a reading, another song, an address, a space for personal testimony . . . yet this too may shift so that the elements can happen in any order or be left out. Some prayers may be used which most people are familiar with – the obvious one being the prayer attributed to Jesus – and songs drawn from a bank reflecting the preferences of the group. Such an experience may feel inspired, energetic, fresh in its newness, highly appropriate to the moment, yet to some it may be disorientating. It can make people feel disempowered if they do not know what is coming next – even the next verse of a song – because they cannot decide minute by minute whether they assent to the content or not. For a liturgical leader needing to create something new every week, it can also be highly demanding, to be constantly under pressure to come up with meaningful material.

Again, liturgies can vary in the degree of participation and the role of leaders. One extreme is for the majority of people to sit like the audience of a performance, watching and listening to one or more designated people saying and doing things, and occasionally being invited to join in by reading words together from a printed source, a book, sheet or screen, all together. The people's main activities are singing and varying their posture between sitting, kneeling and standing. If there is a Eucharist, they may get up and walk to the altar, for the high point of engagement, eating bread and drinking wine. Such a liturgy requires a leader, competently trained and ordained in some way for the role, acting on behalf of the gathered people, to lead them in a shared experience. This process of being led and fed is what many want. For others, it can feel controlling, or constraining, impersonal or too passive. In contrast, a gathering may have a rotating team drawn from among the people, involving everyone through shared activities, discussion, movement such as dance, and prayer, with a strong emphasis on the importance of individuals bringing their own contributions. This can make participants feel valued, unless of course they would prefer something more peaceful and contemplative . . .

Within the extremes described above, there are many permutations. People come to liturgical experiences for different reasons. It is very difficult to satisfy everybody within a congregation. One will leave feeling 'recharged', another will feel 'wound up' by something in the address, another will have been struck by a word or phrase, another will be bored, another puzzled, another irritated, possibly upset, even angry, another uplifted, challenged or inspired. One wants a peaceful, reflective experience that helps them commune with God in their heart, another wants energetic expression that helps them feel love for God through their love of other people. If that were the only liturgy they were ever to attend, their experience may have a lasting effect: the power of the 'one off' is not to be underestimated.

It can be tempting, when faced with people who do not often come to church, to provide an experience that will hook them and make them want more. This is precarious ground; those who do not normally come to church are often very wary of being 'hooked', and with good reason. Someone who attends regularly, however, may be more likely to accept that they will have different impressions on different occasions, depending on their own circumstances as much as on the content of the liturgy. They may also be more prepared to put up with aspects they were less comfortable with, because they are personally involved with the community and the leadership, so the relationship is as important as the liturgy. Creating liturgy, then, is challenging, and most satisfying when a group have similar interests and preferences.

There are many who want unusual new liturgies and rituals. *The Book of Uncommon Prayer* is aimed at those who like some sense of structure and leadership, but who also expect to engage fully. It provides some elements which could be used regularly, or learned by heart, and also material which is specific to a theme.

It does not attempt to replace extant church liturgies; these serve a satisfying purpose for many. The resources in this book offer alternative language, variety of ritual and active participation, and an expansion of the areas of life which could be addressed through liturgical process.

Is this Christ-centred?

There is an understandable concern among many Christians who are wondering whether to come to an 'alternative' liturgy, about whether it is 'Christ-centred' – centred on Christ and a Christian outlook. My hope is that people from a broad spectrum of Christianity, and also people who feel themselves to be 'outside' or marginal, will be happy to engage with the material in this book, although being 'Christ-centred' means different things to different people.

Christ is a Greek title of Jesus, meaning Messiah, or Anointed One of God. Messiah is a Jewish concept, referring to an awaited leader who will come to the people and liberate them in a spiritual or temporal sense, creating a divinely sanctioned rule of justice and peace. The first followers of Jesus were Jews who became convinced that Jesus was the Messiah. Most Jews did not and do not share this opinion (one reason being the distinct absence of a realm of global justice and peace), and Christianity moved away from Judaism to became a new religion in a Gentile or non-Jewish world – that is, a pagan world – commonly using the Greek word 'Christ' rather than the Hebrew word 'Messiah'. The exploration of 'Christ' among early believers drew on Jewish scripture and also on Classical Greek philosophy, especially in the intermingling of the concepts of Wisdom and Word: Sophia and logos. Wisdom is/was highly valued in both Jewish and

Ancient Romano-Greek thinking, often personified as a beautiful woman, and this well-known concept of Divine Wisdom was used to convey something of the sense of the new term 'Christ' to pagans and Jews alike (see the first three chapters of Paul's First Letter to the Corinthians).

I have tried to respect the diversity of contemporary views about the meaning of Christ-centredness, but all the same there will be some liturgies in the book which could seem not to tick the box because they do not explicitly mention Christ but, rather, imply something of the concept in a more subtle way. My feeling is that stepping back from explicit assertion allows space for participants to form their own impressions.

So, if we find ourselves talking about one who gives of themself, sacrificially, for the benefit of others, I would suggest we are talking about a Christic quality, even if some prefer not to label it as such. Likewise, if we talk of the intelligent wisdom of God, delighting in creation at the very beginning, this could, to a Christian, be understood as Christ (Colossians 1:15-20). If we reflect on birth, on a child born of a mother, nursed by a mother, loved by a mother, this reflects something of Christ incarnate – Jesus – and his mother Mary; likewise if we reflect on the wonder of dying but then returning to life, 'resurrecting', regenerating somehow, then this relates to the nature of the risen Christ. In the Gospels, Jesus frequently uses imagery to explain himself in terms of the dying and rising grain cycle, as a bridegroom, a mother hen . . . John's Gospel especially gives us direct metaphors: 'I am bread', 'I am the true vine', 'I am the gateway', 'I am the light'. Christian tradition also makes use of the rising sun as a metaphor of the resurrection – traditional churches often have their altars at the east end. The idea of Jesus as our mother also exists in Christian tradition. Reference to a mother hen sheltering her chicks, then, might not mention Jesus or Christ explicitly, but might nevertheless explore and unpack what Jesus or his early followers may have been thinking of.

What about praying in the name of Jesus?

It has to be said that, even within Christianity, I believe there are as many views on Jesus as there are Christians, and nobody has a monopoly on how to understand him, his life and his words as they have been reported. This is a book for Christians looking for alternative expressions of spirituality, but also for the growing numbers of people who are outside the Christian tradition and exploring their identity and spiritual journey, asking, often tentatively, whether there are any ways at all in which they can relate to biblical expressions of divinity, according to their own perspectives. There are people, and this can come as a surprise to some Christians, who have experienced the idea of 'Jesus is Lord' as undermining to self-worth and self-identity, and who are very wary of such language even though they may have some respect for the person described in the Gospels. One historical example of this is where Christianity has been imposed on people of other cultures through colonialism. There is a growing sense of discomfort with this imposition today, as people increasingly explore the spiritualities of their heritage, reclaiming lost or suppressed identity and the reconnection with ancestors.[3]

Most of the Bible does not mention Jesus because it is made up of Jewish scriptures. One of the most widely used books in the Bible is the Book of Psalms, an ancient collection of prayers or hymns used in Jewish worship and then also in Christian worship. Christians using the psalms and other texts such as prophetic writings, where Christ is not explicitly referred to, often read Jesus into them, concluding that 'Lord' always refers to Jesus (believing that Jesus is God), and that the words of the prophets often point to Jesus. Others see this as an imposition onto a pre-Christian root which has an integrity of its own,

---

[3] An interesting book on this subject is *A Native American Theology* by Clara Sue Kidwell, Homer Noley and George E. 'Tink' Tinker (Orbis Books, 2001).

preferring to address the God of Jesus, or to pray to God with or through Jesus, believing that Jesus provides a way for non-Jews to enter into relationship with biblical divinity. In this book, I have followed this latter approach. Jesus, during his ministry as a rabbi or teacher, taught people to pray to the God of his and their own scriptures.

I recognise that, for some, faithful prayer needs to be in the name of Jesus and I have no objection to anyone adding this privately to prayers I have written if it supports personal worship. I would ask anyone praying with others, however, to respect the endeavour of the book and not to re-insert traditional and faith-assertive vocabulary that I have deliberately 'translated' or omitted, but to respect that the liturgies and prayers offer a 'safe space' for people who may feel ambivalent, to reflect on the possibility of relationship with the Divine Being.

Can it be Christian, if it does not use the language of 'Father, Son and Holy Spirit'?

My short answer is 'yes, but . . .' Much has been written on this subject over the last few decades, especially by feminist theologians – or *thea*logians.[4] The ancient formula for membership of the worldwide Church is baptism in the name of 'Father, Son and Holy Spirit'. If these words are not used during the rite, membership in the eyes of the worldwide Church remains questionable, so this is clearly a place where contemporary and traditional values meet. It is up to individuals to reflect on their position. If we wish to belong, we can assent to the use of age-old language because the history and sense of communion is important, but we can also spend time reflecting

---

[4] *Theo(s)* means 'God' in Greek, and has a masculine ending; Thea has a feminine ending, and ology comes from *logos*, meaning 'study of'. Thealogy, study of the feminine divine, has had growing support in recent decades.

on what the words mean to us: we can translate terms into our own 'language'. There have been a number of interpretations of the Trinitarian formula, such as Augustine's 'Love, Lover and Beloved', and the widely used 'Creator, Redeemer, Sustainer'. All words and human constructs inevitably have limitations, when trying to communicate about the divine. In this book I do not advocate any one particular alternative formula but a few possibilities emerge in the context of the liturgies. The whole book is an exploration of how we might 'translate' traditional language with integrity in a way that helps us in our own spiritual journeys, and in the spirit of the Christian message, without demanding or asserting that the whole Church needs to use the same language. The blessing of Pentecost, after all, was that people of all languages and backgrounds heard and understood the words of the apostles in their own languages – the sacred breath of God speaks to the heart and soul.

How does the Bible talk about God? And what does 'God' mean anyway?

There are many strands in the Bible, just as a rope is made up of many fibres, twisted together. Different strands favour different words for God, but all are essentially inadequate. Using a variety of language reminds us of the constant search for meaningful metaphors.

'God' is an Old English word that would have been recognisable to Anglo-Saxon and Germanic forbears but appears to have even older roots in Sanskrit, meaning 'one who is invoked'.[5] Its closest biblical equivalent is the Mesopotamian word El. El could just mean strength or power, its pictogram a cow or bull's head, with a shepherd's crook representing strong leadership, but it could also signify divinity.

---

[5] http://www.etymonline.com/index.php?term=god

El is used in human and angelic name compounds (Michael, Samuel, Bethel, Gabriel, etc.), and to form titles or descriptors of God, as we see below.

We can talk descriptively about a god or gods – and goddesses – as presumed divine beings or powers, but 'God' as a proper noun denotes, as far as Christians are concerned, the God of Jesus and of his people, the children of Israel. For Jews, Christians and Muslims, united as 'people of the Book' through the biblical character Abraham, there is but one Supreme Being. Christianity is sometimes misunderstood as worshipping three gods because of the concept of the Trinity, traditionally expressed as 'Father, Son and Holy Spirit', but this is not the case; those Christians who accept the concept of the Trinity still believe in One God, the 'three persons' being variously described as aspects, personas or qualities of God. The Trinity is a notoriously difficult concept to express and many who identify as Christian actually have a non-orthodox (even heretical) understanding of the concept, such as the simplified and popular view that Jesus is God, rendering the 'God of the Old Testament' obsolete. In *The Book of Uncommon Prayer*, I explore God as transcendent, incarnate – 'in the flesh'– or earthly, and energetic, in different ways, rooted in a Trinitarian approach to Christianity. As far as I am concerned, God, who is one, embraces, manifests and transcends all gender distinctions and other divisions that confound our thinking.

This book explores diverse ways of talking about God while recognising that, according to biblical tradition, the Ultimate Being is unnameable and indescribable. Naming implies a degree of control, the ability to call someone, even to summon them. According to Exodus 3:14, we cannot know God's name and we cannot control God. The nearest we get is the cryptic description of the divine nature as YHWH, often given vowels to make a pronounceable word, 'Yahweh' (although there is no evidence that this is the correct pronunciation): 'I AM', or 'I will be what

I will be'. Some Christians might disagree about knowing the name of God and say that the name of Jesus is 'the name', but 'Jesus' is a Europeanised form of the Hebrew *'YH suah'*, which means 'the Divine Being (of Exodus 3:14) helps, rescues or saves'. The name 'Jesus' is thus a statement of faith in the power of the biblical God.

The Bible uses many ways of talking about God.[6] The titles tend to get lost in translation, but they include compounds with the ancient word El, expressing power, or divinity:[7]

- El Shaddai: probably God of the Mountains, possibly Breasted God, as the Hebrew for breast is *shad* (Genesis 17:1; 49:25), often translated 'God Almighty'

- El Roi: God of seeing, or God who sees (Genesis 16:13), used by Hagar – an Egyptian woman

- El Olam: eternal or everlasting God (Genesis 21:33)

- El Elyon: God Most High (Genesis 14:19)

- El Rachum: God of motherly tenderness – *rahum* being related to the word for womb (Deuteronomy 4:31)

- El Echad: the One God (Malachi 2:10).

As a mark of respect, Jews do not pronounce the tetragrammaton, that is, the four Hebrew letters representing the name of God, YHWH, but when reading aloud in worship, say something else – traditionally, *Adonai*. Adonai, too, is a word used only with respect, and of God. In everyday speech, to avoid saying even this word, Jews may say '*Ha Shem*', the Name. Adonai means something like 'Lord' in English, and English translators often follow the convention by writing LORD in capitals, instead of YHWH.

---

[6] An interesting site with details of these and other ancient Hebrew names is http://www.hebrew4christians.com/Names_of_G-d/El/el.html
[7] El was also used as the name of the Father god of the Canaanite pantheon.

Through use of 'Lord', masculine gender is thus ascribed to the Ultimate Being, with the intention of showing great respect. It is the sign of respect that is the point – so titles which convey respect are in the spirit of Adonai, whether they are masculine, gender-neutral or feminine. Those who believe it is disrespectful to use a feminine title of God might want to ask themselves why – do we still believe the feminine to be less good, less powerful, less holy?

Interestingly, in the Old Testament, the main Canaanite deity described as in conflict with the God of Israel (for example, in 1 Kings 18:20-40) is called *Baal*, and Baal simply means 'Lord'. It was a title wives in the region sometimes used for their husbands.

Use of 'Lord' to show respect to a powerful man occurs in the New Testament too. In particular, 'Lord' – *kirios* in Greek – is often used of Jesus. It can simply mean 'sir', but it can also be a divine title: Greek translations of the Old Testament use *Kirios* of the God of Israel. Sometimes, there is ambiguity in a New Testament passage, concerning who or what the writer means. This ambiguity can get edited out through translation, depending on the theological position of the translator. One example of ambiguity over the use of 'Lord' is in Mark 5:18-20: is Jesus attributing the healing to God, or is he referring to himself? Does the man who has been healed understand Jesus correctly and obey, or does he misunderstand and go against Jesus' wishes?

> As he was getting into the boat, the man who had been possessed by demons begged him that he might be with him. But Jesus refused, and said to him, 'Go home to your friends, and tell them how much the Lord has done for you, and what mercy he has shown you.' And he went away and began to proclaim in the Decapolis how much Jesus had done for him; and everyone was amazed.
>
> *Mark 5:18-20*

Kirios is used of God in the Bible, but in the Roman Empire, which controlled the Holy Land at the time of Jesus and the early Church, *kirios* was also used of the emperor. New Testament writings that declare 'Jesus is Lord' might be understood as making a dangerously subversive statement of allegiance to an authority other than the emperor – a statement that could result in persecution and even death. This element of subversion tends to get overlooked these days by many who use the word 'Lord'.

The concept behind 'Lord' is of great authority and power. We can use words that express respect for authority without ascribing gender. In Jesus' case, since he was a man, we may feel that 'Lord' is still appropriate – especially if we wish to make a counter-cultural statement of allegiance to Jesus as a superior authority to our human authorities. In this book, while I am sympathetic to 'Jesus is Lord' on these grounds, I have not used 'Lord' on account of its exclusively masculine gender, and because it is a statement of faith that not all readers and participants in the liturgies may wish to make.

Another title ascribed to Jesus in the New Testament is 'Son of God'. In Jewish tradition, there are instances of people described as children or sons of God, and in the Romano-pagan world, emperors were elevated to the status of Son of God and worshipped accordingly. Again, this is a (gendered) statement of faith that not all readers and participants in the liturgies may wish to make, so I have not used it, but I do sometimes use 'the Beloved' to mean Jesus. 'The Beloved' is used in the New Testament, synonymously with 'Son' – for example, at Jesus' baptism ('you are my Son, the Beloved' (Mark 1: 11)) and at the transfiguration. It is also used on its own as a title, in Ephesians 1:6.

There are a few instances where I use 'Christ'. From a cosmic perspective, I would argue that Christ, as the wisdom and power of God (1 Corinthians 1:24), transcends gender. 'Christ' is a title not a name, and means 'anointed, chosen one', one set apart as special and with a special role ordained by God. It is the Greek equivalent of the Jewish term 'Messiah', which is strongly associated with a leader of the Jewish people who will inaugurate a reign of justice, mercy and peace – one who might be known as a son of God. There is a curiously feminine dimension to Jesus' anointing, in that it is described in the Gospels as being performed as an act of devotion by a woman (Mark 14:3-9; Matthew 26:6-13; Luke 7:36-50; John 12:1-8). For Christians, Jesus is the Christ. The term is strongly equated with concepts of Wisdom by early followers of Jesus, Wisdom being a spiritual quality (with a feminine persona) familiar both to Jews and pagans of the first century. Wisdom, in turn, is strongly linked to the Greek philosophical idea of 'logos' or the 'Word' which we find especially in John 1:1-18.

There is some debate about whether Jesus attained this status through his exemplary life and death (Philippians 2:1-11) or whether he was pre-ordained into the role, or held this status since before creation, pre-existent in a very similar way to Wisdom in Proverbs 8:22-31 (compare Colossians 1:15-20).

It has become Christian practice to call God 'Father', even to the exclusion of all other titles. For some, this says all it needs to say about loving relationship; for others, it causes a monumental stumbling block to faith because, for whatever reason, it is difficult to think of God in such terms. (There are of course many for whom it is difficult to think of God as a mother.) This title, perhaps above all the others, has been literalised – even by non-Christians. Plenty of people outside the faith assert quite confidently that Christians believe in a 'male, sky-Father God', and cite this as a reason for seeking a 'female, earth-Mother Goddess,' instead or as well. My feeling is that this is an over-simplification and misunderstanding of biblical imagery, as I hope this book illustrates.

Jesus is said to have called God 'Abba' (Mark 14:36), and told his followers they could do likewise. This is a warmly respectful term used by children and adults towards their fathers, not unlike 'Dad'. The feminine equivalent is 'Amma'. Both words are Aramaic, related to Hebrew, and they, like Jesus himself, come from the context of first-century Mediterranean Jewish culture, which is not easy to translate into our own context. My feeling is that Jesus would encourage his followers today to talk to God in respectful ways that lead to an experience of intimacy and would understand that, for some, 'Father' does not induce such a feeling of intimacy,[8] and that other expressions would evoke greater feelings of love and trust.

---

[8] For an exploration of difficulty with the use of 'Father', see my earlier book, *Rejoice with Me*.

Part 2
The Prayer Bank

Prayer Bank Introduction

This is a bank of prayers, with related biblical texts and explanatory notes, which provide the key building blocks for the liturgies comprising the second part of the book and offer material for anyone wishing to create their own liturgies and prayer experiences using inclusive language. Many prayers in this section have their roots in biblical Christian tradition; they are inspired by and closely related to prayers which have been important in worship for centuries.

There are words in Christianity that mean different things to different people – and mean nothing to others. Using them without explaining what we mean, or using them and assuming everyone thinks like we do, can lead to misunderstandings. As an example, 'Christ' is one such word – the first followers of Jesus worked hard at trying to help their listeners understand what this new term meant, explaining it in relation to ideas people were familiar with at that time: concepts such as wisdom and divine power (1 Corinthians 1:24), and the loving, self-giving and self-emptying nature of Jesus (Philippians 2:1-11). Some terms, which have carried great weight through the ages, and which are inextricably bound up with the essence of Christianity, such as addressing God as 'Father', while beautiful and appropriate for some, are a stumbling block to spirituality for others. Those of us who, for reasons of our own, do not find 'Father' a helpful way of thinking about God can feel excluded from Christianity unless we are supported in finding acceptable alternatives. (See previous chapter.)

I have unpacked some words that have a multiplicity of meanings and have offered 'fresh expressions' of concepts for people who do not want to use, or are not familiar with, standard Christian vocabulary. In so doing, I have inevitably expressed my own interpretation, but hope that I have done so in a way that is respectful of and resonant with the root tradition.

Amen and Awen

Amen is a powerful word, not to be overlooked. It is a key opportunity for a congregation to speak together, expressing agreement with the prayers which have been offered by themselves and on their behalf. *Amen* is an ancient Semitic word, arising in ancient Judaism, used also in Islam, and expresses faith or confidence in the truth of something: affirmation, assent. It is widely understood today as a closure to prayers. In Christianity, there is a particularly special Amen following a prayer called the Doxology, a prayer giving glory to God, traditionally said by the priest during the Eucharistic rite. It is the moment in which everybody gathered expresses their sense of inclusion in the ceremony, and is supposed to be said robustly. There are many beautiful sung and chanted versions of the Amen – and many simple ways of enjoying a spontaneous sung or chanted Amen, so be creative!

For some exploring an Earth Spirituality path, *Awen* is an important alternative word for reflection, closure and conclusion, from the Welsh, referring to divine inspiration, particularly the creative inspiration of the bards.

Intercessions: prayer on behalf of others

Intercessory prayer is prayer offered on behalf of others. It is an important part of liturgy and, although it can be pre-written and delivered in a non-participatory way, it can also be a time for people to voice their own concerns or at least name them in their hearts. Ideally, intercessions are relevant expressions of current concerns, regarding issues of justice and mercy, a reminder that prayer is not just about personal relationship with God but extension of love out into the world. Composing them helps us to try to reach beyond ourselves, exercising our capacity for compassion, respect, integrity and humility. Sentiments expressed, and feelings aroused, aim to mirror the love of God for the world. Because intercessions work best when they reflect the immediacy of circumstances, they need to be produced freshly for an event, albeit following guidelines on structure.

People of faith throughout the ages offer hope that prayer can make a difference, and it is in this spirit that people make petitions and raise concerns, but there is also advice in the Scriptures about praying with wisdom, not for our own will but that God's will be done, trusting in divine wisdom and mercy.

The normal framework is for a leader to describe a theme, with a petition for divine help, pause while people reflect and offer their own prayers aloud or in silence, then conclude this theme with a sentence and response before moving on to the next theme. Things to avoid are intercessions which start to sound like 'to do lists' for God, or polite prompts about problems God seems not to have noticed, or even 'open mike' opportunities for people to make a little speech about their views on the world!

Intercessions: free prayer and inclusive language

Some of the liturgies later in the book do not include intercessory prayer. This section offers some suggestions on how to add intercessions, should you so wish.

The prayers of intercession are often the point at which people are invited to pray about what is on their minds. How this develops depends very much on the kind of group. In this book, which explores alternative language about God and inclusive language generally in worship, 'free prayer' is where I have to let go! As soon as we invite people to pray aloud, we need to be ready for whatever comes out.

I do not know how many liturgies exploring non-gendered language about the divine I have led, in which, once we get to 'free prayer', people simply revert to the language they are familiar with – 'Dear Lord; loving Father' and so on – and this is fair enough. We each need to communicate with the divine in ways that help us feel close.

A liturgy might prompt someone to reflect on how they want to address God, and start looking for ways to avoid saying 'He', but this is something that will be worked out over time – maybe years. My own journey from *wanting* to use conventional language to feeling very uncomfortable with some conventional language about God has lasted for some 30 years or more, with much soul-searching and prayer. In the end, I decided that since I believe I am wholly known by the One who loves me, my reasons for my discomfort in ascribing an exclusively anthropomorphic male gender to this 'One' are understood, accepted, and – if needs be – forgiven. This is my journey, my struggle, and while I am keen to share the thinking that has come out of it, I have no wish to impose it on anybody. This becomes particularly important when praying with people who are in a vulnerable or distressing situation. If, for example, a poorly or elderly person wanted me to join him or her in saying the 'Our Father', this is exactly what I would do, glad to be asked. It is not about me, but about loving this individual who wants to reach out to God *her* way, in companionship with me as a guest in her sacred space.

Two suggested formats for Intercession

Concentric circles:

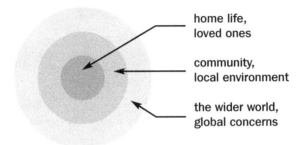

home life,
loved ones

community,
local environment

the wider world,
global concerns

The idea of this structure is to start close to home, then move gradually out – for example:

- personal, home
- loved ones/close contacts
- extended family, neighbours, groups, local environment
- workplace, community, community facilities and wider environment
- others we encounter or are linked to day to day, especially through the caring professions and those who meet our needs, such as farmers
- leaders, wider environmental issues
- global concerns, the earth
- eternal concerns, the universe, 'eternal life' – those who have died.

It would be overwhelming to try to cover all these things on every occasion. Work within the theme of the liturgy, so that prayers are mainly on that theme – for example, environmental concerns, relationships, wellbeing, animals, and so on.

Web of prayer:

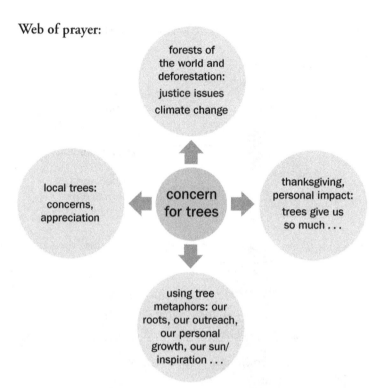

This structure is based on a 'mind map' layout, with a central idea and related thoughts radiating out. It could take the form of a cross as in the diagram or, for more complex ideas, a spider's web.

Both of these forms of intercession can be represented visually – draw rings or a web on paper. Invite people to draw or write on the paper or to place objects meaningfully.

You can make a re-useable version by placing the paper under a table-top layer of glass or by painting on board, safety glass or a metal tray. Depending on the surface, this will also mean you can place votive candles on the prayer-board. An example of intercessions can be found in the 'Liturgy of Outdoors'.

The Prayer Bank

Prayers inspired by Christian liturgical tradition

Glory

A version of the 'Glory be to the Father and to the Son and to the Holy Spirit...', which is used often after prayers, psalms and readings, in some denominations.

> Glory to the One who brings all to birth
> and to love's embodiment
> and to the sacred breath of life,
> primal, present and eternal.
> Amen.

Divine Praise

This is inspired by the *Te Deum*, a widely used Christian hymn of praise dating to the fourth century. The full title in Latin is '*Te deum laudamus*' which is the opening line and means 'You, O God, we praise'.

> Sublime Source of All,
> by your perfect desire,
> all the universe unfolds,
> and all that breathes
> lives in your love;
> so we honour your goodness,
> we wonder at your power,
> and we join with the voices of so many through the ages,

and so many around the world,
expressing the awe
that stirs our hearts.

So too, we stand in awe of you,
revealed as mortal life on earth:
as the one who embodies timeless wisdom,
the one who lives and dies in self-giving love.
We give thanks for the outpouring of yourself,
we give thanks for the outpouring
which sustains all life;
we give thanks for the outpouring of abundant life,
for you who die that we may live.

So breathe through us,
so flow through us,
inspire and delight us,
and lead us in confidence,
sure of your goodness.
Help us and guide us,
support us and comfort us,
give us reason to live
and hope beyond death;
give us reason to feel safe
in the eternity of love,
for in you we trust,
O most lovely One.
Amen.

Blessedness

This is inspired by the sense of past, present and future conveyed
in the *Benedictus,* or the blessing uttered by Zechariah, a Jewish
priest and father of John the Baptist (Luke 1:5-25, 57-80).

We bless you, O God, as Source of All,
as we look back to the roots of trust in you:
firm roots support and give strength,
embedded in the living soil,
firm roots are like ancestors,
named grandmothers and grandfathers
of a chosen people,
Sarah and Abraham, Rebekah and Isaac,
ancient stories of faith in you;
from them we draw wisdom,
from them we draw courage
as we find our way today.
As a tree trunk grows firm and tall,
lifting up its leaves to the sky,
so we strive for the light, the meaning, the truth,
we aim to live well,
and falling, we hope in the power of life
to let new shoots grow from the old.
We look to the one who lives fully in your light,
perfect and true, with leaves of healing for all the world.
So, we face the future,
the fruit of our works and words,
and we ask your blessing,
that it be your own goodness that flowers in us,
your own loving kindness that bears fruit in us,
our seeds a blessing to the world,
and a source of peace,
a source of deep peace.
Amen.

Exultation

This is inspired by the *Magnificat*, Mary's song of praise on meeting her cousin Elizabeth (Luke 1:39-56). This is a women's

song and is derived from an older woman's song, that of
Hannah, mother of Samuel (1 Samuel 2:1-10). These were
Jewish women with great confidence in God's concern for justice
and freedom.

My heart is full of gladness
at the many blessings in my life;
I do not pretend to understand
why I, above others,
have been gifted with all the ripeness of the harvest,
when there is such suffering in the world,
yet sun and the rain give freely like the Holy One.
So despite my own gratitude
I cry out for the sake of those with no voice,
those who have been crushed,
those whose pain destroys their hope;
I cry out for them in solidarity,
because my own life convinces me
that there is one who loves us all
and who is present with us in our most difficult times,
even though we may feel alone.
My own heart tells me there is one who suffers with us
and who knows our grief,
and one who passes through the fearsome gates of death for us,
and rises like the green shoots in the springtime,
to show us the way to everlasting life.
So I will live in hope
and walk as humbly as I may
and pray that trials, when they come,
may lead me deeper into love,
not lead me to despair.
Amen.

A Statement of Hope

A church service often includes a declaration of faith or belief, called a creed, which participants can say together. The Apostles' Creed dates from the fourth century, a time when church leaders were consolidating what it meant to be a follower of Jesus. The following is not a creed, but an expression of hope, which participants can choose to join in with.

> I believe there is reason to hope,
> for there is love in the world,
> and beauty and joy;
> an impulse that inspires those it touches to do good,
> to dream up dreams and create wonders,
> to heal wounds and spread peace.

> I believe there is reason to hope,
> to hold out for eternity,
> for the Source of All,
> to act with courage,
> to be gentle and true,
> and by watching and listening, to increase in wisdom;
> to trust that a seed can grow, in time,
> into a fruitful tree.

> I believe that the earth needs me to care,
> though I often fail,
> and am daunted by the task.
> Yet I need the earth to give herself to me,
> hourly and daily, year by year.
> All that dies that we may live,
> I believe is making a noble sacrifice,
> and I honour the life,
> by striving to live

in hope and in gratitude,
as well as I can.

I believe that I am little but stardust and breath,
yet supported by forces I cannot comprehend,
I journey through life like a river to the sea;
rough ground and smooth, all teaches me,
I believe that my life is about more than myself,
and I search and I wonder,
and ask how best to love.

O Beloved

This is loosely inspired by the prayer attributed to Jesus, of which there are two versions: Luke 11:1-4 and the more familiar Matthew 6:9-13.

O beloved Source of the river of my life,
rain from the sky and wellspring from the earth,
I cannot name you or contain you,
but only delight in your ceaseless flow.

Wash the world with healing grace,
touch the dry land and make it green,
let your fruits be shared by all,
your harvest an eternal joy.

May all who thirst make their way to you
and may all in need find their dry wells filled,
and may all who fear life's raging storms
be sheltered and guided to safe refuge.
Amen.

Or, here is a version which stays closer to the prayer as it appears in Matthew's Gospel, but using inclusive language.

O God, most loving of parents,
residing forever in a blissfulness which lies beyond us,
your name is a holy mystery.
May your power be known,
your desire made manifest on earth,
as in your most perfect realm.
Give us our bread, day by day,
and release us from our bonds,
as we set free those who are bound to us,
and keep us from temptation;
rescue us from harm.
For your realm, your power and your glory abide forever.
Amen.

Going in Peace

This is based on the words of Simeon, who, according to Luke 2:25-35, took the baby Jesus in his arms and praised God, knowing the child to be God's awaited chosen one. 'This man was righteous and devout, looking forward to the consolation of Israel, and the Holy Spirit rested on him. It had been revealed to him by the Holy Spirit that he would not see death before he had seen the Lord's [God's] Messiah.' (Luke 2:25-26) Having seen Jesus, he felt he could now die in peace. It is traditionally used in evening or night prayer.

Holy One, now, you let me go in peace,
according to your word.
for I have seen a sign of hope,
the promise of your help,

which you have prepared for all to see:
a revelatory light to the nations,
your people Israel's glory.

Luke also says: 'There was also a prophet, Anna the daughter of
Phanuel, of the tribe of Asher. She was of a great age, having
lived with her husband for seven years after her marriage, then
as a widow to the age of eighty-four. She never left the temple
but worshipped there with fasting and prayer night and day. At
that moment she came, and began to praise God and to speak
about the child to all who were looking for the redemption of
Jerusalem.' (Luke 2:36-38)

The following imagines Anna's words, as a parallel to
Simeon's, drawing on Hebrew scripture, as a prophet immersed
in temple worship could well have done.

Praise to God Most High,
maker of heaven and earth,[9]
who remembers us with compassion,
as a mother remembers her own children;[10]
for a child has been born for us,
a new hope given to us:
wonderful counsellor, potentate of peace.[11]

Psalm-inspired prayers

The Psalms are a collection of 150 Jewish prayers and hymns,
some of which date back over 3000 years, expressing a wide range
of human emotions and situations that we can still relate to
today. They have been the bedrock of Jewish and then also

---

[9] See Genesis 4:19
[10] See Isaiah 49:15
[11] See Isaiah 9:6

Christian liturgy over the centuries. Some cycles of liturgy revolve around the reading of all the psalms over the course of a week or month, while others just use extracts or make use of the same psalms for specific occasions. It is difficult to conceive of a liturgy without something like a psalm!

The biblical psalms of course are hymns and prayers to the Most High God, maker of heaven and earth (Genesis 14:22), whose name is so holy it is not to be spoken (Exodus 3:14), as explored in the Hebrew scriptures and beloved of Jesus, who told his followers to love God, in accordance with the scriptures (for example, Mark 12:28-34, referring to Deuteronomy 6:4-5). They express devotion to a single God, the God of Israel. Devotion to the biblical God did not develop in a vacuum; people were aware of, influenced by and told to avoid a variety of gods, goddesses and other entities, throughout the emergence of the scriptures. Some of the oldest psalms, such as Psalm 93, have parallels in neighbouring cultures, addressed to different deities, and some ways of talking about God, such as 'rider on the clouds' were also ways of talking about other deities at that time.

The following are not translations of the psalms, but contemporary prayers inspired by a selection of individual psalms, which may be used in a similar manner.

Trust in the Future (in the style of the psalms)

I do not know where next the river of my life will flow,
I do not know what obstacles lie ahead,
what dangerous rapids and what sleepy pools,
deep gorges cut through rock, and waterfalls;
I only know that rivers flow until they reach the sea
and then the waters mingle, all is one,
as it always was and ever will be,

as long as the skies give their rain.
I do not know where next the river of my life will flow,
but flow it must, drawn on and ever on,
and with the constant flow I find my confidence grows strong,
that rivers flow on and on until they reach the sea.

On Contentment (inspired by Psalm 1)

Contentment lies in discerning the Divine desire
and, in discovering it, surrendering to it,
as lovers to one another,
for such is the way to Oneness.
The one who learns to live in love,
is like a tree by a flowing stream:
verdant and fruitful in their season,
a joy to all who draw near.

A comforting refuge (inspired by Psalm 3)

O Holy One, may you be to me,
a shield, a shelter, a cave, a hiding place,
where I may take refuge for a while
from those who seem to set themselves against me.
Let me retreat into you, my rock,
and feel your safe, surrounding strength,
and calm my breath, renew my spirit,
and may your comforting quietness hold me,
let me rest and sleep in peace, to wake renewed,
to see more clearly by the light of day
how best to live, how best to understand
the ones who disturb me most,
and so find ways to walk in peace.

In urgent need (inspired by Psalm 6)

O Eternal One, let me feel your presence;
for I am in need, full of pain,
and the only reality is in this experience,
moment by moment as my breath comes and goes.
If you can help me, O Love on whom I call,
then help me now.
If you are with me and within me,
then touch me somehow.
Gone is the past, and uncertain the future;
in this moment of need, find a way to me now
and speak in a way that I can hear,
for I am weary and do not know where else to turn,
if not to you, O Holy One.

The Rock, our Mother (inspired by the opening of Psalm 7 and Deuteronomy 32:18)[12]

O my Mother Rock,
in you I take refuge,
save me and protect me.
Let me find shelter in you,
let me find comfort in you,
for I remember you
in my time of need.

In awe of the Creator (inspired by Psalm 8)

O Power beyond all powers,
Intelligence beyond all human thought,
how awesome is the notion of your Being,

---

[12] See also section at end of Prayer Bank.

73

the possibility of your presence:
an incomprehensible wonder.
Yet how magnificent, too, is the universe,
how incredible the beauty and the complexity of all that is!
How could it be that such a wonder could unfold
if not through infinite, joyous creativity,
intent upon exploring every possibility for love?
And what are we, within this web of life?
What is humanity? What is our role, our place in all of this?
The power we have on earth,
how should we use it well and wisely
in accordance with your greater will?
For every forest, every ocean,
every bird and beast is subject to our whim,
yet we like children hardly know what we are doing.
Eternal One, Power beyond our human power,
Intelligence beyond all human thought,
how awesome is the notion of your Being,
the possibility of your presence:
an incomprehensible wonder.

Crying out for help (inspired by Psalm 12)

Help me, O Holy One, for who else can I trust?
There is so much confusion and deceit,
so many lies, manipulation and duplicity,
schemes of self-advancement,
set to undermine the unwary and exploit the vulnerable.
Who is honest and true?
Who can I turn to, who will help me in my need,
and speak for justice, stand alongside
those who have no voice or power?
Help me, O Holy One; I cry out to you,
for you alone are true,

as silver, seven-times refined by fire is true
and pure and strong and beautiful;
so rise up and shine in the night of my despair,
a perfect, silver moon-like presence in my heart,
to strengthen me.

Trust in the Power of the Infinite One (inspired by Psalm 16)

I call on you, the power of the Greatest Good,
I call on you, the presence of the love of all loves,
I call on you, the perfection of the Infinite One,
to protect me and all who trust in you.
To me, you are God: sublime source of all,
the cup from which I drink,
and the guide to my path;
my life has been graced by many blessings,
and all these I ascribe to you.
When sleep eludes me, I reflect on you,
the dark night is lit by remembering your words,
and by day and by night,
the thought of you cheers my heart.
So, I have courage and confidence in you,
that you weave all together in wondrous ways,
you lead me along the path of life
and in your presence is true delight.

In time of trouble (inspired by Psalm 17)

I feel a crisis building and see no way out;
the words I spoke, the things I have done,
are being taken and twisted and used against me
and I am afraid that everything is beyond my control.
If I have been unwise, then teach me now;

if I have caused pain, then let me seek forgiveness.
I was only doing what everybody does:
trying to survive in a difficult world.
But my limitations, now, have formed a barrier,
my way ahead is compromised,
so help me, O Perfect Power beyond all Powers,
and show me a window in the wall,
a side-road, a new way, a calming word,
a solution that will help us all,
and will help me to grow in wisdom and gratitude.
Most of all, though, O Holy weaver of life,
I ask that you protect those around me from harm;
shield them from the consequences of my mistakes,
hide them as a mother bird nestles her chicks,
for I have no wish for the innocent to be hurt
        through my fault.
So help me, O Perfect Power beyond all Powers,
and help us all, for the sake of love.

God is a Shepherd (inspired by Psalm 23)

God is a shepherd,
all shall be well.
We rest in green meadows,
and walk by calm waters;
in peace, lies healing for my soul;
and the best paths become clear.

Even though I walk
a valley of pain,
I fear no harm,
for you are with me, Beloved,
and your staff reassures me,
with protection and strength.

You prepare a meal for me,
when others seem against me;
you honour me and delight in me,
and fill my cup to overflowing.
Surely goodness and tenderness will not cease,
and I shall dwell with the One who loves me,
my whole life long.

Concerns about the world (inspired by Psalm 36)

It troubles me, O God, that some seem
to have no regard for justice or compassion at all,
but spend their days in self-promotion and exploitation
    of others.
I do not understand why you seem to tolerate them,
and I wonder what my own response should be.

I balance this with my firm belief
that your love is unflinching,
your concern for your creation boundless,
and your goodness and mercy limitless.
Following your way is a path to peace,
for animals and humanity alike.

How precious is your love, O God!
Anyone is free to take refuge
in the shadow of your wings,
drawing on your abundance,
drinking from the river of your delights,
for the fountain of life springs up from you
and it is by your light that we see.
So let me never doubt your goodness,
and never withdraw your love from me.

Let the arrogant and heartless lose their power,
and let me not behave like them.
Show me how best to understand the world,
and how to live according to your wishes.

On anger and confusion (inspired by Psalm 39)

I promised myself that I would hold my tongue,
thinking this was the way of peace,
so I said nothing to those I think are in the wrong
and even in their presence,
in the sight of injustices, I said nothing.

But the anger grew inside me,
my silence masked an inner struggle.
This was not peace, for a fire burned within me
that was starting to consume me.
So I turned to God, asking for wisdom.
I said, 'Life seems so unfair, so short, so full of pain,
the wicked profiting and the vulnerable suffering
    without help,
and we live from one day to the next,
not knowing which will be our last.'

But all the same, I cling onto the hope of God's love,
I cry out in my suffering, asking for mercy.
If I am silent now, it is because I do not wish
    to speak foolishness
or show my ignorance.
Help me, O God, for I hope in you,
I trust that your goodness is greater than all the wickedness
    of the world.

Gratitude (inspired by Psalm 40)

I waited patiently for you, O God,
and you found a way to reach me;
I was stuck in a pit, a treacherous marsh,
and you pulled me out,
you set me back on firm ground.

You made me so glad I sang for joy;
I wanted to tell everyone how you helped me.
It is your power alone that I know I can trust,
it is a delight to follow your way
and reflect on your words.

There are other troubles in life, O God;
guide me on a wise path
and let me not be discouraged or destroyed
by what unfolds around me,
help me to stay true to you all the days of my life.

God's protection (inspired by Psalm 46)

Even though the world seems to be falling apart,
we will not fear;
though mountains tremble and oceans roar,
nations wage war and whole peoples struggle to survive,
we will not fear.

There is a city with a river of life,
a radiant place, a place where God resides,
a city of peace, where all can live in harmony,
where any, from all directions, can come and live in peace.

Come together, all you peoples;
let this God of love draw conflict to a close.

Be still and know that God is peace;
may peace be proclaimed in all the earth,
may peace be proclaimed in every heart.

Remorse and reconciliation (inspired by Psalm 51)

Have mercy on me, O most loving God,
have mercy on me, and wipe away my guilt.
I am tortured by a sense of shame;
I know I have done wrong and it haunts me day and night.
I have agonised over this, I have been through hell.
Many would say I deserve it, and more punishment besides.
I fear the judgements of society,
condemnation from the community in which I live.
You alone, O God, know all our hearts,
and can have pity on me as well as on those I have wronged –
yet with you too, lies the final judgement.
So have mercy on me, O God,
for I am desperately sorry and do not know where else to turn.

If you cleanse me, holy One,
I will be purer than the freshest snow.
If you purge me, I will be cleansed through and through,
fresh and good as new, ready to begin again.
It is truth that you want, I am convinced –
my own honesty, my willingness to humble myself –
so teach me wisdom, help me to learn from my past
     and change,
so that I can walk your way
and lead others to your loving kindness.

Help and betrayal (inspired by Psalm 55)

O God, you know everything,
so you must know how I feel!

How I wish I could fly away from this situation, free as a bird,
to some quiet countryside retreat and find my peace,
but I cannot escape the reality,
the problem will not go away.
The hardest thing is that this is so personal;
I feel betrayed and let down,
and I feel foolish for trusting in the first place,
when many would have advised more caution.
It is my generosity of spirit, O God, that has caused the problem,
my good nature, that wants to see the best in others.
Now, what do I do? Where can I turn, if not to you?
Throughout the day and night I plead with you,
I ask you to mend what I am powerless to mend
and heal what I am powerless to heal,
for I put my trust in you, that your goodness can change all.

Feeding the world (inspired by Psalm 67)

May God be gracious to us and bless us,
beaming down on us like the sun,
glowing within us like a comforting hearthfire.
May your way be revealed on earth, O Holy One,
so that all may be touched by your transforming power;
may all peoples be glad and sing for joy,
finding freedom through your justice and mercy.
The earth pours forth its abundance;
give us reason, O God, to give thanks.
Teach us to extend your justice and mercy
so that all the world may be fed.

God's magnitude and human frailty (inspired by Psalm 90)

In you has all life existed since the beginning;
there is nothing which exists beyond your presence

or outside of your love.
For you who are infinite, our timescales are as nothing;
our lives are like a breath, a blade of grass,
a fleeting dream in the night;
all too soon we return to the earth of which we are a part,
like a flower, withering and dying.
We are powerless before the grip of death,
which comes to us all.
Teach us to value every single day,
and to grow in wisdom,
that we may find reason to give thanks,
marvelling that you know each of us and love us,
in all our fragility.

God's Comforting Wings (inspired by Psalm 91)

You who live in the shelter of the Most High,
who dwell in the shadow of the mountainous One,
will say to God: 'My refuge and my protection;
my God in whom I trust.
For you set me free from fears that ensnare me;
you soothe me in time of sickness;
you cover me as a bird spreads her wings over her little ones,
and amongst the feathers of your care I find comfort.
Night-time holds no fears for me,
and through the day, the arrows of trouble glance off me,
for your love is my shield.
I see turmoil all around,
all creation groans under her oppression,
yet I trust that your love is stronger than death,
you show us a path of life.
I have made you my refuge, O Holy One,
and to you I turn.

Send messengers of your love, O God;
let my soul be awake always to the vision of your glory
and to words of truth;
may your angels lift me up when I fall,
and guide me when I am lost,
may they show me always the wisdom path
which leads to peace,
the humble path of the Beloved.'
Amen.

Joyful praise (inspired by Psalm 95:1-7)

Let us sing to the Eternal One,
let joyful sound resound,
let us draw together gladly,
our spirits unbound.

For the Source of All fills everything
and everyone with grace
and nothing lies beyond the reach
of everlasting peace.

From the soaring heights of mountains
to the gloomiest abyss,
the sea, the field, the forest, all
are held in perfect love.

Then let us pause in quietness
and listen for the sound
of the Eternal One singing back to us,
in melodies profound.

Creation's praise (inspired by Psalm 96)

Sing to the Eternal One,
sing a new song from the heart,
tell of the majesty and wonder of the Holy One,
the way of wholeness, of gladness and peace.
Some have confidence in material wealth
and many trust in forces that cannot help them,
but true wisdom and insight are a rare treasure
to be sought after, a jewel of great worth.
Truth lies in obedience to the divine call
to live with simplicity and integrity,
with compassion for all and gratitude in the heart.
Trusting in God, who is supreme in goodness,
is a path to peace, the way of humanity;
by so doing we join our voices with all creation,
which puts its trust completely in God,
our songs mingling with the ocean's roar,
the forest's vibrant voice,
the field's and mountain's hymns of praise.
For nature knows that God comes to judge with justice
and all creation longs for harmony to be restored.

A time of hardship (inspired by Psalm 102)

A time of real hardship is upon me,
I am bowed down with worry and pain,
I see no way out of this nightmare
and call on the God I remember from my childhood,
when they told me to trust and to pray
and taught me holy songs to sing.
I hardly know how to ask;
I hardly dare imagine why God may be interested in me;
I hardly understand how there can be a God at all,

that allows such hardship for so many;
yet this is my hope, my sincere hope,
that the words of my teachers were not in vain
and there is one who loves me and who is with me,
beside me in all my suffering and understanding my pain.
So I call out to God, I call out to a power beyond me,
daring to hope for a power of love and goodness,
that can restore happiness to my life
and I ask for help, for I am bowed down with worry and pain.

In awe of creation (inspired by Psalm 104)

Holy One, I stand in awe of you;
I am humbled by your majesty, yet I long to draw closer to you.
Although I cannot comprehend your magnitude,
the smallest detail of creation
reveals your wonder.

*I could marvel at your works, one by one,
all my days, and never reach an end.*

From the delicacy of a feather
to the precision of a crystal,
from the mysterious journey of the moon,
to the flight of the wild birds.
How can such wonders exist,
except for a perfect mind, first envisioning them?

*I could marvel at your works, one by one,
all my days, and never reach an end.*

When I look at the earth and out at the stars,
the universe beyond us,

all this must surely come from your desire
to make something of unutterable beauty.
Then, I marvel at the trees and plants,
the diversity, the colours and scents, the foods they yield,
and the little insects which love them,
and I marvel at all your creatures,
the interconnectedness of the great web of life,
which surely owes its existence to you.
Even the mountains, the forests and plains, the great oceans,
all these things reveal the splendour of their creator.

I could marvel at your works, one by one,
all my days, and never reach an end.

You even made humanity, greatest of all,
yet also most foolish and most able to damage
this pristine earth that you have made,
most capable, most intelligent and loving,
but also most self-serving and unwilling to consider
the consequences of our destructive acts.

I could marvel at your works, one by one,
all my days, and never reach an end.

Yes, if you made this universe you made us too
and love us, as you love the whole,
so let us learn to humble ourselves before our maker,
and submit ourselves to Wisdom's voice,
aligning ourselves to the way you want humanity to live,
that we may play our part in this your world
as lovers of peace and caretakers together of this living jewel.

God's protection and help (inspired by Psalm 121)

I lift up my eyes to the hills –
where will help come from?
My help comes from God,
who made heaven and earth.

May the Holy One keep your footsteps sure;
never resting, never sleeping,
the Eternal One of Israel
keeps constant watch.

May God be your faithful guardian;
a shade for you from the glare of the sun
and a shelter at night
while the moon lights the sky.

May God keep you from all harm,
may God help you to delight in life,
watching over all your travels,
from this time forth and for evermore.
Amen.

In humility (inspired by Psalm 131)

Holy One, my heart is humble
and my gaze is modest and meek;
I know little, and understand less
of the ways of the world;
many things fill me with wonder.
I sit quietly in your presence,
calm and at peace,
like a child who no longer cries for milk,
like my own child, content on my knee.

On mystical knowing (inspired by Psalm 139)

You, O Great Mystery, are the One who knows me;
you know my thoughts
and my words before I speak them,
you see me from within,
knowing the feelings of my heart
and the dreams in my mind;
you know my aches and pains,
my worries and my joys.
There is nowhere I can go to escape you;
you are ahead of me,
closer than my next step,
and far beyond the horizon.
If I had wings to fly to another land,
even there you would be with me,
and in death, you will not leave me.
You knew me as I was growing in my mother's womb;
from you came my breath,
from you came my form,
my body shaped from the earth's own substance.
In the night, you are with me and within me;
the darkness is not dark to you,
nothing impedes your sight
for dark and light are both alike to you.
Sometimes I am afraid lest you judge what you see in me,
for you know my imperfection better than I know myself.
Sometimes I am angry; I want to break free,
to be alone and find a path of my own choosing,
yet without you I am nothing.
Sometimes I judge others harshly,
I hate what I see, the violence and greed around me
make me rage.
All this you know, just as you know the hearts
    of each and everyone;

you hear the footsteps of the ant,
the wing beats of a moth,
you see the fall of every raindrop, the unfurling of every leaf,
and so you watch me too and know the whole of me,
and I give thanks because I believe you love me
    and the whole of creation.
To me, although I cannot fathom you, you are God.

An evening prayer (inspired by Psalm 141)

I reach out to you, O Holy One,
may you hear me when I call.
Let my prayer be like incense rising up,
let my lifted hands surrender all that I am,
as an evening sacrifice.

Guard my speech, O Holy One,
keep watch over my lips,
shield my heart from hatefulness,
let me not be seduced
by schemes which lack love.

Let me be open to correction
by those who are wise,
but let me not be persuaded
by wicked words and false motives,
which draw me away from your path of peace.

I turn my whole being towards you, O God,
I seek you deep within and far beyond me,
I wrestle and strive to live with integrity
yet see pitfalls all around, and my own weakness,
but in you I take refuge, O Holy One, so protect me
    and guide me.

Natural praise (inspired by Psalms 148 and 150)

Praise God!
Praise the Holy One from the far reaches of the universe;
sing praises from the mountain tops!
Praise God, all you angels,
sing praises, you who do God's will.
Praise the Holy One, sun and moon,
sing praises, all the stars of heaven!
Praise the Eternal One, you rolling clouds,
sing praises, you oceans and flowing rivers,
for God is your source, the one who loves you.
Praise the Holy One from the ends of the earth;
sing praises, you sea creatures and all you birds of the air!
Praise God, rain and snow, fire and stormy wind,
sing praises, you who are wild and free.
Praise the Holy One, you gardens and fruit trees
and all the trees of the forest,
sing praises, you creatures, wild and tame!
Praise God, you peoples of the earth,
leaders and followers, folk of all kinds, old and young alike,
sing praises and make delightful music
to the Holy One who fills the universe;
let all that has breath unite to sing in praise of God.

Prayers of the Rock

These prayers draw directly on the passage in Deuteronomy
32:18 which uses the metaphors of rock and mother together.
Rocks in the Bible often mean large rocky outcrops and cliffs
riddled with networks of caves, hiding places for fugitives from
oppressors or shelter from the strong sun. Caves in the Judean
wilderness were used as dwellings at various times, some with
pigeon holes and lamp shelves carved into the walls. The idea of

sheltering, giving refuge and protection, is echoed in images of a mother bird nestling her chicks and a bear protecting her cubs. Caves are often carved out by underground rivers and there is an association in the Bible between rocks and springs of fresh water. Moses is told by God to strike a rock in the desert, whereupon water gushes out. The flow of water from a rocky cave mouth can be seen as a maternal image of the waters of birth bursting from the womb.

My God, my rock, in whom I take refuge,
my shield and the horn of my salvation,
my stronghold and my refuge,
my saviour; you save me from violence.

2 Samuel 22:3

Let all who take refuge in you rejoice;
let them ever sing for joy.
Spread your protection over them,
so that those who love your name may exult in you.

Psalm 5:11

O my Rock,
in you I take refuge.
The storms of life rage outside
but in you I find shelter.
Holy One, you surround me,
the cave of your love welcomes me,
it draws me within to find the rest that I need.
In your safe-holding let me find peace.
In your strong embrace let me find renewal.
Amen.

O my Rock,
I have come to you for retreat.
Give me the inner healing
that only time in your presence can give,
and in time, let me return to the world,
bearing your peace.
Amen.

Holy One, who labours in love
to bring each of us to life,
Self-giving One, who knows in full
the pain that bearing, birthing life can bring,
give me endurance,
give me courage and love
to push on with my own labours
for the sake of life.
Let me feel that my striving is known,
my labour blessed by you,
and that joy will transform all, by and by.
Amen.

Mothering God,
help me to see the worth of waiting,
to let things take shape and grow in their own time,
help me not to rush things,
but give as needed, gently, wisely,
patiently.
Amen.

Mothering God,
compassionate one,
tenderly loving one,

all-forgiving, all-accepting one,
strongly protecting one,
let me feel your presence,
for I need your love.
Amen.

Dear Mother of us all,
our source, our beginning place,
the one to whom we will return,
let us not forget you.
Call us into your shelter,
remind us of your protection,
comfort us with your kindly presence,
your unconditional love for each of us,
no matter what.
Amen.

Oh my Mother,
in you I live and move and have my being,
my whole world, your all-encompassing womb,
my comfort, your heartbeat.
Let me remember the safe, warm darkness of my beginning,
and return in my mind, to your total embrace.
My all you provide, my very life you support;
by your own self-giving,
by your own acceptance and transformation
of all that is impure within me,
you make me whole,
and your cherishing love is my balm.
Amen.

Holy Mother, the sacrifice you made for me
is beyond my grasp.
In your generosity
you do not need me to understand,
you simply ask that I remember you.
You do not ask for me to repay your giving,
you simply hold your arms out wide
and offer up your love.
Amen.

Mother, your mystery disturbs us;
your cloak seems dreadful,
your way, a way of death,
your presence weak and silent in the face of suffering.
Loved ones suffer and we call on you,
confident that you love them too,
yet no help comes – or so it seems.
We cannot see beyond your veil,
we cannot know what reality exists
beyond our final breath,
we cannot know the purpose of so much pain we bear,
yet still we live in hope
and in the glorious fungi and the new green shoots,
rising from the damp, dark earth enriched by layers of decay,
we trust that all is well and all shall be well,
despite our brokenness, and because of it,
for by dying, surrendering to the soil,
a seed will bear its fruit.
Amen.

A Simple Ritual of Bread and Wine

(This can be incorporated into other liturgies, placed towards the end. If concerned, consult those with responsibility in your church about suitability for use in different contexts.)

Preparation

You could display bowls of earth, grain, flour and grapes and pictures of sun, rain and agricultural tools and workers to illustrate the essential growth stages of bread and wine, but as a minimum you need bread and red grape-based drink in vessels suitable for sharing. In church, wine is usually shared from a large pottery or silver cup, passed round with a serviette for wiping the rim after each use. If hygiene is a concern, consider using small individual cups filled from a jug (shot-size cups are ideal) but weigh up the environmental factor of creating plastic waste. See notes in the first section regarding sensitivity towards individual needs, in deciding whether to have wine or non-alcoholic equivalents, and whether you need gluten-free bread. If you want a simple song, consider the Grain Song, which follows.

Some Earth Spirituality traditions use a different alcoholic drink and reflect on respective ingredients and qualities. Favourites are mead, made from honey made by bees, and whisky made from barley. If you want to use these, take time to adapt the ritual and words accordingly.

The Ritual

The earth gives of herself, ceaselessly, that we might live.

Grain seeds buried in the earth grow in the sun and rain; they sprout seeds of their own, become ripe, then are cut down, the new seeds ground into flour for our bread.

We thank the earth for her generous self-giving, our fellow sisters and brothers for their labour, and God for the wonder of life itself.

Lift up the bread.

Jesus likened himself to the grain, and his body to a loaf of bread.

As the grain is cut and Jesus died, bread is broken and many are fed.

So we give thanks and share this bread.

Bread is passed around so all can take and eat.

In giving, use words such as:
'bread of life', 'blessings to you' or 'eat and rejoice'.[13]

In receiving, use words such as:
'thanks be to God', 'blessings to you', or 'blessings of life'.

The earth gives of herself ceaselessly, that we might live.

Vines grow up from the soil, nurtured by sun and rain, pruned and tended with care. Ripe grapes are harvested, their juice crushed out of them, for us to enjoy.

---

[13] See Part 1, concerning avoidance of faith-based assertions concerning Jesus. I do not consider this to be a formal Eucharist and have deliberately not included the familiar Christian statements, 'Christ's body, broken for you' and 'Christ's blood, shed for you' – a conceptual step further than some present may be willing to take. What sharing bread and wine or grape juice means to different people present may be something to reflect on together afterwards.

We thank the earth for her generous self-giving, our fellow sisters and brothers for their labour, and God for the wonder of life itself.

Lift up the wine.

Jesus likened himself to a vine, his followers, the branches, and God, the gardener. He likened the red juice of the grapes to his own blood.

As the juice flows, and Jesus died, wine is fermented and many a heart is stirred.

So we give thanks and share juice/wine.

Juice/wine is passed round so all can drink.

In giving, use words such as:
'fruit of the vine', 'blessings to you', or 'drink and rejoice'.

In receiving, use words such as:
'thanks be to God', 'blessings to you', or 'blessings of life'.

We close with the 'Glory' and a prayer based on the one Jesus taught:
Glory to the One who brings all to birth
and to love's embodiment
and to the sacred breath of life,
primal, present and eternal.
Amen.

O God, most loving of parents,
residing forever in a blissfulness which lies beyond us,
your name is a holy mystery.

May your power be known,
your desire made manifest on earth,
as in your most perfect realm.
Give us our bread, day by day,
and release us from our bonds,
as we set free those who are bound to us,
and keep us from temptation;
rescue us from harm.
For your realm, your power and your glory abide forever.
Amen.

The Grain Song

This is the only song I have included in this book; I wrote it for a Lammastide service some years ago and it has been used at simple Eucharistic rites since then. It is sung meditatively and can be repeated as a whole, or verse by verse.

I am grain, I am grain,
fruit of earth and sun and rain.

I will sow, I will sow,
in your heart my seeds will grow.

You are earth, you are earth,
in you I will come to birth.

I am grain, I am grain,
cut me down, I will live again.

I will reap, I will reap,
Love's great harvest of all who sleep.

I am yeast, I am yeast,
raising dough for the kingdom feast.

I am wine, I am wine,
drink my cup for you are mine.

I am vine, I am vine,
you my branches intertwine.

I am bread, I am bread,
break me till the world is fed.

I am love, I am love,
bread of heaven, from above.

The Grain Song

Annie Heppenstall

Moderato

I am grain, I am grain,

fruit of earth a - nd sun and rain

I will sow, I will sow,
in your hearts my seeds will grow.

You are earth, you are earth,
in you I will come to birth.

I am grain, I am grain,
cut me down, I will live again.

I will reap, I will reap,
Love's great harvest of all who sleep.

I am yeast, I am yeast,
raising dough for the kingdom feast.

I am wine, I am wine,
drink my cup for you are mine.

I am vine, I am vine,
you my branches intertwine.

I am bread, I am bread,
break me till the world is fed.

I am love, I am love,
bread of heaven, from above.

Part 3

Holy Hours and Days

Prayers and texts specific to hours, days, months and seasons

This section is a continuation of the Prayer Bank.

It is based on the ancient tradition of praying through the hours of the day, the days of the week and the seasons of the year, in a great cycle or spiral, always moving on in both the spiritual and temporal journey through life, yet revisiting the familiar, over and over again. This kind of prayer is known as saying 'the Daily Office'; it is particularly a monastic tradition with links to Jewish prayer practice, but has expanded into the lives of many outside of religious communities, particularly through observing morning and evening prayer. Many following an Earth Spirituality path today find natural moments to pause each day, for prayer, ritual and/or meditation, and as in the church cycle, the pattern of sunrise, midday, sunset and midnight offers a meaningful structure. There are examples of how such prayer could be woven together using different elements of this book, later on.

One of the great benefits of participating in the daily prayer patterns of particular spiritual communities is the sense of connection with the community and its history. Through sharing prayer in our own homes or in small groups we can find ourselves mysteriously connected in the 'communion of saints' in ways that allow us to feel we belong to something bigger than ourselves, which can nourish and support us. The suggestions for daily prayer practice in this book may allow you to feel connected with others who are seeking alternative ways to express their spirituality in inclusive, earth-centred ways, in a variety of traditions. There is a growing network of people across the denominations and faith groups, so even if you feel isolated in your own community, you are not alone spiritually.

With many of the prayers and blessings that follow, I have added suggestions for contemplative scripture reading or texts for meditation. Inclusive language translations of the Bible do exist (such as the New International Version published in the United States in 2011) but there are also passages in the Bible that already meet criteria for inclusivity concerning reference to God, which I have used directly from the New Revised Standard Version (NRSV).

Some church traditions provide visual enhancement to the liturgical cycle, through symbolic colours and icons or images for meditation. Purple, for example, is often associated with the weeks before Christmas (Advent) and with the weeks before Easter (Lent), and white or gold with the days of celebration themselves. If you have an altar, shrine or prayer corner at home, you may like to decorate it in ways that reflect the season and other factors meaningful to you, with candles and incense if this supports your contemplation, and of course, as always, include your own preference in music, whether recorded or live.

The Seasons

Although one option is to go straight to the relevant prayer for the day or time of day (which of course you are free to do), a primary consideration in a liturgical office is often the big picture: what season is it? What is the overarching time of year? In the Christian calendar this relates to the cycle of holy days and seasons – Advent, Christmas, Easter, Pentecost and so on – but these in turn correspond in interesting ways with the seasons of the natural year, particularly those of the northern hemisphere where Christianity first developed.[14] While I have maintained the traditional connection between church year and northern

---

[14] For more on this see my earlier book, *Search Me and Know Me: Spiritual Accompaniment through Reflection on the Celtic Cross* (KM Publishing, 2015).

hemisphere cycle, this book provides resources for those in the southern hemisphere to draw seasons and events on the Christian calendar into more appropriate alignment to suit context.

The seasons section comes in two parts:

1. Natural seasons and elements: The seasons speak for themselves but, for some people on a spiritual journey today, the seasons also correspond meaningfully with the traditional elements, earth, air, fire and water, so I have included a blessing reflecting these too. This blessing could be used as an opening sentence at the start of prayer, or on its own. The four elements each have a themed reflection of their own.

2. Special days and times of the solar and Christian cycles: This section includes explanatory information and comment on possible links with aspects of wider contemporary spirituality as well as a suggested biblical text and prayer.

Natural seasons and elements

Spring

> Springtime blessings of new life,
> of growing warmth, and growing light,
> blessings of joy and great delight!

or

Air

> Blessings of the Sacred Breath,
> blessings of air and blowing wind,
> blessings of clear mind and clear insight,
> the interconnectedness of all that lives.

Suggested colours and symbols for the season: yellows and bright greens, other springtime flower colours, flowers, bulbs in pots, catkins, pictures or sculptures of new life.

Summer

> Blessings of summertime,
> of earth's increase,
> of warmth and brightness,
> sun's strength and rain's balm.

or

Fire

> Blessings of fire, the devouring flame,
> blessings of a God whom we cannot contain,

blessings of the one who gives and takes,
whose power is manifest for love's sake.

Suggested colours and symbols for the season: sun, blue skies,
rain water, deep greens and summer flower colours, sunshine
colours – light golds and yellows.

Autumn

Blessings of autumn,
of timely release,
blessings of harvest,
earth's generous yield.

or

Water

Blessings of the water of eternal life,
welling up, within our hearts,
blessings of sea and river and rain,
blessings of tide, of ebb and flow.

Suggested colours and symbols for the season: harvest produce,
water, fallen leaves and seeds, earthy colours – reds, browns,
burnished gold, or watery colours – blues and greens, silver, grey
and white.

Winter

Blessings of endurance and timely retreat,
wintertime inner work,
companionship and peace.

or

Earth

Blessings of earth, of rich, humble soil,
birthing and reclaiming each living thing,
blessings of wisdom and patience and hope,
blessings of cave and safe hiding place.

Suggested colours and symbols for the season: whites, greys, black, silver, red berries and evergreen leaves (beware yew which is beautiful but poisonous), bare twigs and branches that you can hang prayers or decorations from.

Special days and times of the solar and Christian cycles

The cycle of both the solar and liturgical years describes a journey, where there is a great deal of interconnectedness. In Christianity, a key belief which set early followers of Jesus apart from their Jewish contemporaries was the conviction that he had risen from the dead, which was evidence of his Messiahship or Christhood – one chosen by God. Resurrection was and is something that some Jews believe in; writings from the centuries before Jesus' life, during a time of persecution of Jews, express ideas about resurrection of the martyred righteous and the wise faithful (writings such as the Books of Daniel and the Maccabees). Accounts of Jesus' resurrection, then, did not happen in a void. Woven alongside such thoughts of God's restoration of the just and true, we also find elements of a wider Gentile (non-Jewish) interest in resurrection, expressed through natural imagery, especially that of sun and grain. The Apostle Paul and, according to the Gospels, Jesus himself, frequently used the imagery of the dying and rising sun and grain to explain the mystery of Christ to an audience embedded in the natural world.

The following liturgical and solar cycle material draws especially on this natural dying and rising pattern, interwoven with our own human experience.

As a variation in this section, instead of providing prayers, I have suggested a short biblical text and a quality for personal reflection. The text can be used at the opening of prayer or separately.

Advent

traditional associations: purple, candle wreaths

Advent, which means arrival or the coming of something or someone who is expected, is a period of four weeks before Christmas and marks the beginning of the church year. With Luke's Gospel as inspiration, we journey with Mary, who is pregnant, and moving ever on to the place of birth, the ancestral home of her partner Joseph's people. They were required to go, in order to be registered by the Roman authorities. Weary and heavy-laden, yet strong and determined, she keeps moving on, her loyal companion at her side. The whole time is summed up in a few verses from Luke's Gospel: 'All went to their own towns to be registered. Joseph also went from the town of Nazareth in Galilee to Judea, to the city of David called Bethlehem, because he was descended from the house and family of David. He went to be registered with Mary, to whom he was engaged and who was expecting a child.' (Luke 2:3-5)

A well-established tradition is to make a ring of four candles with a fifth in the centre, to light on the Sundays leading up to Christmas. The candles are often purple, with a pink one on the third Sunday for 'gaudete' or 'rejoice', a lightening of mood; the central one is white for Christ and is lit on Christmas Day. Each represents an aspect of the story: the first often represents the patriarchs and matriarchs of the faith, such as Abraham and Sarah; the second represents the biblical prophets; the third, John the Baptist; and the fourth, Mary, Jesus' mother.

In the northern hemisphere, this is a time of journey into colder, darker times, requiring endurance. It is the approach of the winter solstice, time of deepest darkness. The anticipation of a feast might keep flagging spirits up, but the journey at this time can be hard work, especially for the vulnerable. In the southern hemisphere, Advent falls during the approach to the summer solstice or midsummer; you can find midsummer prayers on page 129.

Prayers

Accompany us in our journeys, O God,
help us to travel light and in good faith,
to be brave and kind companions to one another
and to value the journey itself
as much as the destination.
When we are weak, be to us a strong support;
when we stumble, lift us up;
when we take a wrong turn, call us and guide us;
when we lose heart, give us hope.
Amen.

Give us peace, O God;
in our waiting, let us not miss the moments as they slip by;
in our longing, let us not forget to appreciate the present.
Living in hope of a future touched by grace,
a gift greater than we can imagine,
let us live out our time
immersed in your goodness, day by day and hour by hour.
Amen.

Holy One,
take away my fear of failure and inadequacy;
soothe the tensions that grip my poor body;
let me breathe deep and feel your power,
let the balm of your love flow through me and change me.
Amen.

A seasonal text

Lead me in your truth, and teach me,
for you are the God of my salvation;
for you I wait all day long.

Psalm 25:5

A suggested quality for personal reflection is *patience.*

Christmas and winter solstice

(for summer solstice please see page 128)

traditional colours: white and gold – or red and green

The journey is over, Mary and Joseph reach Bethlehem and find a place of shelter, poor but safe, and Mary's labour begins. Conditions are far from perfect – we imagine animal-soiled straw for a bed, an innkeeper and an inexperienced husband for midwives, flickering light and smell of olive oil-burning lamps, and cries of pain, yet in the darkness of night a healthy baby is born, a baby who will come to be called the light of the world. The birth is summed up briefly in Luke's Gospel: 'While they were there, the time came for her to deliver her child. And she gave birth to her firstborn son and wrapped him in bands of cloth, and laid him in a manger, because there was no place for them in the inn.' (Luke 2:6-7)

Jesus' birth is traditionally celebrated within days of the winter solstice, the time of year when the nights are at their longest and the days at their shortest, the sun at its weakest. The sun could be seen, figuratively, as ebbing away or dying, to be rejuvenated in the days following, as the light gradually increases. This is a natural time of gathering indoors around a fire with plenty of food, drink, song and story to share. For some, the baby Jesus is represented by the newborn sun as it gradually regains strength after the longest night. For those celebrating at the time of the summer solstice, the full strength of the sun, again, offers a metaphor for the power of God shining in the world.

There are of course other wintertime faith celebrations around this time, characterised by the prominence of lamp, candle, firework and firelight in the darkness, and there is thus much opportunity to communicate with people of other traditions, and learn how the world finds ways to express hope and joy in challenging times. One celebration we know very little about, but which the Venerable Bede referred to in his writings of the history of the British Isles, and which is of interest to a growing number exploring an Earth Spirituality path, is the ancient northern celebration of 'Mother-night' on the same night as Christmas Eve. It was, it seems, a night to honour significant aspects of the feminine divine from pre-Christian traditions, an invitation today, perhaps, to remember all mothers, figurative and literal, expressed especially for Christians in the figure of Mother Mary and her birthing of the Christ child.

Prayers

Enter the imperfection of our lives, Beloved;
come amongst us as the vulnerable one,
the one who invites nothing but kindness and love,
drawing goodness out of us, despite ourselves.
Amen.

A strength you are, to us, O Light,
strength of mind, strength of spirit.
A gift you are to us, O Light,
gift of life, gift of hope.
A joy you are to us, O Light,
joy of newness, joy of delight.
Amen.

A warming fire you are, O God, in the chill of winter,
a comfort you are, O Love, in the coldest night,
a bright flame of hope you are, O Holy One, a growing light,
a joy you are and a ray of sunshine, piercing the gloom.
Thanks be to you for the blessings you bring.
Amen.

Mothering God, you who labour to bring us
    and all creation to life,
nurturing us ceaselessly, from your own self-giving,
we honour you now and always, in your power and goodness,
in your strength and your willingness to endure all
for the sake of undying love, and we honour our own mothers,
the mothers, nurturers, protectors and carers amongst us
and the capacity within each of us for bringing forth
what is good into the world.
So too we honour you for your little one,
the child you bring forth of your own self,
given to the world for the sake of all that is good:
a gift of power, a gift of gentleness and grace.
Amen.

A seasonal text

And suddenly there was with the angel a multitude of the
heavenly host, praising God and saying,
'Glory to God in the highest heaven,
and on earth peace, goodwill among people!'*

Luke 2:13-14

Suggested qualities for personal reflection are *the aspiration
towards peace on earth and goodwill towards all people.*

Epiphany

Epiphany is on 6 January, following the 12 days of Christmas,
and celebrates the arrival of the magi or wise ones who knew of
a special birth by studying the stars and who travelled from their
homeland far to the east, to seek the newborn baby. The magi
are of interest, as people probably coming from the region of

---

* The NRSV has 'on earth peace among those whom he favours' in the main text and 'goodwill among people' as an alternative in the footnotes.

what is now Iran and Iraq, the heart of the old Persian empire, where the influential religion of Zoroastrianism emerged, and also the western approach to astrology. The event is described in Matthew 2:1-12; here is an extract: 'When they saw that the star had stopped, they were overwhelmed with joy. On entering the house, they saw the child with Mary his mother; and they knelt down and paid him homage. Then, opening their treasure-chests, they offered him gifts of gold, frankincense, and myrrh.' (Matthew 2:10-11)

Prayers

Loving God, be a lamp to our feet,
the brightest star in our sky;
guide us to what is of true worth,
and give us courage and diligence to keep searching
until we find for ourselves
that which draws forth our delight and our awe,
the revelation of your presence among us.
Amen.

Holy One,
draw from us true adoration,
in the wonder of your vulnerability,
draw from us true praise,
in the glory of your gentleness,
draw from us true humility,
in the mystery of your helplessness,
draw from us true love,
in the tenderness of your incarnation.
Amen.

A seasonal text

Where is the way to the dwelling of light,
and where is the place of darkness,

that you may take it to its territory
and that you may discern the paths to its home?

Job 38:19-20

A suggested quality for personal reflection is *generosity* – of spirit, time and effort as well as the gifting of 'things', time, hospitality and kindness.

Candlemas, St Brigid and Imbolc (2 February)

traditional colours and symbols: candles and lamps, white, snowdrops, lambs, milk

Jesus, born in a stable, and his young mother Mary, have survived the first, dangerous weeks after birth, and 40 days later, journey on with Joseph to the splendour of the holy temple in Jerusalem, not far from the place of birth. Here, the new family perform their prayers and rituals according to tradition, and receive unexpected blessings from two elders of the temple community, Simeon and Anna, who speak with great tenderness and insight, recognising the child's uniqueness. Candlemas was traditionally a time when the batch of candles made for the year ahead was blessed and can be seen as a time to dedicate new projects, things and commitments, not to mention babies, to God.

In the northern hemisphere, this is the time when ewes begin to give birth, and the first hardy shoots push up through the chilled soil. This makes it a natural time to celebrate the beginnings of new life in the flow of mothers' milk and the first signs of sprouting in the grain fields. For many following an Earth Spirituality path, this time is honoured under the ancient name of Imbolc which relates to the ewes' milk. Some grains are sown in early spring, others in late autumn or early winter, to lie waiting in the earth until conditions are right. The blessing of the ewes' milk and the sprouting grain are connected, for some, in the thriving child Jesus, nursed by his mother. In the wheel of the Earth Spirituality year, Lammastide and the blessing of the first loaf of the harvest falls opposite Imbolc, and may be a more suitable festival to reflect on in the southern hemisphere – see page 130.

For those interested in 'Celtic' Christian tradition, this is also a time to honour St Brigid or Bridget, one of the most cherished of Irish saints, from the sixth century, about whom there are many legends. One story – and it clearly is a story rather than an attempt at historicity, since Brigid lived some 500 years after Jesus – is that Brigid went to the Holy Land to act as midwife and nurse for the holy family, and then led them to the temple with a flaming torch which stayed alight despite the wet and windy weather. There is some permission-giving in this idea, for us to imagine ourselves into the gospel stories – as with Ignatian contemplation – as people long ago imagined their favourite holy woman into the story of the nativity.

Prayers

> Give your blessing to our work, O God,
> may our time and effort be a sacrifice of love,
> for the good of all.
> Amen.

> Candlelit peace we seek, O Source of all Light,
> peace of fire's friendliness,
> peace of warm companionship in your presence,
> peace in your sanctuary, the still centre of refuge in you.
> Peace we seek, O Source of all Light,
> peace in our hearts, peace in our world.
> Amen.

God of all goodness, we give you thanks
for the delights of this time,
and the signs all around us of newness and hope.
Let us not forget our place in creation,
let us not forget the cycles of life on which we depend,
the web of wonder which you weave,
of which we are but a part.
Even now as the first strong shoots push through
    the frosty ground,
and the lambs come, innocent, into the world,
help us to protect new growth, and rejoice in
    springtime's blessings,
allowing new beginnings in our own hearts too.
Amen.

A choice of seasonal texts

Like newborn infants, long for the pure, spiritual milk, so
that by it you may grow into salvation.

1 Peter 2:2

As a mother comforts her child, so I will comfort you.

Isaiah 66:13a

Suggested qualities for personal reflection are *nurturing, supporting
or protecting the vulnerable, and tender compassion.*

The Annunciation (25 March), spring equinox (usually around 22 March) and the beginning of Lent

colours: blue for Mary, white or gold for Gabriel, a lily for Mary, a dove for the Holy Spirit, feathers or light-catchers for angelic presence, contrasts of light and dark colours in balance for the equinox

At this time, we hear how the archangel Gabriel appeared to a young village woman, Mary, with the news that she would become pregnant by the sacred Spirit of God, and bear a child who would be called 'God saves' or Jesus. She is surprised, mystified, but accepts the conception, saying 'let it be'. From this time on, in the story of the Mother, we begin the count of nine months to birth at Christmas.

The Annunciation falls days after the spring equinox, the time at which days and nights are of equal length, moving towards longer days and shorter nights of summertime. This is a significant time for many following an Earth Spirituality path, and some see this as the pre-Christian Eastre or Oestre, which is referred to by the Venerable Bede, as an Anglo-Saxon festival in honour of an aspect of the feminine divine. In the northern hemisphere at this time, spring is now well underway and the daylight hours are lengthening – as in the south they are diminishing and autumn approaching (see autumn equinox on page 132). This lengthening of days is where the English word 'Lent' comes from. It is a time of gladness and hope, appreciating the power of sun and rain to bring forth vital greenery from the earth, although in the days before global food supply, there would still not be a great deal of fresh produce to eat. The preparation time for Easter requires that Lent be a time of soul-searching, fasting, penitence, self-discipline and humble openness to deeper wisdom, a time of austerity amidst the blossoming – yet not necessarily without joy.

Prayers

O Most Holy One, giving breath to all that lives,
inspire us and fill us with a spirit of joy,
that we may grow in love for you and all that you have made,
knowing your presence deep within us
in the intimacy of our inner being.
So, may your love embolden and empower us,
that we may never be ashamed or afraid
of bearing you in the world.
Amen.

Send your messengers of peace, O God,
that we may hear good news and be transformed within,
for we live in a world groaning with pain
and the struggle for justice and mercy weighs down our souls.
Amen.

As the year rolls on, Eternal One,
grant us the wisdom to hold all in balance,
our measures fair and true,
and like the increasing light of this time,
may we err on the side of generosity.
Save us from hasty judgements, O God,
and grant us wisdom to kneel in the light of your truth
that we may witness to your grace in the world.
Amen.

Guide us through this time, O Holy One,
as we walk our narrow path,
ever deeper into the mystery of your self-giving love.
Humble us and help us to simplify our lives,
that we may find all our needs met in you,
our Beloved, our teacher, our guide and our friend.

Amen.
Humble us, Beloved,
as you humbled yourself,
pouring yourself out as a gift to all the earth,
your surrender of life, a sign of hope,
that after brokenness comes healing
and after sorrow comes joy;
after the pain of death comes life
and after fear and doubt comes consolation.
Amen.

A seasonal text

[Jesus] also said, 'The kingdom of God is as if someone would scatter seed on the ground, and would sleep and rise night and day, and the seed would sprout and grow, he does not know how. The earth produces of itself, first the stalk, then the head, then the full grain in the head. But when the grain is ripe, at once he goes in with his sickle, because the harvest has come.'

Mark 4:26-29

Suggested qualities for personal reflection are *wonder and humility.*

Easter
(see comment in the previous section, about the origin of the word)

This most holy time for Christians recalls the accounts of Jesus' last days among his disciples, in the city of Jerusalem. It falls at the time of the Jewish festival of the Passover. Jesus is cruelly executed by the occupying Roman military dictatorship and his disciples enter a bleak and fearful period, suddenly interrupted by women's accounts of seeing Jesus alive. Incredulous at first, the disciples also have experiences which convince them that Jesus has been raised from the dead, transforming their despair into joy. Belief in the resurrection and what this implies about the status of Jesus and the significance of his death is seen by many as the primary distinguishing feature of Christianity.

The time when Easter falls each year is calculated according to the moon's cycle in relation to the spring equinox. In biblical lands, this is a time when some crops are already ready for harvest; Passover celebrates the start of the barley harvest as well as the freeing of the Hebrew people from oppression in Ancient Egypt. For some, it is significant that Jesus is 'cut down' at the time of the barley harvest, and that in the Gospels Jesus talks of the need to die like a grain of wheat, in order to gain new life (John 12:24-26).[15]

Prayers

Self-giving one, your love knows no bounds
and we stand in awe of your willingness to suffer
that we may have abundant life.
Help us to understand what your sacrifice means
for us and for the world,
and break open the closed stone tombs of our hearts,
that we may be free of the fear of death.
Amen.

Holy One, lift us up and shine into our lives,
touching us and enlivening us at the heart of our being,
that we may find reason to rejoice, reason to love,
reason to live with courage and hope,
finding your transforming presence wherever we go.
Amen.

---

[15] I explore this idea in more depth in my earlier book, *Who do you say that I am?: a Lenten journey into the world of Jesus* (Kevin Mayhew, 2013).

A choice of seasonal texts

> But for you who revere my name the sun of righteousness shall rise, with healing in its wings. You shall go out leaping like calves from the stall.
>
> *Malachi 4:2*

> Set me as a seal upon your heart,
>   as a seal upon your arm;
> for love is strong as death,
>   passion fierce as the grave.
> Its flashes are flashes of fire,
>   a raging flame.
> Many waters cannot quench love,
>   neither can floods drown it.
> If one offered for love
>   all the wealth of one's house,
>   it would be utterly scorned.
>
> *Song of Songs 8:6-7*

Suggested qualities for personal reflection are *love, hope and joy*.

Pentecost and later springtime (or the onset of winter)

Fifty days after Easter, according to the Acts of the Apostles, Mother Mary and the followers of Jesus are gathered in a room, when they experience a powerful force like fire or rushing water, around and within them, lighting up their hearts. They feel this is the gift of the Holy Spirit, a gift of the risen Jesus, and it gives them a compulsion to speak about Jesus in public, with such animation that people wonder what has come over them. Curiously, the multi-cultural crowd of Jerusalem can understand what they say, in their own languages.

Some in the church have come to focus on Mother Mary at around this time, especially in the month of May. According to Luke, following the annunciation by the angel Gabriel, she visits her older cousin Elizabeth at this time, who is also pregnant. This is a meeting of two holy and empowered women, who recognise the spiritual significance of their shared condition and support one another. This can provide a focus for women's groups, working on peace issues, mutual support and self-development. The song of praise Mary sings echoes the words of Hannah, a woman reaching far back in the people's history (1 Samuel 1–2), and so this time draws together the maternal ancestors, the young maiden and the mature or older woman.

Pentecost, also a Jewish festival, for Christians is linked directly to the date of Easter. It always occurs in later springtime in the northern hemisphere, a natural time of exuberance and fecundity, as more food becomes available, energy levels are higher and the desire to procreate – or just to enjoy the sensuality and joy of intimacy – warms the blood. Ancient pastoral festivals at this time celebrated moving the livestock to pastures, out of the by now stinking barns. A festival at this time, enjoying a revival or re-creation in many Earth Spirituality traditions, is known as Beltane. Fresh air, pungent, cleansing fires, journeys up the hillsides driving the flocks, outdoor camps and a loosening up, a greater freedom for young couples to find some privacy among the blossom-laden thickets, all make it a naturally feisty time. In the southern hemisphere, the corresponding Earth Spirituality festival at this time is Samhain, and the onset of winter, a time of testing, reflected in the endurance required by women facing birth (see page 134).

Prayers

Most wise, kindly mothering God,
thank you for the support we can give one another.

Teach us to be of genuine help as we seek to listen
    and to walk alongside,
to wonder at our common ground and tread gently
    over our differences.
Guide us towards what is constructive and life-enhancing,
what is merciful yet honest, peaceful but strong,
allowing us to be true to ourselves while finding the strength
to be who we need to be, for those we love.
Amen.

O most Holy One,
power of rushing wind
and flickering flame,
speak to us, breathe through us,
enlighten and enliven us
that all may know us changed
by the joy in our eyes,
the love in our deeds,
the wisdom in our words.
Amen.

Loving God,
all that you made is good
so may springtime exuberance
lift our spirits, that we may dance and sing,
free of the constraints that diminish our lives,
free of the voices that hold us back,
that we may love all with confidence
and find our true fulfilment in our love of you
and your delight in us.
Amen.

A seasonal text

> My beloved speaks and says to me:
> 'Arise, my love, my fair one,
>   and come away;
> for now the winter is past,
>   the rain is over and gone.
> The flowers appear on the earth;
>   the time of singing has come,
> and the voice of the turtle-dove
>   is heard in our land.'
>
> *Song of Songs 2:10-12*

A suggested quality for personal reflection is *delight*.

St John the Baptist (24 June) and summer solstice (approximately 21 June) (or midwinter in the southern hemisphere)

This is a celebration of the birth of John the Baptist, to Elizabeth and her priestly husband Zechariah. Elizabeth is said to be a cousin to Mary, and her pregnancy is seen as miraculous since she is an older woman. Zechariah was informed that this would happen in a vision, while serving in the temple. John is described as a cousin of Jesus and a respected prophet in his own right, calling people to change their ways and be baptised into a new way of life of justice and integrity. When they are both adult, John baptises Jesus in the river Jordan and acclaims him as the 'lamb of God'. This prominent birth falls six months away from the birth of Jesus.

Just as Christmas falls at the time of the winter solstice (in the northern hemisphere), the birth of John the Baptist falls just after the summer solstice – the time at which the sun is at maximum strength, days are at their longest and nights shortest.

Midsummer is a natural time to celebrate outdoors with fairs, feasting and ritual, and there are many ancient traditions concerning the solar cycle, the power of the 'hero' or deity represented by or identified with the sun, and from that point on, his (often male) gradual demise. While it is a joyous time, it is bittersweet, as from this point on, the journey back into wintertime has begun. In some traditions, there is conflict between a hero of the light half of the year, and another (or anti-hero) of the dark half, an expression of the balance between light and dark – but not necessarily the popularly associated dualism of good and evil. While in the Christian tradition, John yields to Jesus with great grace and without competition, the celebration of John's birth, as with that of Jesus, is tinged by the knowledge of his violent death at the hands of a tyrant (Mark 6:14-29). A wintertime celebration of John the Baptist might focus on his asceticism or the bleakness of his role as a lone voice crying out in the desert.

Prayers

The full might of your power, O God, who could withstand?
Teach us humility to stand before you with reverence,
confessing our own weakness and limitation
in the face of your supreme glory.
Touch us with the depth and breadth and full reach
    of your love,
stop us in our tracks, fill us with awe
that we may witness to your wonder in the world.
Amen.

The world around us, O God, is full of conflicting powers;
it can be hard for us to see you here at all.
Give us wisdom to recognise the tracks of your passing,
the scent of your presence,

the sound of your call,
that we may know you and follow you,
our true love, now and always.
Amen.

A seasonal text

By the tender mercy of our God,
the dawn from on high will break upon us,
to give light to those who sit in darkness
and in the shadow of death
to guide our feet into the way of peace.

Luke 1:78-79

Suggested qualities for personal reflection are *justice and integrity.*

Lammastide: 1 August

At this time, it was traditional to gather the first sheaf of corn and make it into bread, which was blessed and shared as the first loaf of the season: the loaf-mass. Some Christians still practise this rite today. There are many medieval folk legends associating Mary with the ripening grain; her presence passing by cornfields was said to hasten their development. There are also traditions concerning the cutting of the corn, which connect European Christians with Jesus' death, in a way that makes regional sense – the significance of the Mediterranean harvest at Easter time is missed for those who are still watching green blades growing.

There is an older northern hemisphere festival at this time, also celebrating the summer's abundance, and the continuing vitality of the light, which is of importance to some following an Earth Spirituality path. This is sometimes called Lughnasadh.

In the southern hemisphere, the corresponding Earth Spirituality festival at this time is Imbolc and the emergence of spring (see page 118).

Prayers

God of rainfall and sunshine and the ripening grain,
God of fleeing hares and harvest mice,
of pollinating bees and hedgerow flowers,
and of labouring teams at work all day;
bless the fields and bless the grain,
bless this bread and all who eat it.
Let none we know go hungry today,
and may all be welcome here at our table.
So break open our hearts with the broken bread
and may the harvest to come bring gladness to all.
Amen.

Holy One, reveal your love
in flour and yeast and kneaded dough,
your reign in the hands of she who grinds the grain.
Amen.

Seasonal text

And again [Jesus] said, 'To what should I compare the Kingdom of God? It is like yeast that a woman took and mixed in with three measures of flour until all of it was leavened.'

Luke 13:20-21

A suggested quality for personal reflection is *trust*.

St Michael (29 September) and the autumn equinox (usually around 21 September)

The archangel Michael was seen by many in times past as the most important of all angels, chief of the angelic host – a powerful mustering of warrior angels – but also the psychopomp, that is, the one with care over souls in sleep and in the journey through death. Michael protected the souls of the faithful and brought them to heaven. There is a treasury of prayers to St Michael, seeking his guardianship, especially among the people of the Scottish highlands, among whom the celebration of the day involved complex and rich traditions, including the gifting of carrots to one another, and the visiting of ancestral burial grounds.[16]

This festival comes close to the autumn equinox, which some now call Mabon, a time when once again dark and light are in balance and signs of autumn are evident. It makes sense to invoke a guardian angel or spirit at this time, facing the onset of winter and the need to prepare food, warm clothing and safe shelter. This time falls around the period in which many now celebrate the close of the harvest, the abundance and generosity of the earth and the huge human expenditure of labour, in order to survive the year ahead. It is thus a natural time of thanksgiving and rest, but also of the need for wisdom and experience in planning ahead.

In the southern hemisphere, St Michael's festival falls close to the spring equinox and the increase in light. Michael is associated with restoration to wholeness and the triumph of good over evil, the name meaning 'who is like God?' – themes which might be appropriate for springtime reflection.

---

[16] See Alexander Carmichael, *Carmina Gadelica Vol. I & II: Hymns and Incantations* (Forgotten Books, 2007).

Prayers

Loving God,
we thank you for the glorious abundance of the earth,
and we thank you for all that we receive;
help us to be honest stewards of your goodness
and diligent caretakers of your world,
that all may be fed and none go hungry,
all may know justice and none be exploited,
all land be respected and none desecrated
by our greed and self-interest,
by our negligence and ignorance,
for which, O God, we seek your forgiveness
and your guiding wisdom.
Amen.

Each night as we settle to sleep, loving God,
cradle us in your infinite arms,
hide us safe in the shadow of your wings.
And as we enter our final sleep,
so too, watch over us and guard our souls;
bear us gently to your eternal love,
all fear and pain washed away.
Amen.

A seasonal text

And now, our God, we give thanks to you and praise your
glorious name. But who am I, and what is my people, that
we should be able to make this freewill-offering? For all
things come from you, and of your own have we given you.
1 Chronicles 29:13-14

A suggested quality for reflection at this time is *gratitude.*

All Saints and All Souls days (1 and 2 November), Samhain or All Hallows Eve: 31 October

At this time, it has become traditional in the Church to honour the souls of the faithful holy ones who have died (all saints) and also the souls of loved ones, people in family and community who have died (all souls). It is a respectful weekend, sometimes sombre, for many, an opportunity to reflect on their own mortality and to perform rituals of loving remembrance.

For many following an Earth Spirituality path, this is a significant time known as Samhain or Halloween (All Hallows' Eve), a northern hemisphere time of mystery and mischief, when the veil between this world and the 'other' or the next world is, or was said to be, at its thinnest. For many, this marked – or marks – the end of the year. There is an element of topsy-turvy role reversal and confusion on this night, and various traditions in which people would celebrate a degree of licence to behave differently, even wildly, and in which the spirit world was and is respected, honoured and/or treated with due caution. It was also a bonfire time, or bone-fire perhaps, when unusable parts of animals slaughtered to provide winter meat were destroyed. That some animals were butchered before the winter was often a necessity, with limited fodder and indoor space, suggesting also an opportunity for a feast around the fire and ritual associated with blood and death of livestock – a thanksgiving for dependence on domestic creatures of the community.

The corresponding festival for the southern hemisphere, according to Earth Spirituality tradition, is Beltane, the mid-spring festival – see page 126.

Prayers

At this most solemn time, O God, we hold in our hearts the memories of our loved ones who are no longer with us. We live in hope that they are held as always in your undying love, and pray for their peace. We ask for them whatever is best, whatever is most loving, according to your wisdom, O most merciful One. Amen.

Holy One,
touch us with the mystery of this time,
and draw close to us,
the veils between us gently lifted;
shelter us from mischief
and let love melt our fears
as we contemplate your greater mystery,
our souls entrusted to your everlasting care.
Amen.

A seasonal text

Your dead shall live, their corpses shall rise.
O dwellers in the dust, awake and sing for joy!
For your dew is a radiant dew,
and the earth will give birth to those long dead.

Isaiah 26:19

A suggested quality for personal reflection is *peace*.

This brings us to the close of the 'Seasons' section. We can now go on to the days of the week.

135

Days of the Week

The days of the week have themes based mainly on the traditional order of creation as described in Genesis. This allows a daily focus on aspects of the natural world and helps us to remember our embeddedness in the great web of life. I have also provided information on the names of the days of the week which may be of interest – it is an interesting fact that in the English language, and indeed in many other languages, we still have names for the days of the week relating to pre-Christian deities and celestial bodies. We can of course choose to ignore this – a name is just a name – but since both are of interest to many today exploring an Earth Spirituality path, we can also explore potential in the names for meaningful reflection. For each day, I have suggested relevant texts to look up for personal reflection.

Sunday

The first day of the week is the day in which God (according to Genesis) creates light in the watery, primal darkness. In Christian tradition it is a weekly celebration of Christ's resurrection. In English, this day is named after the sun, provider of all our energy, without which there would be no life on earth, and for many (including the psalmist) a symbol of God.

> Source of Light, dwelling in deep darkness,
> make your home in my heart,
> like a bird in a nest,
> free to go out and come in,
> working your goodness in the world,
> your calming of chaos, your offering of hope,

your life-giving breath.
Amen.

Texts for reflection

1 Kings 8:12 – God chooses to live in darkness

Genesis 1:1-5 – the first day, primal darkness, first light

John 12:35-36 – walking while we have the light

James 1:17 – 'Father' of lights, that is, the inseparable source, origin and will for light

Psalm 139:12 – to God, dark and light are alike

Psalm 84:11 – God is a sun and shield

Monday

Monday, the second day, is the day in which the atmosphere, clouds, rain and the water cycle are said to have come into being, according to Genesis – but not water itself, which, as we read in verses 1-3, existed already. The English name for this day relates to the moon, second most prominent of the celestial bodies, with its monthly orbit around the earth. The moon, as the Venerable Bede worked out, exerts a gravitational pull on the earth's expanses of water, controlling the rhythm of the tides. People have long observed that the moon also exerts an influence on the behaviour of living things, and some say on our own moods too. There are several prayers and liturgies reflecting on the moon elsewhere in this book, so the prayer provided here focuses on the atmosphere and water cycle.

> O Holy One, with a voice as subtle as rain on grass,
> and as mighty as rumbling thunder,
> breathe through us, as the air we breathe,
> flow through us, as a surging river,

that we may be emptied of all that obstructs you,
to be channels of your power in the world.
Amen.

Texts for reflection

Genesis 1:6-8 – creation of the sky: atmosphere, clouds and rain

Psalms 68:4; 104:3 – God, the rider on the clouds (this was also an attribute of the rival Canaanite deity, Baal, associated with weather and fertility)

Deuteronomy 11:10-12 – a land watered by God

Job 37:1-5 – God thunders

Matthew 5:45 – God makes sun shine and rain fall on good and bad alike

Matthew 16:2-3 – you understand what a red sky means, but not the signs of the times

John 4:13-15 – a spring of water welling up to eternal life

Revelation 22:17 – an invitation to the thirsty to drink

Psalm 42:1 – a deer longs for flowing streams

Tuesday

On the third day, Genesis describes God's drawing together of the seas, emergence of land and all kinds of vegetation. The name 'Tuesday' derives from a pre-Christian hero-deity of the Germanic traditions, Tiw, or Tyr, and came to us through the Anglo-Saxons who settled in the British Isles. (In other languages, it is more common for the third day to be named after the planet Mars, classically associated with a male warrior deity.)

Gardener God,
let the seeds of our potential unfurl by your tender touch,

to blossom and bear good fruit in the world,
pruned vines from an ancient root, and trained in love,
to honour the green earth and the miracle of life.
Amen.

Texts for reflection

Genesis 1:9-13 – the creation of sea, land and vegetation

Ezekiel 31:8-9 – cedar trees in the garden of God

Psalm 52:8 – the worshipper is an olive tree in the temple grounds

Jeremiah 17:7-8 – the faithful one is like a tree by a river

Ezekiel 47:6-12 and Revelation 22:2 – trees of healing along the river of life

Genesis 2:9 – another creation account, of a beautiful garden, Eden

Song of Songs 2:1-15 – the delights of nature

Mark 4:1-9 – the parable of the sower, one of many references to the grain cycle by Jesus in the Gospels

Luke 12:22-31 – Jesus' advice on not worrying, with nature as an illustration

John 15:1-11 – God the gardener, Jesus the vine, his followers the branches

Romans 11:17-24 – Christians are a wild olive branch grafted onto a tree with a 'rich root' in Judaism

Wednesday

On the fourth day, according to Genesis, God created the celestial lights: sun and moon, stars and planets. They were to give light, to distinguish between day and night and 'for signs and for seasons, for days and for years' (Genesis 1:14) – signs for interpretation and for measuring the passage of time. In biblical times and regions, as throughout much of European history, studying the stars was a recognised science, illustrated in the account of the magi who learned of the birth of Jesus through observing a star. In many languages, this day is named after the planet (and classical deity) Mercury, a messenger, perhaps not unlike some aspects of a biblical angel, skilled in poetry and music. In English, the name comes from Woden, the Anglo-Saxon version of Odin, a Norse deity associated, among his more benign traits, with wisdom, poetry and the origin of a form of writing.

> Eternal One,
> whose starry skies proclaim
> the wonder of your mysteries,
> deepen our insight, sharpen our vision,
> that finding meaning in your universe beyond,
> we may find too, your wisdom deep within.
> Amen.

Texts for reflection

Matthew 2:1-12 – the star of Jesus' nativity

Genesis 1:14-19 – creation of the celestial bodies

Genesis 15:1-6 – Abram's descendants as numerous as the stars

Genesis 37:9-11 – Joseph's dream of sun and stars

Psalm 8:3-4 – the wonder of the heavens

Psalm 104:19 – the moon and sun

Thursday

On the fifth day of the week, God is said to have called all the creatures of sea and air into being, telling them to 'be fruitful and multiply'. The day is named after thunder or the old Norse deity associated with thunder, Thor. In other languages the name of the fifth day is often associated with the planet and classical deity Jupiter.

> Holy One,
> you who know every sparrow
> and every fish in every shoal,
> you whose wide wings give shelter,
> who subdues the greatest monsters of the deep,
> let me rest in your shade,
> you who know me through and through;
> let me be content in you,
> as a bird in the air, a fish in the sea.
> Amen.

Texts for reflection

Genesis 1:20-23 – creatures of sea and air

Mark 1:9-11 – the Spirit came down like a dove

Matthew 6:26 – birds of the air fed by God

Matthew 10:29-31 – God knows when even sparrows fall

John 21:6 – Jesus knows where to catch fish

Psalm 8:8 – birds of the air, fish of the sea

Psalm 50:11 – God knows all the birds of the air

Ezekiel 47:6-12 – many fish and water birds in the river of life

Psalm 91:4 – refuge under God's wings

Friday

On the sixth day, according to Genesis, God created land animals of every kind, including human beings who, male and female, were made in the 'image of God'. The name of this day, Friday, comes from the Norse female deity Frige, but other languages equate the day with another feminine aspect of the divine and related planet, Venus, often associated with love and fertility. Sometimes this planet is known as the morning star, the day star and the evening star. Venus is often to be seen close to the moon.

> Loving God,
> whose concern reaches out to all your creatures,
> teach me to live gently and with regard for all life,
> knowing each belongs to you.
> Give me a compassionate heart
> and a will to tread lightly on this earth,
> harming none, now and always.
> Amen.

Texts for reflection

Matthew 10:16 – Jesus uses the qualities of animals to send his disciples out

Mark 1:12-13 – Jesus is in the desert with wild animals

Genesis 1:24-31 – the creation of land animals including human beings

Psalm 8 – humans in relation to wider creation

Psalm 104 – the wonder of the natural world in relation to God

Psalm 50:9-15 – all the wild creatures are known to God and belong to God

Numbers 22:22-35 – a donkey defended by an angel is given voice

Job 39 – wonders and mysteries of the animal world

Daniel 4:28-33 – the humbling of Nebuchadnezzar

Saturday

The seventh day of the week is, according to Genesis, the day on which God rested from creating the universe and, as a reflection of this holy rest, the children of Israel are also to rest, along with all who work for them, including animals. This came to be called the Sabbath (in ancient times a moon observance), and is still practised in Judaism. Many Christians too choose to respect this as a day of rest although others transfer this to Sunday.

The name for this last day of the week comes from the planet Saturn and classical deity of the same name, in keeping with many other languages.

> Holy One, who calls us to pause and take our rest in you,
> free us for a while from the pressure to be productive,
> and let us find simple joy in your presence,
> delighting that you come to us and dwell amongst us
> as our most dearly beloved.
> Amen.

Texts for reflection

Exodus 20:8-10 – the commandments on keeping the Sabbath day holy

Isaiah 56:1-8 – blessings on those who keep the Sabbath

Amos 8:5 – abuse of the Sabbath for profit

Matthew 12:1-14 – two well known and controversial incidents on the Sabbath, when Jesus justifies picking heads of grain to eat and healing a man's hand

Mark 15:42–16:1 – Jesus' women followers observe the Sabbath before going to anoint his body

Acts 16:13 – spreading the good news to women on the Sabbath

Time of day

balance of activity and rest, engagement with the world

In the monastic tradition of Christianity, praying through the hours of the day and night in a continuous cycle is important. The bulk of prayers come from working through the psalms, of which there are 150, and this in turn derives from Jewish tradition, as the psalms were compiled for temple worship long ago and are still an important part of synagogue worship. There are psalm-inspired prayers in the Prayer Bank, for you to choose those most appropriate for your needs. In this section I have also provided a short prayer for each of the hours. For more information on the significance of the hours, see another of my books, *Search me and Know me*.

Midnight

Text for reflection

> My soul is satisfied as with a rich feast,
>   and my mouth praises you with joyful lips
> when I think of you on my bed,
>   and meditate on you in the watches of the night;
> for you have been my help,
>   and in the shadow of your wings I sing for joy.
>   *Psalm 63:5-7*

Eternal One,
for whom day and night are both alike,
open my eyes and ears, my heart and mind,
that I and all your creatures may pause to sense your presence

here among us, now and always,
and in you find our consolation.
Amen.

The small hours, 3am

Text for reflection

My soul waits for the Eternal One*
more than those who watch for the morning,
more than those who watch for the morning.

Psalm 130:6

Ever-watching One,
be with me now and with all whom you love,
whether waking or sleeping, far or near;
be with us as a guardian, attentive through the night,
that we may know ourselves safe,
and rest in our belovedness.
Amen.

Early light, 6am

Text for reflection

Arise, shine; for your light has come,
and the glory of the Eternal One* has risen upon you.

Isaiah 60:1

Glorious God, who warms and gladdens the world,
let us each grow in your light,
our potential unfurling ever more fully,
blessed by the rays of your all-inclusive love.
Amen .

---

* 'the Lord' in NRSV

Morning, 9am

Text for reflection

So, whether you eat or drink, or whatever you do, do
everything for the glory of God.

1 Corinthians 10:31

Creative God, who constantly pours forth the wonders
　　of your works,
inspire us, enthuse us and energise us
as we set about our daily life,
and give us hope that what we do builds up
　　the common good,
and makes the world a better place.
Amen.

Midday, 12 noon

Text for reflection

Yours is the day, yours also the night;
you established the luminaries and the sun.
You have fixed all the bounds of the earth;
you made summer and winter.

Psalm 74:16-17

O God, our Sun and Shield,
origin and purpose of all,
let us find you in all we encounter,
for you fill heaven and earth
and there is nowhere we can hide from your love.
Amen.

Afternoon, 3pm

Text for reflection

A new heart I will give you, and a new spirit I will put
within you; and I will remove from your body the heart
of stone and give you a heart of flesh.

Ezekiel 36:26

Beloved, self-giving one,
pouring yourself out ceaselessly that we may live,
break open our hard hearts and closed minds
that we may find reason to love,
and to let your generosity flow through us.
Amen.

Evening, 6pm

Text for reflection

Do you not know that you are God's temple and that
God's Spirit dwells in you?

1 Corinthians 3:16

Holy One, beyond, around and within us,
remind us of the sanctity of what you have made,
the world in its goodness
and our own selves, temples to your Spirit,
and let us honour you in every way.
Amen.

Night-time, 9pm

Text for reflection

Ask, and it will be given to you; search, and you will find;
knock, and the door will be opened for you. For everyone

who asks receives, and everyone who searches finds, and
for everyone who knocks, the door will be opened.

Matthew 7:7

God of peace and true wisdom,
calm us and free us from the burdens of the day,
that we may find our rest in you,
fully known and fully loved in all our unique unfinishedness.
Amen.

Moon phases, feelings, moods, intuitions, self-awareness

The moon is an ancient way of measuring the passing of time, as it moves through its monthly cycle from thin newness to fullness, shrinking back until there is nothing to be seen. The moon has an influence on the earth's seas and oceans, and is often associated with the fluidity of our emotional lives. In this section, each lunar phase has a prayer reflecting the stage in the cycle itself – a time of growth or fullness, decline or absence – and also a prayer exploring how this can help us reflect on our inner feelings. There are further prayers and liturgies concerning the moon, later in the book.

Dark moon

In times of darkness, we remember you, O God,
and we wait with as much patience as we are blessed with,
for clarity to return.
Give us courage and hope,
endurance and peace of mind,
for when we feel far from you, fears creep closer.
Though we cannot see the way,
all is known to you.
Though we cannot know what lies beyond us,
all is held in your love.
So let us learn to trust, by day and by night,
longing for an end to the feeling of absence,
longing to rediscover love's embrace.
Amen.

or

Let this be a sacred time, O God,
for me to look within,
to learn to see myself as you see me,
to understand myself more deeply;
that your wisdom may guide me,
and spread peace in the world.

New moon

In times of new beginnings we remember you, O God;
bless our times of celebration,
our times of brightness and gladness,
togetherness and connection with those we hold dear,
whether far or near.
Help us work for reconciliation, and mutual respect,
that peace may reign supreme
at your great feast.
Amen.

or

Let this be a sacred time, O God,
for me to celebrate renewal,
letting go of the past,
stepping into the present moment
in peace and hope.
Amen.

Waxing (growing) moon

In times of increase we remember you, O God,
asking your blessing that all will go well,
help us play our part with patience,

directing our effort where it is most helpful,
not just for ourselves but for the common good.
Amen.

or

Let this be a sacred time, O God,
in which I let what has begun, gradually grow,
finding within me the patience and trust
that allows me to tend my concerns with wisdom.
Amen.

Full moon

In times of full intensity we remember you, O God,
giving thanks for your blessings of abundance and fruition.
Inspired by your mystery, and strengthened by your goodness,
may we reflect your light, as the moon reflects the sun.
Amen.

or

Let this be a sacred time, O God,
in which I recognise what power I have,
and use it well.
May your enchanting presence influence my very being,
as the moon draws the tides
and the creatures of the sea.
Amen.

Waning (decreasing) moon

In times of decrease we remember you, O God.
With the ebb and the flow, we recognise the timeliness
of letting go, of fading light and gentler power,

of natural, gradual closure and times of withdrawal,
blessed by your grace and held in your peace.
Amen.

or

Let this be a sacred time, O God,
in which I can let go of the past
and all that is not needed,
and be at peace,
knowing that emptiness makes way for fullness.
Amen.

Creating a personal Daily Prayer routine

Building up a pattern of daily prayer can help us in our spiritual journey, day by day. The contents of the Prayer Bank can be woven together in myriad ways, to suit personal preference. Here are some possibilities:

- I pray at 6am and 6pm every day, using the prayers for those hours.

- I am busy and work irregular hours. I turn to the prayer for whatever the nearest 'holy hour' is, when I have time to sit in peace for 10 minutes.

- I often sleep poorly and particularly like the 3am prayer along with the day of the week with its scripture readings. Reflecting on these sometimes helps me get back to sleep.

- I cannot get to church on Sundays but do a full prayer of everything for the day: natural and church seasons, time, day, moon . . . and I have my own altar which I decorate with a coloured candle.

- I take my book outdoors and reflect on the moon 'mood' prayer each week in my quiet place.

- I say the blessing for the season and the prayer for the day every morning, and before I go to bed I pray the 'Divine Praise' or say the Statement of Hope.

- We do the full liturgy for the day whenever one of us has a birthday.

- It is traditional to use the Benedictus in the morning and the Magnificat in the evening so I have followed that pattern, using the equivalents in the Prayer Bank.

Three times a day

There are many patterns of daily prayer: every three hours, morning and evening, three times a day . . . each with a historical precedent. We can adopt any model that suits us and helps us to develop a rhythm of prayer and a sense of continuity, working towards Paul's admonition to 'pray without ceasing' (1 Thessalonians 5:16-18). Here, I offer structure for three times a day, reflecting the practice of Daniel, a Jew living in exile in Babylon, who rises to prominence but remains loyal to the God of his people, despite pressure to abandon the faith.

> Although Daniel knew that the document had been signed, he continued to go to his house, which had windows in its upper room open towards Jerusalem, and to get down on his knees three times a day to pray to his God and praise him, just as he had done previously. The conspirators came and found Daniel praying and seeking mercy before his God.
>
> *Daniel 6:10-11*

Evening prayer

The evening is a time for quiet reflection. Isaac was walking in the fields in the evening, when he saw the camel caravan bringing Rebekah, who had left all she knew to marry Isaac (Genesis 24:10-32). God came to the garden of Eden to walk in the cool of the evening, with the first couple (Genesis 3:8). After a day of teaching, Jesus sends his followers away so that he can pray alone on the mountainside (Matthew 14:23). Temple worship included an evening sacrifice (Psalm 141:2) and the Christian tradition has long had evening liturgies such as Compline, a gentle candlelit service before retiring. For some, the close of day is time to reflect on the day, using a prayerful structure such as the 'Examen'; for others, silent meditation is more helpful. In Jewish practice, the new day begins in the evening at sunset; in

Roman practice, the new day begins at midnight. In honour of Daniel and his courage to pray under persecution, I am beginning with the evening.

This evening prayer is best practised when the day is over, to allow closure on the many things that stimulate our restless minds. I have used normal and bold type to indicate leader and response, but of course the prayer is also suitable for individual use.

Opening:

I will lie down and sleep in peace;
for in your loving presence, O Holy One, my soul is safe.
Return, O my soul, to your rest,
for God* has dealt bountifully with you.
(based on Psalms 4:8 and 116:7)

Choose appropriate prayers from the Holy Hours and Days section of the Prayer Bank, depending on time, season, day of week, phase of moon, including:

Prayer for 9pm

God of peace and true wisdom,
calm us and free us from the burdens of the day,
that we may find our rest in you,
fully known and fully loved in all our unique unfinishedness.
Amen.

God's Comforting Wings (inspired by Psalm 91)

You who live in the shelter of the Most High,
who dwell in the shadow of the mountainous One,
will say to God, 'My refuge and my protection;
my God in whom I trust.

---

* 'the Lord' in NRSV

For you set me free from fears that ensnare me;
you soothe me in time of sickness;
you cover me as a bird spreads her wings over her little ones,
and amongst the feathers of your care I find comfort.

Night-time holds no fears for me,
and through the day, the arrows of trouble glance off me,
for your love is my shield.

I see turmoil all around,
all creation groans under her oppression,
yet I trust that your love is stronger than death,
you show us a path of life.

I have made you my refuge, O Holy One,
and to you I turn.
Send messengers of your love, O God;
let my soul be awake always to the vision of your glory
and to words of truth;

may your angels lift me up when I fall,
and guide me when I am lost,
may they show me always the wisdom path
which leads to peace,
the humble path of the Beloved.
Amen.

Prayer:

Beloved, thank you for being with me today.
For the things I may have said which caused harm, please
forgive me and teach me wisdom.
For the things I may have done which caused harm, please
forgive me and teach me ways to bring healing.

For anything I may have thought which caused me to stray from your way, forgive me and guide me back.

If I have taken for granted the many sacrifices of others for my sake, please forgive me and teach me gratitude.

If I have exploited others, and your beautiful creation, for my own ends, please forgive me and teach me gentleness.

If I have let fear or anger or self-interest govern me, instead of love, please forgive me and let my love grow stronger.

If I have let doubts and worries weigh me down, please forgive me and give me trust, hope and joy.

If I have been complacent in the face of injustices, staying silent when the voiceless needed a friend, please forgive me and give me courage.

If I have let myself down through my own weakness, please forgive me and teach me self-discipline.

All my weakness, my ignorance and my foolishness is known to you, Beloved, who know me better than I know myself. Let me rest in the knowledge that, knowing me, you also love me and patiently wait for me.

So, Beloved, let the light of your love glow warm and strong within me;
let the light of your love glow warm and strong around me;
let the light of your love glow warm and strong around all I love, especially . . . [names];
let the light of your love glow warm and strong in this place;
let the light of your love glow warm and strong in all the earth, now and always.
Amen.

Option: *include the 'Exultation', from the Prayer Bank*

A short visualisation, stilling the mind (choice of three)

In a time of quiet, imagine yourself as a candle (see the fire liturgy) shielded by a glass lantern.

Imagine your flame burning steadily and your light shining in the darkness.

Imagine your thoughts as they come up, as moths, attracted by the light. They come near but cannot reach the flame or disturb it. The glass protects them, but also protects the steady burning of the flame. See each thought-moth come and fly away back into the night, until there is only the stillness of the night, and the gentle light of yourself, the lantern.

or

Imagine a clear garden pool with lilies and fish. This is your mind.

See the fish swimming peacefully, almost silently gliding through the water.

See the lilies resting on the surface, their stems and roots reaching down to the bottom of the pool.

Imagine a child at the side of the pool, feeding the fish, throwing little pellets of bread, one by one. These pellets are your thoughts.

See the fish surging up to eat the food; they take the pellets, one by one.

After a time, the child tires of feeding the fish. The fish go back to gliding calmly through the water.

The pool is calm and beautiful.

or

Imagine you are in a warm and pleasant cave or hut, feeling safe and sheltered from the elements.

See your thoughts as they come up, as little birds flying in and out through an opening – swallows, doves or sparrows perhaps – tending a nest or perching to shelter.

As they calm down and gradually stop flying about, you are left in peace in the quiet of your cave.

(You may fall asleep while doing this visualisation, which of course is fine!)

A choice of closing texts:

> Jesus said, 'Peace I leave with you; my peace I give to you. I do not give to you as the world gives. Do not let your hearts be troubled, and do not let them be afraid.'
>
> *John 14:27*

or

> Ask, and it will be given to you; search, and you will find; knock, and the door will be opened for you. For everyone who asks receives, and everyone who searches finds, and for everyone who knocks, the door will be opened.
>
> *Matthew 7:7-8*

or

> Be still and know that I am God!
>
> *Psalm 46:10*

Close with the 'Going in Peace', either inspired by Simeon or Anna, or with the 'Glory'.

Holy One, now, you let me go in peace,
according to your word.
For I have seen a sign of hope,
the promise of your help,
which you have prepared for all to see:
a revelatory light to the nations,
the children of Israel's glory.

or

Praise to God Most High,
maker of heaven and earth,
who remembers us with compassion,
as a mother remembers her own children;
for a child has been born for us,
a new hope given to us:
wonderful counsellor, potentate of peace.

and/or

Glory to the One who brings all to birth
and to love's embodiment
and to the sacred breath of life,
primal, present and eternal.
Amen.

**As I sleep, my Beloved, cradle me in your infinite arms
and weave your miracles of transformation in my soul,
that I may find rest and peace
and wake strengthened to live your love in the world.
Amen.**

Morning prayer

This prayer is quite short, recognising that many of us need to get up and get on with the day, but wish to do so having dedicated it to God. To extend it, spend any amount of time on personal prayer and choose from the Prayer Bank. It is traditional, for example, to say the Benedictus (Luke 1:67-79) in the morning.

In preparation, make a set of nine or more cards or pebbles with the fruits of the Holy Spirit (qualities listed in Galatians 5:22-23) (see below), one written on each. Add or substitute other qualities if you wish, such as wisdom, humility, courage and grace, and add to the collection of cards when you think of new words.

Opening:

Holy One,
Let me hear of your steadfast love in the morning,
for in you I put my trust.
Teach me the way I should go,
for to you I lift up my soul.

Psalm 143:8

Choose appropriate prayers from the Holy Hours and Days section of the Prayer Bank, depending on time, season, day of week, phase of moon, including:

Prayer of early light, 6am

Arise, shine; for your light has come,
and the glory of the Eternal One* has risen upon you.

Isaiah 60:1

---

* 'the Lord' in NRSV

Glorious God, who warms and gladdens the world,
let us each grow in your light,
our potential unfurling ever more fully,
blessed by the rays of your all-inclusive love.
Amen.

May all I do and say and think today,
be done in the power of your undying love,
and through your Beloved presence.
May I find courage and humility,
patience and strength to carry hope into the world,
your light shining from within.
Amen.

Option: use the 'Blessedness' prayer from the Prayer Bank

A quality for the day:

As I prepare for the day ahead, let me take but one word with me, to keep in my heart and mind.

It is written that 'the fruit of the Spirit is love, joy, peace, patience, kindness, generosity, faithfulness, gentleness, and self-control' (Galatians 5:22-23). So let me choose well from your holy words, O God.

Pause for a moment of peace.

Take one word card from the nine (or more), and meditate on this for as long as you wish.

A reading:

For as the rain and the snow come down from heaven,
and do not return there until they have watered the earth,

making it bring forth and sprout,
giving seed to the sower and bread to the eater,
so shall my word be that goes out from my mouth;
it shall not return to me empty,
but it shall accomplish that which I purpose,
and succeed in the thing for which I sent it.
For you shall go out in joy,
and be led back in peace;
the mountains and the hills before you
shall burst into song,
and all the trees of the field shall clap their hands.

Isaiah 55:10-12

So may I go out in joy and return in peace,
in the spirit of the Beloved.
Amen.

Midday prayer

Choose appropriate prayers from the Holy Hours and Days section
of the Prayer Bank, depending on time, season, day of week, phase
of moon, including:

Midday prayer, 12 noon

Yours is the day, yours also the night;
you established the luminaries and the sun.
You have fixed all the bounds of the earth;
you made summer and winter.

Psalm 74:16-17

O God, our Sun and Shield,
origin and purpose of all,
let us find you in all we encounter,

for you fill heaven and earth
and there is nowhere we can hide from your love.
Amen.

*Pause for as much time as you wish, to focus on breathing. Imagine
the sacred breath flowing into you and out into the world. Imagine the
breath relaxing, inspiring and blessing you. Imagine all beings who
breathe, united by this sacred breath. Imagine everyone you meet,
all people, and creatures, to be interconnected by an underlying and
divine love.*

Natural praise (inspired by Psalms 148 and 150)

Praise God!
**Praise the Holy One from the far reaches of the universe;
sing praises from the mountain tops!**

Praise God, all you angels,
sing praises, you who do God's will.
**Praise the Holy One, sun and moon,
sing praises, all the stars of heaven!**
Praise the Eternal One, you rolling clouds,
sing praises, you oceans and flowing rivers,
for God is your source, the one who loves you.
Praise the Holy One from the ends of the earth;
sing praises, you sea creatures and all you birds of the air!

Praise God, rain and snow, fire and stormy wind,
sing praises, you who are wild and free.
**Praise the Holy One, you gardens and fruit trees
and all the trees of the forest,**
sing praises, you creatures, wild and tame!
**Praise God, you peoples of the earth,
leaders and followers, folk of all kinds, old and young alike,**

sing praises and make delightful music
to the Holy One who fills the universe;
let all that has breath unite to sing in praise of God.
Amen.

Beloved,
let me not be distracted from love;
let me not be tempted from your path;
align me to your holy wisdom,
be clear to me; be radiant within me,
and let no fear or failure dampen my trust in your goodness.
Amen.

Being Creative with the material in the Prayer Bank

The material in the Prayer Bank is a flexible resource. Below are a couple of examples of how to make use of the Prayer Bank.

Example of a Special Day Prayer

You can create a personal liturgy for or with somebody who might appreciate it, to give a spiritual dimension to celebrations of a special day. The following example is based on my birthday. I chose 6pm, the 'holy hour' closest to the time I was born, and checked on the internet to find out that I was born on a Wednesday during a waning moon. There is a sense of balance about it which I quite like: I brought fire and water together for the blessing, and drew a prayer from the depths of winter and Christ's own birth into my summertime celebration, to honour the fact that my birthday is not just about me, but also about honouring my mother and the gifts of mothering and of life itself.

Annie's Birthday Prayer

An opening blessing, combining the fire of summertime and my personal feeling of affinity with water:

> Blessings of fire, the devouring flame,
> blessings of a God whom we cannot contain,
> blessings of the one who gives and takes,
> whose power is manifest for love's sake.
>
> Blessings of the water of eternal life,
> welling up within our hearts,

blessings of sea and river and rain,
blessings of tide, of ebb and flow.

A prayer from Christmas, to honour my own mother:

Mothering God, you who labour to bring us and all creation
    to life,
nurturing us ceaselessly, from your own self-giving,
we honour you now and always, in your power and goodness,
in your strength and your willingness to endure all
for the sake of undying love, and we honour our
own mothers,
the mothers, nurturers, protectors and carers amongst us
and the capacity within each of us for bringing forth
what is good into the world.
So too we honour you for your little one,
the child you bring forth of your own self,
given to the world for the sake of all that is good:
a gift of power, a gift of gentleness and grace.
Amen.

Day of the week: *(I was born on a Wednesday and you can find
out your own day of birth from the internet)*

Eternal One,
whose starry skies proclaim
the wonder of your mysteries,
deepen our insight, sharpen our vision,
that finding meaning in your universe beyond,
we may find, too, your wisdom deep within.
Amen.

Silent meditation

Evening, 6pm *(I was born at about 5pm)*

> Holy One, beyond, around and within us,
> remind us of the sanctity of what you have made,
> the world in its goodness
> and our own selves, temples to your Spirit,
> and let us honour you in every way.
> Amen.

According to information found on the internet, the moon was waning at the time of my birth:

> Let this be a sacred time, O God,
> in which I can let go of the past
> and all that is not needed,
> and be at peace,
> knowing that emptiness makes way for fullness.
> Amen.

Pause for reflection on past, present and future

O Beloved

> O beloved Source of the river of my life,
> rain from the sky and wellspring from the earth,
> I cannot name you or contain you,
> but only delight in your ceaseless flow.

> Wash the world with healing grace,
> touch the dry land and make it green,
> let your fruits be shared by all,
> your harvest an eternal joy.

May all who thirst make their way to you
and may all in need find their dry wells filled,
and may all who fear life's raging storms
be sheltered and guided to safe refuge.
Amen.

Example of a special day: the Watch at New Year

The following is an example of how to draw elements of the
Prayer Bank together for a particular occasion, in this instance
to create a 'Watch' service for the night when the New Year
begins. This is a secular event dependent on the Roman roots of
the Gregorian calendar, and not a Christian or naturally special
time, but we can hallow it with prayer, nevertheless.

To represent the days of the week and the phases of the moon
(which are different every year), I have chosen the prayer for
Friday, which is the day human beings are said to have been
created (Genesis 1), and a New Moon prayer expressing hopeful
new beginnings. You could just miss them out if you prefer, or
substitute the appropriate one each year. (Check on the internet
or a calendar to find out what the correct day of the week and
lunar phase will be.)

Planning Summary:

Midnight on the night of 31 December – 1 January

General intention: ending the old year, blessing the new, a time
of reflection and hope

Christian season: Christmas, leading towards Epiphany

Season (northern hemisphere): winter, after the solstice

Day of week: this changes yearly; I have chosen the prayer
for Friday

Hour: midnight

Moon phase: this changes yearly; I have chosen a New Moon prayer

Suggested colours and symbols for the season: whites, greys, black, silver, red berries and evergreen leaves (beware yew which is beautiful but poisonous), bare twigs and branches that you can hang prayers or decorations from.

Bold font: all join in.
Light font: one voice (leader or designated reader).

Liturgy of the Watch

Suitable music as introduction

An opening winter blessing upon everyone gathered together:

Blessings of endurance and timely retreat,
wintertime inner work,
companionship and peace.

From the seasonal text:

**Glory to God in the highest heaven,
and on earth peace, goodwill among people!**[*]

Luke 2:13-14

A Christmas-season prayer

**A warming fire you are, O God, in the chill of winter,
a comfort you are, O Love, in the coldest night,
a bright flame of hope you are, O Holy One, a growing light,
a joy you are and a ray of sunshine, piercing the gloom.
Thanks be to you for the blessings you bring.
Amen.**

---

* The NRSV has 'on earth peace among those whom he favours' in the main text and 'goodwill among people' as an alternative in the footnotes.

Prayer for Friday

Loving God,
whose concern reaches out to all your creatures,
teach us to live gently and with regard for all life,
knowing each belongs to you.
Give us a compassionate heart
and a will to tread lightly on this earth,
harming none, now and always.
Amen.

Blessedness (based on Benedictus)
(or use Divine Praise, based on Te Deum)

We look back to the roots
of trust in you, O God,
and we bless you as Source of All.
Firm roots support and give strength,
embedded in the living soil,
firm roots are like ancestors,
named grandmothers and grandfathers
of a chosen people,
Sarah and Abraham, Rebekah and Isaac,
ancient stories of faith in you;
from them we draw wisdom,
from them we draw courage
as we find our way today.
As a tree trunk grows firm and tall,
lifting up its leaves to the sky,
so we strive for the light, the meaning, the truth;
we aim to live well,
and falling, we hope in the power of life
to let new shoots grow from the old.
We look to the one who lives fully in your light,

perfect and true, with leaves of healing for all the world.
So, we face the future,
the fruit of our works and words,
and we ask your blessing,
that it be your own goodness that flowers in us,
your own loving kindness that bears fruit in us,
our seeds a blessing to the world,
and a source of peace,
a source of deep peace.
Amen.

Option: an appropriate song

Midnight prayer

Eternal One,
for whom day and night are both alike,
open our eyes and ears, our hearts and minds,
that we and all your creatures may pause to sense
    your presence
here among us, now and always,
and in you find our consolation.
Amen.

Midnight text

My soul is satisfied as with a rich feast,
    and my mouth praises you with joyful lips
when I think of you on my bed,
    and meditate on you in the watches of the night;
for you have been my help,
    and in the shadow of your wings I sing for joy.

Psalm 63:5-7

A prayer from the New Moon phase

In times of new beginnings we remember you, O God;
bless our times of celebration,
our times of brightness and gladness,
togetherness and connection with those we hold dear,
whether far or near.
Help us work for reconciliation, and mutual respect,
that peace may reign supreme
at your great feast.
Amen.

A time of quiet

Option: *lighting of candles for hopes and loves*

A 'psalm'-style prayer: Trust in the Future

We do not know where next the river of our lives will flow,
we do not know what obstacles lie ahead,
what dangerous rapids and what sleepy pools,
deep gorges cut through rock, and waterfalls;
we only know that rivers flow until they reach the sea
and then the waters mingle; all is one –
as it always was and ever will be,
as long as the skies give their rain.

We do not know where next the river of our lives will flow,
but flow it must, drawn on and ever on,
and with the constant flow we find our confidence
    grows strong,
that rivers flow on and on until they reach the sea.

We close by saying together a prayer inspired by the one Jesus taught:

O God, most loving of parents,
residing forever in a blissfulness which lies beyond us,
your name is a holy mystery.
May your power be known,
your desire made manifest on earth,
as in your most perfect realm.
Give us our bread, day by day,
and release us from our bonds,
as we set free those who are bound to us,
and keep us from temptation;
rescue us from harm.
For your realm, your power and your glory abide forever.
Amen.

Part 4

The Liturgies

1. Liturgies of the Feminine Divine

Introduction

Using feminine language about God remains a minority pursuit in Christianity as a whole, despite the writings of mystics such as the thirteenth-century Julian of Norwich (the first woman to write in English, with her remarkable *Revelations of Divine Love*), and indeed, despite the material available in the Bible. Because of this, I suggest that the prayers and liturgies in this section be explored with sensitivity, perhaps within the context of an open but interested group over a series of weeks, with at least one session devoted to the four aspects of God below, so that participants have time and support for reflection. Christianity is not a faith of esoteric teachings; it is not *'gnostic'* – involving hidden knowledge – to explore the feminine, but is simply an articulation of what is clearly written in the Bible for all to find and use.

Part of the difficulty, in my opinion, in exploring feminine expressions of the divine stems from forgetting that all language is inherently inadequate to express the ineffable. It also stems from a blurred distinction between idols and icons. Wanting to have a comfortable 'picture' of God that makes sense to us – a king on a throne, an affable father with a big beard, a tanned and kindly-looking young man in homespun clothes – may help some of us to feel in relationship with God, but we also move towards doing what the first commandment tells us not to do: making idols to worship (Exodus 20:4-6). Making a feminine image, it seems to me, is no worse than making a male image (Deuteronomy 4:15-16). It is still an image. As long as we can appreciate the symbolic, the metaphorical, the meaning behind or beyond the image, then we might say it is an *icon*, a window onto the divine. Our gaze does not stop at the object but goes deeper or higher, or further into our own souls; our devotions are still directed towards the divine rather than towards the thing we have made. But if our gaze stops at the thing we have made and attaches faith to the object, we are behaving in a way that the prophets of the Bible warned us against. For someone following a biblical faith path, this is a subtle but important distinction. The prophet Isaiah, for example, asks the people who they can compare God with:

> To whom then will you liken God? ...
> An idol? – A workman casts it,
> and a goldsmith overlays it with gold,
> and casts for it silver chains.
> As a gift one chooses mulberry wood
> – wood that will not rot –
> then seeks out a skilled artisan
> to set up an image that will not topple.
> Have you not known? Have you not heard?
> Has it not been told you from the beginning?
> Have you not understood from the foundations
>   of the earth? ...
> To whom then will you compare me,
> or who is my equal? says the Holy One.
> *Isaiah 40:18-21, 25*

How we feel about images, idols and icons may well depend on our religious upbringing; for centuries, there has been debate and at times destructive, bitter hostility between those who would eradicate all images, and those who would promote the use of imagery as a visual expression of devotion. There is no 'right' answer. But it is worth remembering that images are not always statues or paintings. We also construct images out of words and form images in our minds, using our imagination. Our dreams are full of images – they are the language of our wordless inner world or unconscious mind.

Always, reflecting on an image, including a word-image or a mental picture, we need to remember that there is infinitely more to God than anything we make; we cannot contain, constrain or construct God to suit ourselves. Neither an image nor an icon ever tells us all there is to know about the divine. In contemplation, the wonder and also the humility lies in the realisation uttered by Job, on encountering the vastness of God:

'Who is this that hides counsel without knowledge?'
Therefore I have uttered what I did not understand,
things too wonderful for me, which I did not know.

Job 42:3

While it is hoped that this section will delight some, it may challenge others. It is one thing to omit masculine expressions of the divine, such as Father, Lord, King and Son, and quite another to replace them with feminine terms. Why this is so challenging is an interesting question with a multitude of possible answers. Personally, I do not consider exclusion of either masculine or feminine to be adequate in addressing or describing God, and see gender binaries as limited in themselves, which is why in most of this book I use gender-neutral expressions – but then, no language is adequate in describing God. As long as people mistakenly (in my opinion) continue to assume that Christianity stipulates a male deity (and this includes many people outside of the faith), it seems worth exercising the feminine, lest we inadvertently forget the God who gave us birth (Deuteronomy 32:18).

It has to be said that a feeling of exclusion is the real experience of countless women over the centuries, obliged to use male-only language about God, so the reversal is, at least, an interesting exercise. I hope that the following prayers are more than this, and can be used as a spiritual resource for the increasing numbers who hunger for the feminine to be acknowledged within Christianity.

Aspects of the Divine

Four aspects of divinity used in this section draw on significant feminine ways of thinking about God. Four, rather than three, is deliberate: I am not in this instance seeking to propose alternatives to the traditional expressions of the Trinity as such. Aspects, qualities, titles and concepts are fluid; they interweave or melt into one another. I have used feminine expressions which are all valid and biblically rooted concepts.

Mother

The Bible contains images of God bringing forth and birthing (Deuteronomy 32:18), of caring for nursing babies and having 'womb-love', the (idealised) tender compassion of a mother for her offspring (for example, Deuteronomy 4:31; Isaiah 49:15 and 66:13; Genesis 49:25; Luke 1:78 and 13:34). In Deuteronomy 32:18 we read:

> You were unmindful of the Rock that bore you;
> you forgot the God who gave you birth.

In the Old Testament, fathering and mothering references often occur in close proximity (see Deuteronomy 32:6 for the nearest father reference to Deuteronomy 32:18 above). There is a sense of respect for both parents. Examples of this unity of motherhood and fatherhood range from the fifth commandment: 'honour your father and your mother, so that your days may be long in the land...' (Exodus 20:12) to the poetic:

Has the rain a father,
>   or who has begotten the drops of dew?
From whose womb did the ice come forth,
>   and who has given birth to the hoar-frost of heaven?

Job 38:28-29

When we encounter 'Father' in worship, then, as an alternative to replacing it immediately with 'Mother', we might like to add *'and Mother'*, or refer to the parenting qualities of God: 'O mothering, fathering God'. This practice reminds us of the balance, and of the metaphorical nature of language about God.

Concerning Jesus, the prologue of John's Gospel talks of being born of God (John 1:13). Jesus, according to John, likens his coming death to a woman's labour (John 16:21), and he likens himself to a mother hen (Luke 13:34). In medieval thinking, for example in the writings of Anselm and Julian of Norwich, Jesus was referred to as a mother labouring on the cross and suckling his children with his own milk – it was thought that milk was a by-product of blood.

Jesus is said to have called God 'Abba' (Mark 14:36). This is a warmly respectful term used by children and adults towards their fathers, not unlike 'Dad'. The feminine equivalent is 'Amma'. Both words are Aramaic, related to Hebrew, and they, like Jesus himself, come from the context of first-century Mediterranean Jewish culture, which is not easy to translate into our own context. My feeling is that Jesus would encourage his followers to follow his example in talking to God in respectful ways that lead to an experience of intimacy and would understand that, for some, 'Father' does not induce a feeling of intimacy.[17]

---

[17] For an exploration of difficulty with the use of 'Father', see my earlier book, *Rejoice with Me*.

Ruach

Ruach is a Hebrew word expressing the wind, breath or spirit of God which animates and effects changes in the world and in people's hearts and minds. *Ruach* hovers over the primal waters at the beginning of creation: 'In the beginning when God created the heavens and the earth, the earth was a formless void and darkness covered the face of the deep, while a wind from God swept over the face of the waters.' (Genesis 1:1-2)

Ruach is the living breath that keeps mortals alive (Genesis 6:3). She is the ecstatic spirit that comes upon the future king Saul, when he meets a band of musical prophets (1 Samuel 10:6), and the inspiring spirit that causes Isaiah to speak of 'good news to the oppressed', proclaiming God's liberating justice in a passage which Jesus is said to read from, during a visit to a synagogue (Isaiah 61:1-3 and Luke 4:16-30).

Ruach being a noun with a feminine gender, we can say 'she', even though the word was later translated into Greek, *pneumatos*, as a neuter word – 'it' – and into Latin, *spiritus*, as a masculine word – 'he'. The Latin-derived term 'Spirit' has dominated our thinking for a long time, but there is no reason apart from convention why it should continue to do so.

Jesus, as a speaker of Aramaic and Hebrew, is far more likely to have thought in terms of *Ruach*: she. After the resurrection, according to John, he conveys the 'Holy Spirit' or the Ruach to his followers by breathing on them – the act of someone who associates the divine breath with spiritual power: 'When [Jesus] had said this, he breathed on them and said to them, "Receive the Holy Spirit."' (John 20:22)[18]

---

[18] John's Gospel is written in Greek, so the text actually says, 'pneuma hagion'.

Shekhinah

Shekhinah is another word from Hebrew, emerging in the Jewish Rabbinic tradition possibly as early as the earliest Christian writings. It is also used in some denominations of Christianity. *Shekhinah* derives from the Hebrew word meaning 'to dwell' (which has a consonant root SHK) and refers to God's presence dwelling among or within us, often as a cloud or in a cloud. The *Shekhinah* is traditionally associated with the glory of God, with divine light and loving presence (for example, in Exodus 40:34-38, Exodus 24:16, Numbers 9:15 and Ezekiel 1:28). 'Then the cloud covered the tent of meeting, and the glory of God* filled the tabernacle. Moses was not able to enter the tent of meeting because the cloud settled upon it, and the glory of God# filled the tabernacle.' (Exodus 40:34-35)

The divine presence is often thought of as feminine. In Judaism she is sometimes equated with the Sabbath, envisioned as a longed for and beautiful bride to be welcomed joyfully into the home.

In Christianity, the *Shekhinah* could be seen as an expression of the Holy Spirit or perhaps of Christ, suggested by the account of the 'transfiguration' of Jesus, when he meets Moses and Elijah from his people's past, and shines with a dazzling brightness (Mark 9:2-13; Matthew 17:1-13; Luke 9:28-36). In this account, Peter seems to reflect the 'dwelling' nature of the *Shekhinah* by offering to build shelters:

> Six days later, Jesus took with him Peter and James and John, and led them up a high mountain apart, by themselves. And he was transfigured before them, and his clothes became dazzling white, such as no one on earth could bleach them. And there appeared to them Elijah with Moses, who were talking with Jesus. Then Peter said

---

* 'the Lord' in NRSV
# 'the Lord' in NRSV

to Jesus, 'Rabbi, it is good for us to be here; let us make three dwellings, one for you, one for Moses, and one for Elijah.' He did not know what to say, for they were terrified. Then a cloud overshadowed them, and from the cloud there came a voice, 'This is my Son, the Beloved; listen to him!' Suddenly when they looked around, they saw no one with them any more, but only Jesus.

Mark 9:2-13

There is also an association with birds and spiritual presence, and the passages in the Gospels where the Holy Spirit is described as a dove or like a dove are highly evocative of the concept of Shekhinah.

In those days Jesus came from Nazareth of Galilee and was baptized by John in the Jordan. And just as he was coming up out of the water, he saw the heavens torn apart and the Spirit descending like a dove on him. And a voice came from heaven, 'You are my Son, the Beloved; with you I am well pleased.'

Mark 1:9-11

The Hebrew Scriptures contain many references to the sheltering mantle of God's wings, especially in the psalms, although much of this literature is ancient (including the texts about God's presence in clouds of glory) and may predate more personified concepts of the Shekhinah as developed by the Rabbis. The Shekhinah, of course, is borrowed from and still alive in Judaism and needs to be respected as such.

Wisdom, Sophia

Wisdom is a personification of one of the most important divine attributes and at times seems to be God or God's holy word. Wisdom is that which the faithful should seek:

Happy are those who find wisdom,
  and those who get understanding,
for her income is better than silver,
  and her revenue better than gold.
She is more precious than jewels,
  and nothing you desire can compare with her.
Long life is in her right hand;
  in her left hand are riches and honour.
Her ways are ways of pleasantness,
  and all her paths are peace.
She is a tree of life to those who lay hold of her;
  those who hold her fast are called happy . . .

Get wisdom; get insight: do not forget, nor turn away
  from the words of my mouth.
Do not forsake her, and she will keep you;
  love her, and she will guard you.
The beginning of wisdom is this: Get wisdom,
  and whatever else you get, get insight.
Prize her highly, and she will exalt you;
  she will honour you if you embrace her.
She will place on your head a fair garland;
  she will bestow on you a beautiful crown.

Proverbs 3:13-18; 4:5-9

Wisdom appears in the Old and New Testaments and also in the inter-Testamental or Apocryphal writings,[19] as a powerful and attractive woman. We find her especially in Proverbs 8:1–9:6 and in the Wisdom of Solomon, a book known to the writers of the New Testament but appearing only in the Apocrypha. A

---

[19] A collection of Jewish writings from around the third century BCE to the first century CE, written in Greek rather than Hebrew and of lesser liturgical value, accepted as inspirational but not authoritative by the Anglican and Roman Catholic Churches, and not to be confused with the 'Gnostic' gospels.

comparison of a number of Paul's letters with the text of the Wisdom of Solomon reveals how Paul draws on and dialogues with this earlier writing and perhaps expects others to be familiar with it.[20] Paul says, for example, in 1 Corinthians 1:24, that Christ is 'the power of God and the wisdom of God'.

Jesus is said to have called himself Wisdom's child (Luke 7:35). The New Testament writers, well aware of the importance of Wisdom in both contemporary Judaism and the pagan Romano-Greek world, drew many parallels between Jesus and Wisdom.

In the Old Testament, King Solomon is said to have desired and sought Wisdom and to have been the wisest of kings (1 Kings 4:29-34), having asked God for understanding to govern well rather than for power and wealth (1 Kings 3:1-15). The Queen of Sheba comes to visit him, to test his fabled wisdom for herself (1 Kings 10:1-13). When we read in Matthew 12:42 that Jesus is greater than Solomon, this is a significant claim to make: 'The queen of the South will rise up at the judgement with this generation and condemn it, because she came from the ends of the earth to listen to the wisdom of Solomon, and see, something greater than Solomon is here!' Wisdom is described differently in different texts, but shares the pre-existent nature claimed for Christ (Proverbs 8:22-31), and deep love for humanity (Proverbs 8:31), suggesting that Wisdom, for Christians, *is* Christ (Colossians 1:15-20), the perfect reflection of God or emanation of God.

For wisdom is more mobile than any motion;
because of her pureness she pervades and penetrates
  all things.

---

[20] For an in-depth analysis, see 'God's Design: The Death of Creation? An Ecojustice Reading of Romans 8:18-30 in the light of Wisdom 1-2', by Marie Turner in *The Earth Story in Wisdom Traditions*, The Earth Bible Vol. 3, ed. Norman C. Habel and Shirley Wurst (Sheffield Academic Press, 2001).

For she is a breath of the power of God,
and a pure emanation of the glory of the Almighty;
therefore nothing defiled gains entrance into her.
For she is a reflection of eternal light,
a spotless mirror of the working of God,
and an image of his [God's] goodness.

Wisdom of Solomon 7:24-26

The ancient identification of Holy Wisdom with Christ is demonstrated in the huge sixth-century Orthodox church built in Constantinople, now Istanbul, called Hagia Sophia: Holy Wisdom. The name is meant to signify Christ as referred to in John 1:1-18 by the Greek philosophical term 'Logos' or Word. God's word, of course, is wise, and powerful – bringing us back to Paul's statement in 1 Corinthians 1:24 that Christ is the power and the wisdom of God.

She

We can get round quite a lot of gender issues about God by addressing God directly: 'You, O God, are a lamp to my feet; you light my path.' But when we want to talk *about* God, we often want to use a pronoun, and this is where 'he' slips in: 'God is a lamp to my feet, he lights my path.' Avoidance of pronouns is a challenge. It can make language clumsy, to try to avoid saying 'he'. In the following prayers and liturgies, since we are exploring the feminine divine, *She* is appropriate. I like 'She' as a pronoun for God; I think it is better than 'He'. Looking at it carefully, *She* includes: s+he, whereas *He* excludes: (-s)he. To me, this supports expression of God's embrace of and transcendence of gender distinctions. 'Her' and 'hers' also include 'he'.

Using 'She' of God, in a Christian context, can take some courage. It can also cause confusion for those who believe quite literally in a 'Father in Heaven'. This can include children and people young in their faith, and for their sake the usage is to be explored with sensitivity and humility.

I hope the material below provides an introduction to approaching the possibility of God's feminine side, as revealed in Scripture, but it can only serve as an introduction. There is an abundance of writing on the subject by better theologians than myself, some of which is included in the list for further reading at the end of this book.

She

O Great She:
She who brings forth, tirelessly,
newness from the rotting forest floor;
She who nurtures, nourishes,
reabsorbs, reclaims,
breaks down to elemental usefulness
and recreates, nothing wasted,
all knitted back together into life;

O Great She,
of wild strength, raw power,
tempered by a tender love of every little one,
creation's pain rocked and soothed
in the ebb and flow of time,
manifesting her desire in myriad ways,
the ceaseless waves, the diamond fragments of the spray,
the whispered 'be' – or is it sung? –
the sacred sound resonating through eternity;

O Great She,
who bears us, incubates us for new life,
surrounding us, our refuge and our all,

protecting, feeding, animating,
letting go into the world,
but never losing touch,
a cobweb-fine connection to the Source of All,
our mother and our midwife,
and guardian of the gate,
where each must go, when death draws near;

O Great She,
She of the threshold and of safe passage,
She of choice, of freedom,
and the love that conquers death,
She of limitless compassion,
and the laughing, weeping knowledge of our souls,
her brokenness our hope;
She who lifts us when we fall,
and carries us, or guides our way,
She of wholeness, of Wisdom's origin,
She I seek, and She I invoke.

A daily body prayer routine honouring the divine feminine

At its fullest, the following prayer routine can involve the whole body and environment, and be carried out where there is room to move about freely. It can also be condensed into a form which can be practised sitting or standing in a confined space.

The directions

Turning to the four directions acknowledges the presence of God everywhere, but also the presence of all the peoples and living things of the world, and the sphere of the earth itself. It reminds us that we stand at the centre point of these four directions in our own unique spot, a perspective on the world which nobody else can occupy. Following any direction far enough we would come back full circle to this centre point. Here at the 'centre' of our own circles, we are connected to all that is, all the time. Just recalling these directions can re-connect us with the immensity of creation and creator.

Direction is important in biblical symbolism. For Christians, sunrise in the east speaks of resurrection joy, while the south recalls the midday sun and the time of day when Paul received his blinding encounter with the risen Christ on the road to Damascus. West is the direction of the setting sun, the ancient time of evening prayer, and north is the direction in which the sun does not appear – we might associate it with our experiences of absence and fear, our dark nights, when we wait in hope for a new dawn.[21]

Choose a location where you can be undisturbed. Jesus is said to have told his disciples that when they wanted to pray, they were to go alone into their room and close the door so that they could be alone with God. You can of course do this prayer outside, but in the spirit of Jesus' teaching, you might prefer to avoid a location where your actions attract attention. Matthew 6:6 reads: 'But whenever you pray, go into your room and shut the door and pray to your Father who is in secret; and your Father who sees in secret will reward you.' The writer of Matthew's Gospel uses 'Father' of God very frequently. In drawing on the passage for my opening prayer, I have adapted the language.

Opening prayer:

O most Holy One,
you see my heart and know my innermost thoughts;

---

[21] For a fuller exploration of the symbolism of directions and times of day, please refer to my book *Search me and Know me.*

194

be with me in the intimacy of this time and place,
your tender love surrounding and filling me,
so that I, in turn, may extend your love to the world.
Amen.

Direction to face: north

Optional posture: Kneel, head on the ground, curled in a foetal position reminiscent of a baby, or sit with this in mind, curled up in a way that is comfortable.

Optional symbol of devotion: A rock which you can hold or contemplate, representing the 'rock who bore you' of Deuteronomy 32:18.

Invocation: O Rock who bore me, O Mother of all!

Petition: Let me never forget your love for me and all your children.

Turn clockwise one quarter-turn.

Direction: east

Optional posture: Kneel upright or resting on your heels, arms outstretched as though in welcome or praise – this is the direction of the rising sun, symbol of the resurrection.

Optional symbol of devotion: Light an incense cone or stick and meditate on the psalmist's prayer that the smoke may carry prayers to God (Psalm 141:2), or create simple music – especially with a wind instrument or wind chimes, or, if outdoors, focus on wind in the trees and birdsong.

Invocation: O Ruach, O sacred breath of God!

Petition: Breathe through me and inspire me.

Turn clockwise one quarter-turn.

Direction: south, direction of the midday sun

Optional posture: Stand upright, arms uplifted.

Optional symbol of devotion: Light a candle or other source of light and warmth, or reflect on the sun itself at midday.

Invocation: Oh glorious Shekhinah, oh loving presence of God!

Petition: Be with me, make your home in my heart.

Turn clockwise one quarter-turn.

Direction: west, direction of the setting sun

Optional posture: Stand, sit or kneel with hands across chest or cupped over heart.

Optional symbol of devotion: Baruch 3:12-13 speaks of a 'fountain of wisdom' equated with the way of God. Use flowing water, or a bowl and jug that you can pour from, meditatively, a water feature or, if outdoors, a stream, spring or fountain.

Invocation: O Holy Wisdom!

Petition: Teach me and guide me, let me learn your ways.

Turning clockwise one more quarter-turn brings you back to the starting position. If you wish, you can now move round again, offering praise for each attribute of God in turn and/or asking each time for specific qualities or gifts, for example:

North: O Mother (or O mothering God), fill me with courage and strength, and let all my actions come from your deep compassion welling up within me. Amen.

East: O Ruach (or Sacred Breath), enliven and inspire me, challenge and comfort me, that I may be changed by your power. Amen.

South: O Shekhinah (or O glorious presence of God), enlighten my life, set my heart ablaze with love for you, that I may shine with your love in the world. Amen.

West: O Holy Wisdom (or O Hagia Sophia), teach me and guide me, and let me grow in wisdom, that I may be of use to the world. Amen.

In a third rotation, you could spread out your arms and ask for blessings upon all who live in the four directions, far or near. You can include loved ones, situations in the news, ecological concerns and anything else on your mind, closing each with an 'Amen'. During this rotation, if you wish you can extinguish the incense and candle, sending the intention behind them out to the world.

Close your prayer where you began, facing north, by placing your hands across your chest and bowing down to God with an 'Amen', acknowledging, if you wish, that even in hardship and darkness, God is still with us and still loves us.

Meditation on the Sacred Breath

This text is for personal reflection or for a leader to read to a group, with appropriate pauses. If leading others in breathing exercises, respect that asthma may be an issue, in which case individuals will know how best to respond to the meditation for their own wellbeing – so avoid being overly prescriptive.

Choose a comfortable upright posture if possible, or lie flat.

You may wish to light a candle and/or incense. If in a group, check this is not an irritant to anyone first.

Meditating on the breath is a well-known practice today. The Bible is permeated with a sense of the spirituality of breath, which emanates from God, the Source of All, animating all living things, mysterious, powerful and empowering. Breathing, we are dependent on God, and somehow one with God, not unlike a baby in the womb, connected to their mother by the placenta, through which they breathe and receive nutrition.

We breathe naturally, but tense breath is shallow and fast. A calm breath is deeper and slower. Our breath can tell us how we are feeling in the present moment.

Pause for a moment and notice your own breathing.

We breathe in the air around us. The air was made breathable long ago, by the forests and all the vegetation that covers the earth. Green things take in carbon dioxide and release oxygen. We could not live without green plants. The atmosphere they have made is precious: it is good (Genesis 1).

Pause for a moment and imagine this air, all around, hovering over the whole planet, circulating in swirls of wind, surrounding us all, entering us all, entering every cell of our bodies, then leaving again, to be cleansed by the trees and breathed anew by other creatures.

In God we 'live and move and have our being' (Acts 17:28).

Pause

The psalmist talks of the divine breath, *ruach*, which is translated here as 'spirit'. The sacred breath is everywhere.

Where can I go from your spirit? (or, 'where can I go from
your breath?')
    Or where can I flee from your presence?
If I ascend to heaven, you are there;
    if I make my bed in Sheol, you are there.
If I take the wings of the morning
    and settle at the farthest limits of the sea,
even there your hand shall lead me,
    and your right hand shall hold me fast.
If I say, 'Surely the darkness shall cover me,
    and the light around me become night',
even the darkness is not dark to you;
    the night is as bright as the day,
    for darkness is as light to you.

Psalm 139:7-12

Pause

In a time of quiet, focus on your own breath. Notice the natural
pause between in-breath and out-breath.

As you breathe in, imagine the air swirling around you, drawing
in, swirling around your body to enliven it, then being released.

As you breathe in, say to yourself, 'You are within me.'
As you breathe out, say to yourself, 'You are beyond me.'

You can simplify these or change them slightly – 'God within'/
'God beyond . . .' or 'life within me, life beyond me', or simply,
'Breath of life', 'She' or 'Ruach', whether breathing in or out.

Practise this meditative breathing for as long as you wish.

When you want to close the session, take time to return your awareness to your environment, and stretch.

Close with an 'Amen' or a suitable prayer chosen from the Prayer Bank.

Liturgy of Remembering Our Mother

Refer to the introductory section above about Mother, and use this with people who are taking part before the liturgy to support meaningful engagement.

Prepare a central feature – large rocks, and smaller ones people can pick up, on a tray with a bowl of water.

If possible, have a drum to beat a steady heartbeat rhythm softly in the background during the visualisation. Practise in advance!

As with all the liturgies provided, 'normal' type indicates the leader and '**bold**' type indicates responses by all.

Opening:

> In the beginning when God created the heavens and the earth, the earth was a formless void and darkness covered the face of the deep, while a wind from God swept over the face of the waters. Then God said, 'Let there be light'; and there was light.
>
> *Genesis 1:1-3*

> The Holy One is here, as in the beginning.
> **She is here, within us and around us.**

> **O Source of All, the Great Mother who gave us birth,**
> **you are the essence of life in us, our very breath,**
> **you know the hearts and minds of all your children.**

**Draw us to you as a hen gathers up her chicks,
and let us dwell in your loving presence always.
Amen.**

These are the words of God, to the children of Israel, according
to Isaiah:

Can a woman forget her nursing-child,
or show no compassion for the child of her womb?
Even these may forget,
yet I will not forget you.
See, I have inscribed you on the palms of my hands;
your walls are continually before me . . .
As a mother comforts her child,
so I will comfort you;
you shall be comforted in Jerusalem.
Isaiah 49:15-16 and 66:13

**So, we pray for our own peace, but also for the peace of all
for whom Jerusalem is holy; may there be peace; peace in
the land, peace between neighbours, peace spreading out
to all the world.[22]
Amen.**

Reconciliation:

Though God does not forget us, all too often we forget God,
as it is written:

You were unmindful of the Rock that bore you;
you forgot the God who gave you birth.
Deuteronomy 32:18

---

[22] Psalm 122:6 asks us to pray for the peace of Jerusalem. The city is often described in feminine imagery in the Bible and in Isaiah 66:6-13 is described as a mother birthing a new beginning for the city.

So, we acknowledge that we have been unmindful of the One who bore us.

Pause

> Mothering God, the Rock who gives all birth,
> you have been forgotten for too long;
> you have been wronged,
> and your many children of the earth neglected,
> knowingly and in ignorance,
> time and again.
> We are sorry for our own forgetting,
> and ask you to teach us better ways,
> reconciling us to one another and to you
> and all the earth in love,
> according to your tender compassion.
> We ask this for our own sake
> and for all who will come after us,
> [and for the sake of Jesus, who laboured on the cross
> that we might have life.]*
> So release us from the past, renew us
> and show us the path to true wisdom,
> and the mystery of your endless love.
> Amen.

The good news of reconciliation to God is to be proclaimed in all the world (Luke 24:47). Jesus said:

'I tell you, her sins, which were many, have been forgiven; hence she has shown great love. But the one to whom little is forgiven, loves little.' Then he said to her, 'Your sins are forgiven.'

Luke 7:47-48

---

* for optional use

So, with humility, let us too accept God's forgiving grace into our own lives.

By the tender mercy of our God,
the dawn from on high will break upon us,
to give light to those who sit in darkness and in the
shadow of death,
to guide our feet into the way of peace.

Luke 1:78-79

Amen.

Say together 'Divine Praise' or 'Exultation' from the Prayer Bank

Opportunity for song

Glory to the One who brings all to birth
and to love's embodiment
and to the sacred breath of life,
primal, present and eternal.
Amen.

A time of meditation. All are invited to take and hold a piece of rock during a time of silence: May we remember the Rock who gave us birth.

Pause in silence.
At the close of the silence, invite participants to join in a visualisation.

A guided visualisation:

Close your eyes, breathe calmly, in … out …

Listen to the drum, a heartbeat … the mother's heartbeat …

Let your breath come from deep within, become aware of your belly, the place where once, the breath, and nutrition too, came into your body, and left again as waste, for the mother to process . . .

Breath from the mother, breath back to the mother . . .

Breathe deep . . .

Feel yourself supported; you float in a bubble of warm liquid.

You float in the darkness.

The warm, liquid darkness is your beginning, your first human home.

Just be, in this warm, watery darkness, with the sound of the mother's heartbeat, the mother's life, the mother who meets all your needs, the mother who is all you know, your whole world . . .

Listen to the heartbeat . . . be aware of your breathing.

Be at peace.

Extended pause

This safe, dark womb world is where you began. The memory of this place is still deep within your inner being. The safety, the way you are wholly surrounded by love, with all your needs met, is something you know.

You can return to this sense of peace by seeking refuge in God, at any time.

In God, you live and breathe and have your being.

Pause

Now, when you are ready, become aware of the light in the room, stretch a little; breathe deep and open your eyes, quietly returning your thoughts to the room and the people around you.

Let us say together:

**O Mothering God,
Let all who take refuge in you rejoice;
let them ever sing for joy.
Spread your protection over them,
so that those who love your name may exult in you.
Amen.**

Dear Mother of us all,
our source, our beginning place,
the one to whom we will return,
let us not forget you.
Call us into your shelter,
remind us of your protection,
comfort us with your kindly presence,
your unconditional love for each of us,
no matter what.
Amen.

and/or

Holy Mother, the sacrifice you made for me
is beyond my grasp.
In your generosity
you do not need me to understand,

you simply ask that I remember you.
You do not ask for me to repay your giving,
you simply hold your arms out wide
and offer up your love.
Amen.

Closing prayer:

O beloved Source of the river of my life,
rain from the sky and wellspring from the earth,
I cannot name you or contain you,
but only delight in your ceaseless flow.

Wash the world with healing grace,
touch the dry land and make it green,
let your fruits be shared by all,
your harvest an eternal joy.

May all who thirst make their way to you
and may all in need find their dry wells filled,
and may all who fear life's raging storms
be sheltered and guided to safe refuge.
Amen.

A Celebration of Holy Wisdom

Refer to the introductory section above about Wisdom, and use this with people who are taking part before the liturgy to support meaningful engagement.

Decide which reflection to use: Tree of Life or Wisdom's Yoke. The Tree of Life reflection needs plenty of fresh (non-poisonous) leaves of different kinds on display in the centre of the circle, and a large tray of earth (an option is to use potting compost which can be re-used). An alternative is to use paper leaves which can be written on – remember the pens!

The liturgy includes a sharing of bread and wine or grape juice, reflecting on a passage in Proverbs 9:1-6 in which Wisdom, in her personification as a woman, invites people to a feast which will help guests to move from a state of immaturity or ignorance, to 'walk in the way of insight'. For Christians, this has clear resonance with Jesus' sharing of bread and wine (Matthew 26:26-30, Mark 14:22-25, Luke 22:14-23, 1 Corinthians 11:23-26), and also with 'the way', a term used since the earliest times to describe following Jesus (for example, Matthew 7:13-14, John 14:6).

Opening reading:

> Happy are those who find wisdom,
>> and those who get understanding,
> for her income is better than silver,
>> and her revenue better than gold.
> She is more precious than jewels,
>> and nothing you desire can compare with her.
> Long life is in her right hand;
>> in her left hand are riches and honour.
> Her ways are ways of pleasantness,
>> and all her paths are peace.
> She is a tree of life to those who lay hold of her;
>> those who hold her fast are called happy.
>>> *Proverbs 3:13-18*

Wisdom says, 'whoever finds me finds life' (Proverbs 8:35).

So let us seek and find our tree of life.
Amen.

Optional: Include prayers of season, weekday, time and moon phase from the Holy Hours and Days section.

207

A choice of psalm-inspired prayer

On Contentment (inspired by Psalm 1)

> Contentment lies in discerning the divine desire
> and, in discovering it, surrendering to it,
> as lovers to one another,
> for such is the way to Oneness.
> The one who learns to live in love,
> is like a tree by a flowing stream:
> verdant and fruitful in their season,
> a joy to all who draw near.

or

Trust in the Power of the Infinite One (inspired by Psalm 16)

> I call on you, the power of the Greatest Good,
> I call on you, the presence of the love of all loves,
> I call on you, the perfection of the Infinite One,
> to protect me and all who trust in you.
> To me, you are God: sublime source of all,
> the cup from which I drink,
> and the guide to my path;
> my life has been graced by many blessings,
> and all these I ascribe to you.
> When sleep eludes me, I reflect on you,
> the dark night is lit by remembering your words,
> and by day and by night,
> the thought of you cheers my heart.
> So, I have courage and confidence in you,
> that you weave all together in wondrous ways,
> you lead me along the path of life
> and in your presence is true delight.
> **Amen.**

Choice of reflections: Wisdom as the Tree of Life, or Wisdom's Yoke

Wisdom as the Tree of Life: A reading for imaginative contemplation

Pause to relax body and mind, close eyes and calm breathing, then listen to the text read two or three times, building up an impression of the scene.

> Then the angel showed me the river of the water of life, bright as crystal, flowing from the throne of God and of the Lamb through the middle of the street of the city. On either side of the river is the tree of life with its twelve kinds of fruit, producing its fruit each month; and the leaves of the tree are for the healing of the nations.
>
> *Revelation 22:1-2*

In a time of quiet, imagine the trees by the river, with their ripe fruits and healing leaves. Who, where and what are *you*, in this scene?[23]

A time of silence

When you are ready, bring your awareness back to the room and the people around you.

Choose three leaves from the display, and let them reflect three healing needs. These might be:

- something within yourself
- something in a situation in your own life
- something in the wider world.

---

[23] A longer healing visualisation on this passage can be found in my earlier book, *Hiding in God* (Kevin Mayhew, 2012) p.145.

Imagine love surrounding these concerns, and bathing them with light.

Bring the leaves and place them on the earth.

Opportunity for song

OR

Wisdom's yoke: reflecting on laying down our burdens

Two readings:

It is written of Wisdom,
'Come to her with all your soul,
  and keep her ways with all your might.
Search out and seek, and she will become known to you;
  and when you get hold of her, do not let her go.
For at last you will find the rest she gives,
  and she will be changed into joy for you.
Then her fetters will become for you a strong defence,
  and her collar a glorious robe.
Her yoke is a golden ornament,
  and her bonds a purple cord.
You will wear her like a glorious robe,
  and put her on like a splendid crown.'

Sirach 6:26-31

Jesus spoke of a yoke too, as though he and Wisdom are one:

'Come to me, all you that are weary and are carrying heavy burdens, and I will give you rest. Take my yoke upon you, and learn from me; for I am gentle and humble in heart, and you will find rest for your souls. For my yoke is easy, and my burden is light.'

Matthew 11:28-30

Pause

In a moment of quiet, imagine your own concerns as heavy loads: reflect on whichever idea appeals to you – that of Jesus' yoke, a wooden one hand-made by a carpenter, which makes light of our burdens, or the golden yoke of Wisdom, which gives rest and joy to the soul.

Pause

Use movements to accompany these words:

> **I unburden my heart.**
> **I unburden my mind.**
> **I unburden my whole being,**
> **and lay my heavy load at the foot of the tree of life,**
> **to claim rest for my soul.**
> **Amen.**

Opportunity for song

CONTINUING WITH THE LITURGY –

A question and answer reflection:
[different voices can read the questions and responses]

Question: Many claim to be wise, yet how do we recognise true wisdom?

Response: Where there is envy and selfish ambition, there will also be disorder and wickedness of every kind. But the wisdom from above is first pure, then peaceable, gentle, willing to yield, full of mercy and good fruits, without a trace of partiality or hypocrisy. And a

211

harvest of righteousness is sown in peace for those who make peace.

James 3:16-18

Holy One, grant us your wisdom from above, to become peace-makers on earth.

Question: What is the beginning of Wisdom?

Response: The voice of Wisdom says,
'Ages ago I was set up,
at the first, before the beginning of the earth.
When there were no depths I was brought forth,
when there were no springs abounding with water.
Before the mountains had been shaped,
before the hills, I was brought forth.'

Proverbs 8:23-25

Eternal One, open our hearts and minds in awe.

Question: What does Wisdom say of our world and our lives?

Response: You have forsaken the fountain of wisdom.
If you had walked in the way of God,
you would be living in peace for ever.

Baruch 3:12-13

Source of All, draw us back to your fountain of wisdom, that we may walk your way and have peace in our hearts.

Question: And what of the Christ?

Response: It is written, that Christ is 'the power of God and the wisdom of God'.
We speak God's wisdom, secret and hidden,
which God decreed before the ages for our glory.

1 Corinthians 1:24b; 2:7

**O Beloved, let us drink of Wisdom's fountain
and welcome her holy power;
let us find peace growing in our hearts,
and share that peace with all the world.
Amen.**

Peace is shared with all, with the words 'Wisdom's peace' and a handclasp or hug.

Opportunity for song

Invitation to the Table

Wisdom stands in the marketplace and invites all to be her guests:
'Come, eat of my bread
and drink of the wine I have mixed.
Lay aside immaturity, and live,
and walk in the way of insight.'

Proverbs 9:5-6

Bread and wine are brought to the central table.

All are welcome to Wisdom's table.

In every generation she passes into holy souls
and makes them friends of God, and prophets.

Wisdom of Solomon 7:27b

213

All raise a hand in blessing, towards the bread and wine.

We bless the bread and wine of Wisdom's feast.
We honour all holy souls, all friends of God throughout the
ages and throughout the world.
We draw near, in gratitude for our own invitation to
Wisdom's table.

A time of quiet as all go to the table to take bread and wine or juice,
or pass it around the circle.

Opportunity for song

Closure:

It is said of Wisdom,
'Come to her with all your soul,
    and keep her ways with all your might.
Search out and seek, and she will become known to you;
    and when you get hold of her, do not let her go.
For at last you will find the rest she gives,
    and she will be changed into joy for you.'

Sirach 6:26-28

So may we walk in the way of God.

May Wisdom guide our steps in peace and joy.
Amen.

Shekhinah – Presence of God

This is simply a prayer. It could be used to open a creative session on the presence of God, expressed in myriad ways. Images can be sought from the Bible, from nature, from poetry or other writings, or from music. Participants may like to respond to verses of the prayer itself, choosing those they resonate with to explore feelings, or they may want to write new verses. The prayer can be illustrated, danced, turned into song, represented with photographs of nature . . . and offered up together at the end of the session for all to see the diversity of ways we can express our intimate experiences of God with us.

For a liturgy reflecting on the loving presence of God with us, see 'Liturgy of loneliness, solitude and aloneness' in the Liturgies of Humanity section. Change the language a little if you wish, to name the Shekhinah in the liturgy. The following prayer appears at the end.

Oh Shekhinah, oh loving presence of God,
be with me and hear my prayer.

When I feel afraid,
swoop down like a mighty eagle
and lift up my soul in praise and prayer,
renewing me,
empowering me to live with courage,
stirred by the beat of your mighty wings.

When I feel vulnerable,
spread your wings around me like a mother hen.
Let your touch be feather-soft,
gentle and comforting,
a hiding place for me to nestle into,
accepted, safe and loved,
your nest my home.

When I feel my love grow cold,
come to me, like a phoenix,

and sit on my shoulder or on my outstretched arm,
and be my companion,
intelligent, bright-eyed,
singing wordless songs to touch my heart,
your fiery plumage re-igniting my delight.

When I feel hurt,
be small as a sparrow
in the tangled hedge of my mind,
plucking out the thorns that cause me pain
and re-weaving them, delicately,
into nests where new life can grow,
softened by your own breast's down.

When I feel doubt,
be like a snow-white dove
that makes her home in the crevice of a rock,
and find a way to come into my heart,
and settle there, and make your nest
and let me feel your love
and know your presence,
undeniable, within.

When I feel lost,
be a star in the night, a lantern way ahead,
a lighthouse beam protecting my fragile boat from rocks,
a rescue dog, a welcome sign,
a kindly stranger with a map,
a friend coming out to me, along the path.
Be the radiant light, the comforting light,
the guiding light,
the glad light of hope.

When I feel angry,
settle around me as a golden, healing cloud
and draw from me all that is bitter,
let it dissipate into the air;
absorb my violence
and leave me with a passion to do good,
your own strength to work with humility
for justice and for mercy in the world.

When I feel bewildered by the complexities of life,
lift up the cloud and let the clarity of light shine through;
draw me higher up the mountain of your majesty
and ever further into mystery,
and there let me surrender to your glorious power,
the power of perfect love,
the brilliance of your presence,
no longer beyond me, but within.

Amen.

2. Liturgies of Nature

This section opens with a set of four meditational liturgies on the theme of the traditional elements, earth, air, fire and water, then goes on to explore other themes, including the expansiveness of God, and prayers concerning animals and trees.

The Elements

Since the elemental theme has such significance for so many today, it could be explored over a series of weeks, each week drawing together visual, tactile and audio resources on one of the elements, to add to the experience. The elements lend themselves to colour and expression of feelings. Bringing fabrics, pictures, natural objects, and so on, can support participants in finding unspoken layers of meaning.

The liturgies could also form part of a longer session, extending into or concluding a creative workshop – such as making a banner, an altar cloth, a community mural, squares for a tapestry – or an outdoor walk, urban or rural, to look for aspects of the element in question and perhaps get involved in related environmental concerns from litter-picking to reviewing carbon emissions.

Liturgy of Earth

There are quite a few texts in this reflection. A storytelling style with different voices and props for illustration would be appropriate. If possible, meet outside and encourage walking barefoot and sitting or lying on the ground, while maintaining sensitivity to special physical needs, especially seating.

If indoors, have soil, earth, in the centre, and/or pot plants. If planting bulbs or seeds, plan resources accordingly.

Choose suitable 'earthy' music for the start as people settle. One option is drumming, even circle-dancing, making a definite connection with the earth under foot.

The colour scheme might include a range of greens for vegetation, and earth colours – browns, reds and yellows.

This could be part of making a community garden or allotment, campaigning to protect local green space or regenerate urban space, spending time appreciating local woodland or reviewing church carbon footprint, considering animal rights issues, ethical food sources, ecology and social justice issues concerning land in other parts of the world . . . or it could lead into a bring-and-share meal.

Opening:

The 'Earth' blessing from Holy Hours and Days section

Option for everyone to chant this blessing several times over, even walking or stamping round in a circle, building up pace and energy – especially with drumming.

Blessings of earth, of rich, humble soil,
birthing and reclaiming each living thing,
blessings of wisdom and patience and hope,
blessings of cave and safe hiding place.

The prayer for the third day of the week (from Holy Hours and Days):

Gardener God,
let the seeds of our potential unfurl by your tender touch,
to blossom and bear good fruit in the world,
pruned vines from an ancient root, and trained in love,
to honour the green earth and the miracle of life.
Amen.

Reading:

> And God said, 'Let the waters under the sky be gathered
> together into one place, and let the dry land appear.' And
> it was so. God called the dry land Earth ... And God saw
> that it was good. Then God said, 'Let the earth put forth
> vegetation: plants yielding seed, and fruit trees of every
> kind on earth that bear fruit with the seed in it.' And it
> was so. The earth brought forth vegetation: plants yielding
> seed of every kind, and trees of every kind bearing fruit
> with the seed in it. And God saw that it was good.
>
> *Genesis 1:9-12*

Leader: The earth is where we get the word humility
from – Latin *hummus*, which is the layer of organic
matter – dead leaves, twigs and so on – that is
gradually decaying and releasing its nutrients into the
soil, enriching it. Soil may seem lowly, dirty, but it
is vital to life. Our needs come from the earth; even
the air we breathe comes from ancient forests, which
grew from seeds embedded in the earth, long ago.

Response: **We are of the earth and the earth is good.**

Leader: The mystery and sacredness of the earth have long
been recognised. In the book of Leviticus, we read
how the blood of all creatures, animals as well as
humans, if spilt anywhere other than in the temple,
must be poured on the ground and covered over with
soil; 'For the life of every creature – its blood is its
life ...' (Leviticus 17:14). Letting the life-blood seep
into the soil in some sense returns it to the source of
all life.

Response: We are of the earth and the earth is good.

Leader: In the Gospels, Jesus often talks about the earth and the way seeds are sown and sprout after a time of hiding away in the soil. He said our hearts are like the soil. Some land can receive seeds and allow them to bear fruit in themselves; others are too full of stones or brambles, to receive the seeds of God's wisdom. (Mark 4:1-20)

Response: We are of the earth and the earth is good.

Leader: In Psalm 139 we read of being 'knitted together' while still in the womb. We are formed from the minerals of the earth itself; we are of the earth, just as our ancestors were. The first human, according to Genesis 2:7, was formed of the 'dust of the ground', and his name is a play on the word meaning 'of the ground or of the earth', expressing a reddish colour. We are of the earth, the earth feeds us and to the earth we return.

Response: We are of the earth and the earth is good.

Opportunity for song

From the earth, all good things grow,
all green plants and fruit trees,
all grain crops, all root crops,
all mushrooms and all flowers,
and creatures eat of them,
or of one another;
and we, creatures too,

we take our fill and eat,
or else we die.
So we give thanks for the One who provides.
We give thanks for the source of abundance.
We give thanks for the lives which sustain our own lives.

A visualisation on being rooted and grounded in love.

See notes on leading a visualisation. Especially if outdoors, people may wish to lie down on the ground or at least take off shoes.

In the letters to the early church communities of the first century, we find a prayer for the followers of Jesus in Ephesus, which draws on the imagery of a tree growing strong, its roots planted firmly in the soil – soil which represents divine love:

'I pray that, according to the riches of [God's*] glory, [God**] may grant that you may be strengthened in your inner being with power through his Spirit, and that Christ may dwell in your hearts through faith, as you are being rooted and grounded in love.'

Ephesians 3:16-17

Stand, sit or lie down and relax your shoulders. Relax your neck, your back, your arms and legs . . . Close your eyes and focus on your breath, flowing in, flowing out . . .

Pause

See yourself as tree-like, growing tall, your arm-branches spreading out towards the sunlight; or as the kind of plant that can send out roots all along its length, like ivy.

Pause

---

* 'his' in NRSV
** 'he' in NRSV

Become aware of the part of you that is in contact with the ground, physically, or in your imagination.

Imagine that roots grow from the part of you that is in contact with the ground.

The roots anchor you to the living earth.

The earth is holding you; it is rich and moist, glowing with goodness and potential. You grew out of this rich, dark goodness, when you were a seed, long ago, and it has always nourished you. Take time to feel your roots enjoying this life-giving soil.

Pause

Your roots grow naturally from you, working their way downwards, seeking moisture and nutrients, to draw up into your body.

Imagine the gentle flow of living water, up from the soil which holds you.

The living water that flows up into you is full of love, liquid love.

Let liquid love flow into you from the earth, warming you, comforting you, relaxing you.

Longer pause

Now imagine your trunk and branches reaching upwards, fine twigs holding leaves up to the sun. Imagine yourself reaching out to catch the sunlight and to be nourished by it. Your roots hold you firmly as you sway in the breeze.

How does it feel, to be rooted and grounded in love?

Pause

Thank the earth, if you wish, before imagining your roots and branches drawing back into your body.

Gradually become more aware of your body, its contact with the ground, the sounds and smells around you. Notice your breathing. Be aware of the sensations in your body, telling you that you are free to move about as usual.

In your own time, open your eyes and return fully to this place.

Opportunity for a song

Touching the earth activity

Some may already have touched the earth, physically, but we now have time for all to connect further with the way the earth supports vegetation.

Outdoors:

There is now [15 minutes] to find a tree to sit with or lean against, or some other vegetation growing from the soil, to reflect on in our own ways – or just lie here in the grass and feel the earth holding you. Try to use all your senses, and to be quiet, stilling the thoughts in your mind too, so you can be receptive to nature.

Please come back when you hear the [drum] beginning to play.

Indoors:

There are pot plants to hold and sit with, and bulbs/larger seeds (such as nasturtium seeds or acorns) to plant in suitable soil or compost.

(Explain what is going to happen to the planted bulbs or seeds afterwards. Can they be taken home? Whilst it is in the spirit of the session to have bare hands, some may appreciate tools or gloves that prevent contact with soil.)

Draw back together using drum, music or song, according to preference.

Closing 'blood' thanksgiving ritual

> We heard earlier how blood is sacred, the life of the creature. We heard how, since ancient times, it is to be poured out on the ground and covered over with soil, for the life-blood belongs to God.

> **We give thanks for the life of every creature.**

> So many creatures are killed, for food and for other reasons. We know that many have died without the thanks and respect due to them. Let us now honour the lives of all creatures that die for the sake of human life, by accident or on purpose, and let us give thanks for them.

> **We give thanks for the life of every creature.**

> For many, red wine has come to represent blood – the blood of Christ poured out in love. Wine is the juice of the grape, life-blood of the earth. We use it here as a symbol of self-giving love, of the death of the innocent, for the sake of others.

> **We give thanks for the life-blood of the earth;**
> **we give thanks for the life-blood of all creatures,**
> **and we give thanks for the power of love,**

love which is stronger than death.

Repeat this prayer as a chant, while passing a cup or jug of wine around the circle so all can engage with it in their own way, perhaps by gazing into it or holding a hand over it in blessing – but not drinking it; this is an act of giving, not taking.

The wine or grape juice is held up for all to see, then poured onto the ground or into the pot of soil, which is to be taken outside at the end of the gathering and put on the soil.

All things come from you and of your own have we given you.

1 Chronicles 29:14

**All things come from you and of your own have we
given you,
O God who fills heaven and earth.
Amen.**

We say together a blessing on all the creatures of the earth, who have given their lives that human beings may eat.

**Most Holy One, maker of heaven and earth,
all creatures owe their lives to you,
and not one sparrow falls without your knowledge.
Every animal of the forest is yours
and the livestock of a thousand hills.
As with humanity, O God, you give them breath
    and nourishment
and when you withdraw these gifts, they die.
In taking the lives of your creatures, O God,
in felling your trees and cultivating your earth,**

we respect and give thanks
for all the lives which are given for human benefit.
May there be no pain, may there be no distress,
may your creatures be at peace
and may we be forgiven the shedding of blood.
Amen.

'Do I not fill heaven and earth?' says God;
so may we search and find the sacredness of the earth.

'Do I not fill heaven and earth?' says God;
so help us to love God through loving the earth.

'Do I not fill heaven and earth?' says God;
so may we take no more than we need,
and return what we can;
may we work for healing, not harm,
for regeneration, for re-greening;
may we cherish the earth
and all creation, now and in the time to come.
Amen.

Liturgy of Air

If possible, meet outdoors where the wind blows through trees.

If indoors, a quiet, gentle fan might add some interest; place
a ribbon or a scarf at a safe distance, to flutter, and perhaps a
windchime.

The liturgy mentions *Ruach*, or sacred breath, which is
described more fully in the Feminine Divine section.

This could be part of a longer session on renewable energy,
kite flying, conservation relating to trees and birds, including
feeding garden birds, clean air campaigns, reducing pollution,
climate change awareness, traffic calming, promoting cycling
routes . . .

Mention beforehand that there will be a focus on breathing, and that people should participate according to their own wellbeing needs.

Opening music:

Live or recorded wind instruments or voices, or a recording of Aeolian harps – harps designed to catch the wind and play eerie sounds without human intervention.

Blessing of Air from Holy Hours and Days:

Blessings of the Sacred Breath,
blessings of air and blowing wind,
blessings of clear mind and clear insight,
the interconnectedness of all that lives.

Prayer for the second day of the week from Holy Hours and Days:

O Holy One, with a voice as subtle as rain on grass,
and as mighty as rumbling thunder,
breathe through us, as the air we breathe,
flow through us, as a surging river,
that we may be emptied of all that obstructs you,
to be channels of your power in the world.
Amen.

Leader: In the Hebrew scriptures, words and concepts to do with wind, air, spirit and breath mingle. *Ruach*, the 'wind of God' which hovers over the primal waters before the beginning of time (Genesis 1:1-3), is not separate from the sacred life breath which animates all living things, and is not separate from the active power of God, filling all, moving, empowering, and uttering words of creativity and wisdom. There are other words too for the spirit, but *ruach* is the first to be mentioned, and is 'She'.

Let's pause for a moment and sense the wind around us, or any signs of the air's movement [or, if indoors, to the sound of wind creating music through song or wind instruments].

Pause

Now, let's talk back to the wind with our own wordless voices. *(Leader and key participants may need to lead this, to encourage others.)*

Some unusual sounds may emerge as we do this; please accept the sounds you hear and support one another gently and calmly.

I invite you to close your eyes and relax your body . . . your shoulders, your neck, your chest and belly . . . Then calmly, when you are ready, begin to make a sound without words, breathing naturally – a hum, a shhh, or a soft whooo . . . Imagine the sound being carried out into the atmosphere beyond us, joining the flow of air, of wind, circulating the earth.

The sounds may well come from high up in your throat and chest at first, as you get used to the experience, but gradually, try to let your voice sink down and come from a deeper place. Let your voice begin to express your heart, your feelings, the depths of your inner being . . .

Take time for voices to emerge. Encourage calm, and a gentle, passing humour rather than laughter.

As the sounds ebb away, a leader introduces the next stage:

Now let's replace the wordless sound with a single word each, repeated over and over, whispering, singing or chanting, a word from the heart, such as 'be', or 'love', 'joy', 'peace' ... each sending their own word out on the wind, into the atmosphere, as a prayer or a blessing to all life.

When the sound ends, pause.

Now let us just focus on our own breathing, the air flowing into our lungs ... and leaving ... breathing in ... and breathing out ...

When we breathe more deeply, it can relax us, but it can energise us too. It can help us to feel more fully alive.

Close your eyes for a moment and imagine yourself up on a hill, the wind blowing all around you, pushing or pulling at you, almost blowing right through you. Imagine the fresh air entering you ... and leaving you ... in ... and out ...

Pause in silence for a suitable time, at least 15 seconds.

Leader: According to the Gospel of John, Jesus told a woman he once met that God is Spirit, and is to be worshipped 'in spirit and truth' (John 4:24). Jesus and his companions grew up with a Hebrew understanding of Spirit as *Ruach*, the sacred breath, the wind of God, that animates all living beings: 'She'.

According to the same Gospel, when Jesus appeared to his frightened followers, after his death, he breathed on them, and they received the 'Holy

231

Spirit', the sacred breath, which empowered and inspired them (John 20:21-22). He also said to them, 'Peace be with you.'

Allow those words 'Peace be with you' to echo in your mind. Close your eyes for a while and hear them resonate deep within. In your own time, whisper or speak or sing these words, 'peace be with you', into the group, over and over again, to bless one another. *(Leader and key participants may need to lead this, to encourage others.)*

When the voices stop, invite everyone to choose whether to move about visiting any who remain sitting, or whether to stay seated and receive 'visitors'. Shake hands, saying, 'peace be with you'. (Hugging may seem appropriate but not everyone may feel comfortable with this.)

Return to circle.

We are told that one of the leading teachers of the new way of Jesus, Paul, quoted a pagan poet from Ancient Greece back at his listeners in Athens. Paul said that God is very close to us all, and that in God 'we live and move and have our being' (Acts 17:28).

It is as though God is the air we breathe.

O God, in you we live,
in you we breathe,
in you we think and move and have our being.
Sustaining One,
Supporting One,
most Intimate One,

source of the sacred breath,
the animating air,
within us and all around us,
uniting all that lives,
we seek to know your presence.
Help us to trust you
and to love you,
to join in praise of you, with all that breathes,
O Holy One.
Amen.

Close at this point or with a return to the music played earlier.

Liturgy of Fire

Use a venue where it is safe to light candles or a fire. Have a central candle, with plenty of small candles to be lit in the course of the liturgy and placed centrally or around the room. This is most effective during the evening, when the light can be dimmed. (Use large print for service sheets.) If outdoors, light a fire at the centre in advance – bear in mind this can take longer than we might hope! Take all due safety precautions.

This liturgy could be part of a wider reflection on energy, the power of the sun, warmth, poverty issues and keeping warm in the winter.

As always, choose suitable music for the beginning. Drumming – such as djembe or bodhran – is one option.

To lead into the theme, begin with different voices reading the introductory passages, each followed by a pause.

Introductory music

Opening:

Blessing of Fire (from the Holy Hours and Days section)

> Blessings of fire, the devouring flame;
> **blessings of a God whom we cannot contain,**
> blessings of the one who gives and takes,
> **whose power is manifest for love's sake.**

> Fire is a divine metaphor: 'God is a devouring fire ...'
> *(Deuteronomy 4:24)*

Kindle your flame in our hearts, O God.

Light a candle

> In the poetry of the Song of Songs, fire is used as a metaphor
> of love.

> Set me as a seal upon your heart,
>   as a seal upon your arm;
> for love is strong as death,
>   passion fierce as the grave.
> Its flashes are flashes of fire,
>   a raging flame.
> Many waters cannot quench love,
>   neither can floods drown it.
> *Song of Songs 8:6-7*

Kindle your flame in our hearts, O God.

Light a candle

Fire is also used to describe the mysterious presence of divine power, as experienced by human beings. Soon after Jesus died, according to the account in Acts, his followers had a strange and powerful experience. The presence of the Holy Spirit, the 'wind' of God's sacred breath, came to them like fire:

'And suddenly from heaven there came a sound like the rush of a violent wind, and it filled the entire house where they were sitting. Divided tongues, as of fire, appeared among them, and a tongue rested on each of them. All of them were filled with the Holy Spirit ...'

Acts 2:2-4

Kindle your flame in our hearts, O God.

Light a candle

According to the Gospels, Jesus himself spoke of the cleansing fire of harvest-time, which burned up chaff and stalks separated from the ripe grain. If we are the grain, this can describe the removal of what gets in the way of us being truly useful, or the removal of what we no longer need to be whole.

Kindle your flame in our hearts, O God.

Light a candle

O love, strong as death,
    and fierce as the grave,
your flashes are flashes of fire,
    a raging flame.
No water can quench you, O love,
    no flood can drown you.

235

It is written that God is love. (1 John 4:16)
O love, O Holy One, set us on fire with your love. (a Franciscan prayer)

What is God's living presence, if not a fire, lighting up our hearts?
O Love, O Holy One, set us on fire with your love.

What is God's power, if not the power to strip us of all that keeps us from our true potential?
O Love, O Holy One, set us on fire with your love.

Opportunity for a song from preferred tradition on themes of love and fire, and/or a chant, preferably with drum and movement, rising to a crescendo then diminishing again, to the words:

Rush of wind,
fire from above,
come, sacred Spirit,
come, O Love!

A time of silence

Invite people to go round the circle and talk about what sets their hearts on fire with love and gladness, using a piece of kindling wood as a talking stick.

If indoors with a central candle display, offer participants the opportunity to light more small candles, to represent their loves. Depending on the location, people might like to light several candles each and place them in safe places around the room, then dim the lights for a while, to enjoy the candlelight.

(Note, if there is a bonfire, it might seem a good idea to burn things you want to be rid of, symbolically. It is worth thinking about this beforehand – there is something healthy about getting rid of old dead matter to make way for fresh growth, but it can nevertheless be quite a powerful gesture. I do not recommend committing anything to the flames that might be regretted later, or that might cause offence, including names or pictures of people.)

Spend some time in silence and, if suitable, use a simple song or chant from preferred tradition, or evocative music, live or recorded. One option is to whisper the chant used above, repetitively:

Rush of wind,
fire from above,
come sacred Spirit,
come, O Love.

A candle visualisation
(allow a pause between each suggestion).

As we sit in the firelight, or candlelight, let us close our eyes for a while and be aware of the sounds, the smells of fire; what it communicates to us deep within.

Be aware of your breath, your body posture. Try to relax. (Use the body relaxation exercise on pages 25-26.)

Close your eyes or keep them focussed on the flame. Imagine a candle – how does it look? What colour and shape is it?

Let this candle represent yourself. See your inner being, the heart of you known to God, as the wick running right through.

See the flame being lit, at the beginning of your life, from the source of all lights.

Watch the little pool of wax melted by the heat. See the wax as God's love, given to you, sustaining you.

Watch the flame. How is it burning? Does it flicker, or burn undisturbed? Does it seem weak or strong? Is it affected by draughts, interference from the world around you, or is it at peace? What does the flame suggest to you?

Imagine a draught disturbing the flame.

Now, if you wish, imagine a glass jar or a lantern around the candle, protecting it. The light can still shine, but undisturbed. You can imagine your inner light sheltered like this, whenever you feel troubled by influences around you.

Imagine this fire warming you and making you glow deliciously, from within.

Imagine the flames to be flames of love's power, giving you energy and desire to live your life to the full.

Welcome the inner glow, as you welcome God within you. Let your light shine out in the darkness, a light for the world, burning with love.

Sit for a while, in the warmth and light of this flame.

Longer pause

In time, become aware of the sounds and smells around you, the presence of other people, the light of flames in the centre of the circle. Give yourself time to stretch and come back to the present company.

Let us pray.

Thanks be to God, the sun of our lives,
and thanks to God, our warmth,
and thanks to God, our light.

Holy One, thank you for the warmth of your love.
Warm me from within, comfort me and enlighten me,
let me shine with your love
and so bring gladness and hope to all around.
Amen.

Liturgy of Water

The presence of a running water feature or a natural spring or stream would support this liturgy. If this is not possible, have a bowl of water in the centre, and/or a picture of a natural spring, and a number of small bowls.

Begin with suitable music playing in the background, which can be phased out.

Opening:

Blessing of Water (from Holy Hours and Days)

Blessings of the water of eternal life,
welling up, within our hearts,
blessings of sea and river and rain,
blessings of tide, of ebb and flow.

'They feast on the abundance of your house,
and you give them drink from the river of your delights.
For with you is the fountain of life;
in your light we see light.'

Psalm 36:8-9

May your fountain of life well up within us
and flow out, in blessing to the world.

All extend a hand or hands towards the water in the centre, saying together:

Be blessed, precious water,
here and everywhere;
may your power work for good,
to support life in abundance.

Leader: We pause now, to reflect on what water means in our own lives.

Pause

Leader: We each have our own experiences of water. While we cannot live without it, and often find it beautiful, it has immense power and sometimes it disturbs or endangers us, reminding us of human fragility.

In a time of sharing, we can tell one another how we feel about water – or we can talk to the water itself.

In groups of [three, four or five], pass round a small bowl of water filled from the central bowl. Each person will use the bowl like a talking stick, saying something of their own experience and feelings. Others support by listening quietly. When everyone in your group has had a turn, please sit quietly until all of us are ready.

As groups fall quiet, draw everyone back together by inviting someone from each group to empty their small bowl back into the larger one.

We say together:
Be blessed, precious water,
here and everywhere;

be blessed, precious water,
within us and beyond us.
May your great power work for good;
by your clarity and gentleness,
teach us of God's love.
Be blessed, precious water,
carrying us on.

Now we settle back into the circle to let the water touch us deep within.

May our minds be open to explore,
and may our hearts be open to adore
the source of the living water,
the source of all peace and love.
Amen.

A guided meditation

(Each stage needs to be followed by a pause of at least 15 seconds, to allow people to form their impressions free from interruption.)

Begin with the relaxation exercise on pages 25-26.

In your mind's eye, imagine a shrine before you. Take time to notice what kind of place it is – simple or ornate, ancient or new, set in a garden or in the middle of a city ...

Approach the shrine – are there steps to ascend or descend? Is there a great gateway, or a simple door?

How does it feel to step within? How do you wish to show your respect?

Is it a simple place or full of colours and decorations? Is there subdued lighting, candles in darkness or bright light? What are the sounds? Is there music? Singing? Is it cool? Comfortably warm? Stonework, woodwork, tiles, textiles, overhanging branches . . . ?

As you grow used to the space, you become aware of the sound of gently bubbling water. Go towards this sound and notice where it is coming from. Is there a well? Is there a pool in the floor? Is it up on a platform or behind a screen, down in a cellar, or in a lovely courtyard? . . .

Watch the spring of water, see how clear and fresh it is, sparkling as though alive. Notice there is a creature enjoying the water somehow, which shows you that it is safe. How do you want to respond to it? Touch it? Drink it? Bathe in it? Spend time experiencing the water.

(Allow a longer pause of at least 30 seconds, up to several minutes.)

In time, you notice that the water is spilling out over the edge of its pool, trickling over the floor. The trickle becomes a sparkling stream which finds its way out through the door of the sanctuary. You can journey out with the water, swimming in it, floating on it, even becoming the water itself . . .

The water flows on and on, and everywhere it goes, life springs up along its banks. Fish leap, birds wade and dive, reeds, trees and flowers sprout, people laugh with delight . . . wherever it flows, there is rejuvenation, healing and beauty.

In a time of quiet, notice where the stream flows, who and what is blessed by its refreshing waters. Imagine loved ones and places being rejuvenated by the living waters, which bring only blessing and cause no harm.

A longer pause

In time, let yourself gently return to this room, allowing the spring waters to recede or withdraw to the well within the temple. Look back at that temple or sanctuary and know that it is within you. Know that you can visit that temple any time you like and draw on that spring of living water welling up within.

Become aware of your breathing, of your body, your seat, your feet on the floor, the sounds around you, and when you are ready, open your eyes and sit quietly for a while.

In silence or by sharing with somebody nearby, take time to reflect on the meditation, and what it suggested to you about being a holy temple from which living water flows.

Opportunity for a song or music from your preferred tradition, on the theme of water

and/or this prayer used as a repetitive chant, with gestures to mind, heart and the wider world, to match the words:

> **May our minds be open to explore,**
> **and may our hearts be open to adore**
> **the source of the living water,**
> **the source of all peace and love.**
> **May your sacred stream well up within**
> **and flow out, in blessing to the world.**
>
> **Amen.**

Liturgy of Outdoors

The theme explores the endless potential for encounter with the divine in the natural world. It needs to be held outdoors, preferably in a place where people can sit or bring seating, if needed.

Opening:

> The Eternal One fills heaven and earth!
> **May we seek and find God's loving presence.**

A prayer:

Eternal One who fills heaven and earth,
God of the open places where we can be free,
we seek to be aware of your presence here with us now.
Yours is the breath of life itself,
so surround us and fill us,
hear us and catch our prayers
as we speak them into the wind.

Let us pause for a moment to take notice of this place.

Pause

Look up at the sky, endless above us.
Feel the movement of air, the temperature, the sun's rays.
Look all around at the lie of the land, the features,
the creatures,
the trees and rocks, water and soil.
Feel the soil beneath your feet,
notice birdsong and scents in the air,
breathe, watch, listen, touch . . .
Let something in particular catch your attention and become
an anchor that connects you more deeply to this place.

A time of quiet

Let us witness to the wonder around us by speaking the names
of things we have noticed – a word or two each, around
the circle.

Listen to one another naming aspects of the natural world.

Say together:

Holy One,
We cannot contain you, define you or control you,
help us to find the freedom we seek;
and understanding of what it means
to be truly alive in this world you have made.
Amen.

A short biblical reflection in a storytelling style

Maybe God who fills heaven and earth does not want to be enclosed either. There is an account in the Bible describing a time long ago, when the first kings and queens of Israel were established in Jerusalem. The warrior-hero King David had built himself a fine palace of cedar wood, as was the fashion among royalty of the region in those days, and it occurred to him that he should now build a palace – a temple rather – for the God of his ancestors, on whom he had depended for his rise to power. As he said, so eloquently, 'See now, I am living in a house of cedar, but the ark of God stays in a tent' (2 Samuel 7:2). It was a very fine tent, when all is said and done, precision-made to divine specifications, by the Israelite ancestors during their desert-days (Exodus 26). Nathan, the king's advisor, told King David he was sure the idea would be as blessed as his other projects, but then in the night had a dream in which God said, 'Wherever I have moved about among all the people of Israel, did I ever speak a word with any of the tribal leaders of Israel, whom I commanded to shepherd my people Israel, saying, "Why have you not built me a house of cedar?"' (2 Samuel 7:7). So Nathan went back to the king and told him this, and for this reason no temple was built in David's day, but only in the days of his son, the mighty King Solomon.

Before the temple was built, the divine presence,[24] God's dazzling glory, would come down as a cloud – or *in* a cloud.

---

[24] God's presence personified as Shekhinah is explored in the section on the feminine divine.

Moses first entered this glory-cloud high up on the mountain Sinai, his followers gazing on in awe. The presence remained with the people, leading them through the wilderness, a pillar of fire by night and a cloud by day. When the tent of meeting was made, the glory of God visited and was present among the people in a cloud which they could see, hovering at the entrance (Exodus 40:34-38). They say that Jesus entered that glory-cloud up on a mountain too and was transformed with dazzling light (Mark 9:2-8).

God of the mountain glory-cloud,
lead us through our own wildernesses,
lighten our steps,
brighten our nights,
and let your brilliance gladden our hearts,
wherever we may be,
O Holy One.
Amen.

Those drawn to Jesus can find confidence to seek God outdoors, in the way he lived.

A different voice can read each of the following:

Jesus slept rough and prayed on his own at night on the mountainsides. During his fasting ordeal, he shared his time with angels and wild beasts.

The Spirit immediately drove him out into the wilderness. He was in the wilderness for forty days, tempted by Satan; and he was with the wild beasts; and the angels waited on him.

Mark 1:12-13

Someone once asked to join Jesus on the way. And Jesus said to him, 'Foxes have holes, and birds of the air have nests; but the Son of Man (or the 'child of humanity' – meaning himself) has nowhere to lay his head.'

Matthew 8:20

'Now when Jesus heard this (that John the Baptist had been killed), he withdrew from there in a boat to a deserted place by himself.' Crowds join him and his disciples and he ministers to them before sending them away again. 'And after he had dismissed the crowds, he went up the mountain by himself to pray. When evening came, he was there alone.'

Matthew 14:13, 23

Jesus of the mountains and wild places,
Jesus of hillsides and flowering meadows,
Jesus of barley fields and wild animals,
be our brother and our teacher,
our guide along the way.
Amen.

Prayer:

In awe of creation (inspired by Psalm 104)

Holy One, I stand in awe of you;
I am humbled by your majesty, yet I long to draw closer to you.
Although I cannot comprehend your magnitude,
the smallest detail of creation
reveals your wonder.

I could marvel at your works, O God, one by one,
all my days, and never reach an end.

From the delicacy of a feather
to the precision of a crystal,
from the mysterious journey of the moon,
to the flight of the wild birds.
How can such wonders exist,
except for a perfect mind, first envisioning them?

**I could marvel at your works, O God, one by one,
all my days, and never reach an end.**

When I look at the earth and out at the stars,
the universe beyond us,
all this must surely come from your desire
to make something of unutterable beauty.
Then, I marvel at the trees and plants,
the diversity, the colours and scents, the foods they yield,
and the little insects which love them,
and I marvel at all your creatures,
the interconnectedness of the great web of life,
which surely owes its existence to you.
Even the mountains, the forests and plains, the great oceans,
all these things reveal the splendour of their creator.

**I could marvel at your works, O God, one by one,
all my days, and never reach an end.**

You even made humanity, greatest of all,
yet also most foolish and most able to damage
this pristine earth that you have made,
most capable, most intelligent and loving,
but also most self-serving and unwilling to consider
the consequences of our destructive acts.

**I could marvel at your works, O God, one by one,
all my days, and never reach an end.**

Yes, if you made this universe you made us too
and love us, as you love the whole,
so let us learn to humble ourselves before our maker,
and submit ourselves to Wisdom's voice,
aligning ourselves to the way you want humanity to live,
that we may play our part in this your world
as lovers of peace and caretakers together of this living jewel.

Amen.

We now take [15 minutes] either to stay quietly here, or to
find a place nearby where we can be still and listen, open to
the wisdom of creation. Please come back when you hear [this
drum beating].

Time for quiet reflection

*On return, invite people to share thoughts and experiences. Allow
plenty of time for this, using a talking stick or stone (see guidance
notes), unless the weather makes it uncomfortable to sit listening for
a long time.*

*Alternatively, to get warm (or after the sharing time), stand in a
circle and stamp or clap in rhythm to this chant, using a drum if
available. Turn the chant into a simple circle dance if you wish:*

**The mountains and the hills shall burst into song
and the trees of the field shall clap their hands!**
(from Isaiah 55:12)

Having engaged with the natural world ourselves,
reminding ourselves of how important creation is, let us
pray for the earth here and beyond us.

Let us pray for the earth,
and our part in caring for the earth,
with thanks for earth's goodness and sorrow for our failings,
asking for divine help in walking the way of wisdom.

Holy One, we pray for our own contact with the earth:
the food we eat, our gardens and pot plants, our own
enjoyment of the natural world.
Especially, we thank you for . . .
We ask for your love to influence . . .

**Protect what we love and teach us to take good care of
your earth.**

Holy One, we pray for the area where we live, and our
local concerns:

Especially, we thank you for . . .
We ask for your love to influence . . .

**Protect what we love and teach us to take good care of
your earth.**

Holy One, we pray for this land, for the woodlands and
rivers, the mountains and farmlands . . .

Especially, we thank you for . . .
We ask for your love to influence . . .

**Protect what we love and teach us to take good care of
your earth.**

Holy One, we pray for the wellbeing of the whole planet,
our home and home to all life.

Especially, we thank you for . . .
We ask for your love to influence . . .

**Protect what we love and teach us to take good care of
your earth.**

**We make these prayers with sincerity,
asking that you accept our good intentions,
and by your love, weave together the greatest good,
in our lives and the lives of all who share this planet,
to become a blessing for the future.
This we ask, recognising our own limitations
and your own all-powerful and self-giving love,
Amen.**

A closing psalm:

Natural praise (inspired by Psalms 148 and 150)

Praise God!
Praise the Holy One from the far reaches of the universe;
sing praises from the mountain tops!
Praise God, all you angels,
sing praises, you who do God's will.
Praise the Holy One, sun and moon,
sing praises, all the stars of heaven!
Praise the Eternal One, you rolling clouds,
**sing praises, you oceans and flowing rivers,
for God is your source, the one who loves you.**

Praise the Holy One from the ends of the earth;
sing praises, you sea creatures and all you birds of the air!
Praise God, rain and snow, fire and stormy wind,
sing praises, you who are wild and free.
Praise the Holy One, you gardens and fruit trees
and all the trees of the forest,
sing praises, you creatures, wild and tame!
Praise God, you peoples of the earth,
leaders and followers, men and women,
   old and young alike,
sing praises and make delightful music
to the Holy One who fills the universe;
let all that has breath unite to sing in praise of God.
Amen.

Liturgy for blessing a place for use (indoors or outdoors), or for reclaiming a troubled place

This can be used outdoors or indoors. Place is important; when Moses encountered the burning bush, the voice told him to remove his sandals because he was on holy ground. The presence of God was tangible through a natural wonder. The Hebrews encamped in the wilderness did not approach the mountain where Moses received his revelations because of an air of immense sanctity. We can feel that a place has natural wonder, and we can also feel that a place is holy because of prayer over generations. For some, the whole of creation is sacred, and every natural place has a sanctity or a 'thinness'[25] about it. We can also feel that a place is troubled in some way. This may be because we know something disturbing happened there, but sometimes we have a 'bad feeling' about a place without knowing its history.

---

[25] For reflection on 'thinness', see my earlier book, *Search me and Know me.*

The 'spirit of a place' means different things to different people. It may mean an actual entity attached to an area, which is an ancient idea we find in many cultures (for example, the wilderness entity Azazel in Leviticus 16), but equally, the term might refer to a sense of atmosphere affected by a microclimate and the way it is used or neglected by humans and other living things, or because of public perception arising from folklore about a place. Whatever our views on the 'spirit of a place', it is widely accepted that it can help to invoke a warm and friendly atmosphere through gathering together in prayer and companionship. Similarly, if committing a place for special use, it can support the intention of the project to say special prayers of renewal and dedication.

Resources needed:

Portable incense and candles (in jars or lanterns), containers of water, small bells or other metallic things that make a joyful ringing sound.

Decide beforehand what mood is appropriate, for example:

- a merry and light-hearted community stroll to bless the neighbourhood, with chat and laughter along the way, perhaps even with refreshments at the stations, not unlike the old rogation-tide processions around the parish boundaries and fields;

- a meditative walk in silence, respecting the atmosphere of the place;

- solemn prayers after something distressing has occurred in a place;

- dedication of a new home or community building.

This liturgy ideally involves walking around. Consider mobility issues within the group in advance. If some need or want to stay at base, try to provide pictures and/or a 'map' of the place to reflect on, with candles and prayers. Try to make the base place significant: a threshold place to bless those who come in and go out, a 'hearth' place of meeting and eating, a 'hub' place of connecting with others. Encourage people who are staying put to support the walkers, and vice versa.

Starting place

Welcome and explanation of the purpose of the gathering. This can be extended into storytelling, with drama, music and/or poetry, involving any number of participants. This could, for example, be an activity for a children's group to plan.

The Holy One is here, as close as the air we breathe.

**The Holy One is here, within us and around us.
In God we live and move and have our being.**

We meet in this place, recognising its past. We think of the people and creatures who passed through and spent time here, the lives interconnected by this place.

The Holy One is here, within us and around us.

We think of the stories about this place, the things that happened here, that we have heard of, and the things that are unknown to us.

The Holy One is here, within us and around us.

We connect with the natural goodness of this place, the earth beneath us, the rocks, water and living things, the sky above, the air we breathe.

The Holy One is here, within us and around us.

Here we meet together, the love in our hearts reaching out to fill this place with goodness, with warmth and kindness, with love and peace.

Pause in silence.
Any who are going to remain in the starting place can say:

> **Here we stay, at peace in this place,**
> **speaking words of gentleness and love.**
> **If once there was brokenness and pain,**
> **may there now be abundant life.**
> **Amen.**

Continue with reflections as appropriate.

Those processing stand and say:

> **Now we walk about this place.**
> **Where others have trod heavily,**
> **let us tread lightly on the earth.**
> **If troubles once filled the air,**
> **let us speak words of gentleness and love.**
> **If others once brought distress,**
> **let us bring peace.**
> **If once there was brokenness and pain,**
> **may there now be healing and abundant life.**
> **Amen.**

A procession is formed and all walk from place to place (decide in advance where to stop), carrying candles, water, incense and bells. Participants may wish to walk barefoot.

At each 'station':

Explanation of why you have stopped here. This could be extended to include dance, drama, music and poetry.

Hold up candles
Blessings of the light: the light of the world!

Sprinkle water
Blessings of the living water that gives renewal and hope.

Wave incense
Blessings and praise by all that lives!

Ring bells[26]
Blessings of dedication to goodness and love!
Amen!

Opportunity for a song, light refreshments or, on a more reflective note, join hands and stand in silence for a minute, ending with an 'Amen'.

Setting off again, repeat the prayer:
Now we walk about this place.
Where others have trod heavily,
let us tread lightly on the earth . . .

and repeat the whole process until the whole place has received attention, then return to the starting point. If people have been waiting here, re-group with sensitivity to the fact that they may still be praying.

---

[26] Exodus 28:33, Sirach 45:9: Aaron's garments were adorned with tiny golden bells to make a sound as he walked, as a reminder to the children of Israel and a protection from harm.

If refreshments have not been shared already, this may be a good time and place to share refreshments and music.

Option of including a ritual of bread and wine.

Animal and plant themes

Breeding for food, killing and eating animals

Recently on a social media site I noticed a question from a Muslim to a Christian, asking what prayers are said at the death of an animal killed for food. The fact that Christianity does not have a ritual or even a traditional prayer to be said on such an occasion seems to be a sad omission, especially as the faith began with two out of three restrictions on behaviour being to do with meat consumption, according to Acts 15:19-20: 'Therefore I (James, brother of Jesus) have reached the decision that we should not trouble those Gentiles who are turning to God, but we should write to them to abstain only from things polluted by idols and from fornication and from whatever has been strangled and from blood.'

This prompted me to write a prayer. I have to say, I offer this prayer as a lifelong vegetarian/vegan with a concern for animal welfare in farming, not wishing in this instance to enter into the politics of the meat industry itself as much as to appreciate that there are those who do find ways to eat meat which has been ethically reared and dispatched according to values which honour creature and creator. The intention is that the prayer may be said for any creature which is to be killed for food, as close to the time of death as possible. If the prayer is being said over a group of animals, change singular to plural. Whatever our views on the whole issue, the intention in religious slaughter is that the act be done with respect, compassion and a high level of skill; without

this, the prayer is diminished. An adapted form of this prayer
has been included in the 'Earth' liturgy earlier in this section, in
which life-blood is honoured.

> Most Holy One, maker of heaven and earth,
> all creatures owe their lives to you,
> and not one sparrow falls without your knowledge.
> Every animal of the forest is yours
> and the livestock of a thousand hills.
> As with humanity, O God, you give them breath
>   and nourishment
> and when you withdraw these gifts, they die.
> In taking the life of this your creature, O God,
> we do so with all respect, giving thanks
> for this life which is given for our nourishment.
> May there be no pain, may there be no distress,
> may this creature of yours be at peace
> and may we be forgiven the shedding of blood.
> Amen.

Animal Companions

In asking what kind of liturgies people would find useful, I found
that many suggestions involved animal companions – pets. This
was not a surprise, having presided over a number of child-
friendly pet burials over the years, and been present at a number
of creatures' final visits to the vet – hamster, guinea pig, cat
and dog. All sorts of strong emotions come up, from guilt and
anxiety about making the right decision, or about the animal's
comfort, to a sense of loss, or of concern for a loved one who is
going to grieve.

It is often said that experiencing the death of a pet is a way of
introducing the fact of mortality to children, and indeed it can

be. Views differ on whether it is more helpful to talk directly about death or to avoid doing so, because it can seem so stark. I used the euphemism 'put to sleep' concerning a poorly hamster, many years ago, which confused my son, who was little at the time. He expected her to wake up again when she was better – so it would be wrong to bury her. I decided to speak more directly after this.

We each have our own views on what may or may not happen after death, for humans and for other creatures, so anything we state about 'whatever next' really needs to be qualified with 'I think that' or 'In my view', or 'What this passage in the Bible means to me, is . . .'. Allowing children to form their own impressions, based on what makes sense to them, supports their emerging spiritual journeys. They are inevitably influenced by significant people in their lives but are also likely to change their minds, just as adults do.

Children of course are not the only ones for whom animal funerals take place; pets touch so many of our hearts, not least the elderly, for whom the loss of a companion animal can be a particular blow.

A prayer for an animal companion that is going to be put down

Loving God,
all creatures owe their lives to you,
and they are all known to you.
Thank you for the life of [name], who has brought us
    so much joy;
we have tried to look after him/her as well as we can,
and now we are sure the kindest thing is to help [name]
    die peacefully.
We want [name] to know that she/he is greatly loved, now
    as always,

and as his/her life ends may your own loving presence
surround him/her
and fill him/her with peace.
Amen.

A pet burial

Pet burials and ash-scatterings are very personal and often the
way children first encounter death. You may feel there are degrees
of intensity – perhaps the long-term companionship of a larger
animal, a cat, dog or horse, might require more thought and
emotional involvement than the passing of a goldfish. Please
adapt the language to suit the participants and the creature.

A suitable spot is located for burial, a hole dug and the animal
placed near or inside – in a biodegradable box if appropriate.

Mourners may wish to bring tributes to place on the grave,
on which they have written and want to read out or sing.

Loving God,
we are here to return [name] to the earth.
Throughout our lives, the earth gives us and all living
things everything we need.
It is natural to give the body of [name] back, with thanks
and love.

Jesus said that not even a sparrow, a little garden bird, dies
without God knowing (Matthew 10:29). In one of the oldest
books of the Bible, there is a story about a donkey who was
being treated badly. An angel told the owner off! (Numbers
22:22-35). So we can trust that God knows all about [name],
how we have loved him/her and how he/she has spent his/her
days – and nights. God knows better than we do, about
[name's] feelings and delights, fears and dreams.

Encourage people to mention memories with gentle humour.

God knows ... what [name] got up to when we were out.
God knows ... what [name] used to dream about when his
paws were twitching ...
God knows ... how she always knew when ...
God knows about the time ...

Let's say a prayer.

Loving God,
thank you for [name], who has brought us so much joy,
we will always have special memories of the times
we shared together.
While this body of [name] is dead and needs to
return to the earth,
the spirit of [name] lives on in our love,
which does not die.
Amen.

Now we share our own thoughts, hopes and prayers.

Start by making some 'I wish' statements. At the end of each, flowers
might be placed or thrown on the ground.

I wish for [name] green fields to run free ...
I wish for [name] a warm fire to curl up by ...
I wish for [name] all the hay she can eat ...
I wish for [name] a safe warm burrow in the ground ...

Now we will cover [name] over with earth because it is time
to let him/her go in peace.

Soil is filled in on top of the body – let children help if they want to.

We place this marker on the grave.

After the marker has been placed, people can also put flowers and other tributes on the grave, then pause for a moment's quiet.

Now the burial is over, let's say one more prayer:

Dear God, you know that we are feeling sad,
please help us get used to living without [name],
and in our memories, to find gladness again.
Help us to be kind and thoughtful to each other,
today and tomorrow, and always.
Amen.

Giving thanks to food

Graces and harvest festival liturgies abound, thanking God for food and 'all good gifts'. What tends to be lacking in the Christian tradition is a thanksgiving directed at living things themselves, which have died to feed us or otherwise meet our needs. Most of us live far removed from the processes that bring us our 'daily bread' and more, and it is easy to see our food and other things as objects, products, rather than as beautiful, complex entities in their own right – indeed, animals such as pigs and chickens are often referred to in the industry as 'products' rather than living beings. We are only just moving away from medieval attitudes, which claimed that animals could not feel pain and had no soul or spiritual dimension. This prayer extends gratitude to the living things themselves – some may see this as a pointless gesture, but we do after all thank one another for making sacrifices for the good of others, and the act fosters a sense of appreciation and respect for our part in the food chain and the greater web of life.

The prayer is in the form of a litany. A litany is a stream of petitions from a leader, with a response from the collective. It has a rhythm and repetitive pattern to it. It is in the spirit of a prayer written by St Francis, who addressed aspects of the natural world such as sun, moon and water directly in his canticle to Brother Sun.

Gentle lambs and sheep of the flock,
grazing in your green pastures,
for all that you give us, by the grace of God,
we thank you and we bless you.

Lowing cattle of field and barn,
of milking sheds and separated calves,
for all that you give us, by the grace of God,
we thank you and we bless you.

Bright-eyed pigs and piglets, lovers of the mud,
so often caged behind bars,
for all that you give us, by the grace of God,
we thank you and we bless you.

Fussing chickens, soil-scratching,
eggs and chicks nestling,
for all that you give us, by the grace of God,
we thank you and we bless you.

Smooth fish, in a water world of your own,
scales and gills so different from us, yet still so alive,
for all that you give us, by the grace of God,
we thank you and we bless you.

Little bees, lovers of the flowers,
dancers in the sun, honeycomb architects,

for all that you give us, by the grace of God,
we thank you and we bless you.

Golden fields of grain, of sun, rain and earth,
swaying in the wind, each seed-bearing head,
for all that you give us, by the grace of God,
we thank you and we bless you.

Apple trees and all fruit trees,
of springtime blossom and autumn abundance,
for all that you give us, by the grace of God,
we thank you and we bless you.

Grapevine of careful cultivation, swelling clusters
through pruning and sunshine,
for all that you give us, by the grace of God,
we thank you and we bless you.

Felling or planting a tree

Felling a tree can bring up strong feelings and is often not done lightly; trees are seen or felt to have a spiritual presence by many, or at least to be natural wonders, living things that need protecting. In the Franciscan order, friars used to be forbidden from chopping down an entire tree without specific permission, and there have been laws concerning respect for and value of trees in different cultures around the world. In the Bible, there are texts which talk about tree felling, including warnings not to destroy fruit trees (for example, Deuteronomy 20:19-20). In today's climate, where whole forests are under threat, one tree can represent all of its kind, and be a focus for prayer. This is a prayer for trees under threat, for occasions when a tree needs to be felled, or if we find a much loved tree has been taken down.

Planting a tree, on the other hand, is a gift to the locality and to the world, a gift to the future, and something to celebrate. Judaism has a special day and ceremony, Tu Bishvat, in which trees are planted and their value to God, to life and to humanity honoured. Planting a tree is sometimes done as a memorial or in thanksgiving for birth. I have included an option to mention this, but have retained a focus on the tree itself rather than on human life – this can be adjusted appropriately.

Meet on location if possible, or if this is not possible, bring some leaves of the tree, or a similar one, and place them in the circle. You might like to meet on a Tuesday, the day, traditionally, on which God made trees.

If this is a felling, ask people in advance to think about something to share about the tree – a memory, a story, a poem, a dance or a piece of music . . .

If you are planning a memorial or birth celebration planting, invite people to bring something to share concerning the person – such as a prayer, blessing or piece of music.

Tree Blessing

In the beginning, according to the book of Genesis, God made all things, day by day over six days. On the third day, dry land appeared.

Then God said, 'Let the earth put forth vegetation: plants yielding seed, and fruit trees of every kind on earth that bear fruit with the seed in it.' And it was so. The earth brought forth vegetation: plants yielding seed of every kind, and trees of every kind bearing fruit with the seed in it. And God saw that it was good.

Genesis 1:11-12

265

The prayer for the third day, Tuesday:

Gardener God,
let the seeds of our potential unfurl by your tender touch,
to blossom and bear good fruit in the world,
pruned vines from an ancient root, and trained in love,
to honour the green earth and the miracle of life.
Amen.

Trees draw together all the traditional elements: they grow out of the earth, which holds their roots; they cleanse the air, making it suitable for animals to breathe; they use the fiery energy of the sun to make food and give us heat and light as they burn; they draw up water from the soil and breathe water vapour out into the atmosphere. So, we say all four of the seasonal blessings in honour of this tree and all trees:

Blessings of the Sacred Breath,
blessings of air and blowing wind,
blessings of clear mind and clear insight,
the interconnectedness of all that lives.

Blessings of fire, the devouring flame,
blessings of a God whom we cannot contain,
blessings of the one who gives and takes,
whose power is manifest for love's sake.

Blessings of the water of eternal life,
welling up, within our hearts,
blessings of sea and river and rain,
blessings of tide, of ebb and flow.

Blessings of earth, of rich, humble soil,
birthing and reclaiming each living thing,

blessings of wisdom and patience and hope,
blessings of cave and safe hiding place.
Amen.

For the goodness of the earth,
for the goodness of all vegetation,
for the goodness of the trees,
we give thanks.

For the abundance of the earth,
for the intelligence and creativity of humanity,
for the wonder of life itself,
we give thanks.

Thanks be to the Holy One,
the Source of All, incarnate on earth,
present within and amongst us,
filling all that is.
Amen.

For a tree felling

For our part in shaping the world,
we seek your guidance, O Holy One.
For our part in damaging what you have made,
we seek your forgiveness, O Holy One.
For our part in managing your creation for the good of all,
we seek your wisdom, O Holy One.

This tree, which is to be [has been] felled,
    is [was] beautiful.
It has grown tall, over many years;
history has unfolded around it,
seasons have come and gone,

and many creatures have come to this tree
for food and for shelter.
It has been a part of our own lives
and has touched our hearts and souls.

Participants are invited to share their own thoughts and
memories about the tree.

Allow plenty of time for sharing music, poetry, memories...

Now let us collect our thoughts and feelings, and take them
to the tree. All are invited to come up to the tree, touch
and hug it, talk to it aloud or silently, and gaze up into
the branches.

Allow time for everyone to engage with the tree.

We now step back from the tree, as we accept we need to let
go of it.

Let us close by saying together a prayer of the waning moon:

In times of decrease we remember you, O God.
With the ebb and the flow, we recognise the timeliness
of letting go, of fading light and gentler power,
of natural, gradual closure and times of withdrawal,
blessed by your grace and held in your peace.
Amen.

Planting a tree

It is said of Wisdom,
'Her ways are ways of pleasantness,
    and all her paths are peace.

She is a tree of life to those who lay hold of her;
those who hold her fast are called happy.'
Proverbs 3:17-18

By planting this tree, we honour life itself,
we honour the path of peace
and the way of wisdom.

Optional, for a planting for a birth or memorial

Especially, we honour [name], for whom we plant this tree as
a symbol of our love and of our hope in the future.
　　All life is interwoven and [name], like this tree, has a
unique place in creation, a place in our hearts, a place in
God's loving embrace.

All are invited to share thoughts and prayers concerning
[name].

*Use an appropriate prayer from the Prayer Bank, depending on
the occasion.*

Say together the Statement of Hope.

Continuing with the planting –

All are invited to stand around the sapling in a circle, and
raise a hand in blessing.

Holy One, source of all,
you who fill heaven and earth,
be here around and within this tree,
in the wind, in the soil, in the sap and the sunlight,

and may there be strong growth,
long life, protection from harm,
for this tree and all its kind, here and around the world.

Although we plant just one little tree,
may it be a sign of our willingness to care,
a sign of our eagerness to bring healing to the earth,
and our desire to honour what you have made.
Help us to understand how best to live lovingly
for the sake of all life and generations to come.
Amen.

*Choose a reading from the following (or find another – there are
many references to a variety of trees in the Bible)*[27]

A vision of healing, from the Book of Revelation:

Then the angel showed me the river of the water of life,
bright as crystal, flowing from the throne of God and of
the Lamb through the middle of the street of the city. On
either side of the river is the tree of life with its twelve
kinds of fruit, producing its fruit each month; and the
leaves of the tree are for the healing of the nations.

Revelation 22:1-2

A tree of love:

As an apple tree among the trees of the wood,
　　so is my beloved among young men.
With great delight I sat in his shadow,
　　and his fruit was sweet to my taste.

Song of Songs 2:3

---

[27] My book *The Healer's Tree: A Bible-based Resource on Ecology, Peace and Justice* (Wild Goose
Publications, 2011) contains reflections and references to a number of biblical trees.

A description of a mighty tree (the context is that the Assyrian nation is likened to the tree):

A cedar of Lebanon,
with fair branches and forest shade,
  and of great height,
  its top among the clouds.
The waters nourished it,
  the deep made it grow tall,
making its rivers flow
  around the place where it was planted,
sending forth its streams
  to all the trees of the field.
So it towered high
  above all the trees of the field;
its boughs grew large
  and its branches long,
  from abundant water in its shoots.
All the birds of the air
  made their nests in its boughs;
under its branches all the animals of the field
  gave birth to their young;
and in its shade
  all great nations lived.
It was beautiful in its greatness,
  in the length of its branches;
for its roots went down
  to abundant water.
The cedars in the garden of God could not rival it,
  nor the fir trees equal its boughs;
the plane trees were as nothing
  compared with its branches;
no tree in the garden of God
  was like it in beauty.

Ezekiel 31:3-8

To close, say together the 'Blessedness' prayer from the Prayer Bank

We bless you, O God, as Source of All,
as we look back to the roots of trust in you:
firm roots support and give strength,
embedded in the living soil,
firm roots are like ancestors,
named grandmothers and grandfathers
of a chosen people,
Sarah and Abraham, Rebekah and Isaac,
ancient stories of faith in you;
from them we draw wisdom,
from them we draw courage
as we find our way today.
As a tree trunk grows firm and tall,
lifting up its leaves to the sky,
so we strive for the light, the meaning, the truth,
we aim to live well,
and falling, we hope in the power of life
to let new shoots grow from the old.
We look to the one who lives fully in your light,
perfect and true, with leaves of healing for all the world.
So, we face the future,
the fruit of our works and words,
and we ask your blessing,
that it may be your own goodness that flowers in us,
your own loving kindness that bears fruit in us,
our seeds a blessing to the world,
and a source of peace,
a source of deep peace.
Amen.

3. Liturgies of Humanity

The times we need a liturgy are often those times when it is most difficult to know what to say. Each situation is unique and, in distressing or challenging circumstances, people find comfort and courage in different ways, so please be ready to be flexible and listen to participants' preferences.

A Penitential Liturgy for Peace

Being penitent is not popular with everyone; there is a place, however, for humility – the acceptance that we are no more perfect than the broken world we see around us. It can actually be quite a relief to admit that we get things wrong. There is a place for inviting God's goodness to transform our own hearts, as well as the world 'out there'. This liturgy may be useful during Lent and Advent, but also in response to world news or community, family and inner discord.

Preparation for the intercessions: if possible, assemble some different representations of the planet for people to engage with. As an example, I have a set of tennis-ball-sized globes of the world which I found at low cost in the children's section of a bargain bookshop. It is surprisingly moving to meditate while holding the world in your hands. I also have a large fabric appliqué earth which I made from cloth scraps, which can be laid on the floor. Over the years people have put candles, flowers and all sorts of other things on it as prayers and blessings, so it has bits of wax and seeds caught up in it.

For a more structured approach to intercessions, as an alternative, see the relevant section of the Prayer Bank.

Opening:

If we say that we have no sin, we deceive ourselves, and the truth is not in us.

1 John 1:8

**Heal us, O God, and we shall be healed;
save us and we shall be saved,
for you are our praise.**

(based on Jeremiah 17:14)

Prayers from the Holy Hours and Days section:

Enter the imperfection of our lives, Beloved;
come amongst us as the vulnerable one,
the one who invites nothing but kindness and love,
drawing goodness out of us despite ourselves.
Amen.

(a Christmas season prayer)

and/or

Humble us, Beloved,
as you humbled yourself,
pouring yourself out as a gift to all the earth,
your surrender of life, a sign of hope,
that after brokenness comes healing
and after sorrow comes joy;
after the pain of death comes life
and after fear and doubt comes consolation.
Amen.

(a Lent season prayer)

A reading:

> They have treated the wound of my people carelessly,
> saying, 'Peace, peace',
> when there is no peace.
>
> 'The harvest is past, the summer is ended,
> and we are not saved.'
>   For the hurt of my poor people I am hurt,
> I mourn, and dismay has taken hold of me.
> Is there no balm in Gilead?
> Is there no physician there?
> Why then has the health of my poor people
> not been restored?
> O that my head were a spring of water,
> and my eyes a fountain of tears,
> so that I might weep day and night
> for the slain of my poor people!
>
> *Jeremiah 8:11, 20–9:1*

Pause

A psalm:

> Have mercy on me, O God,
> according to your steadfast love;
> **according to your abundant mercy**
> **blot out my transgressions.**
>
> You desire truth in the inward being;
> **therefore teach me wisdom in my secret heart.**
> Let me hear joy and gladness;
> **let the bones that you have crushed rejoice.**

Create in me a clean heart, O God,
and put a new and right spirit within me.
Do not cast me away from your presence,
and do not take your holy spirit from me.
Restore to me the joy of your salvation,
and sustain in me a willing spirit.

Psalm 51:1, 6, 8, 10-12

Pause

Opportunity for song

Intercession:

Now we turn our thoughts to the world beyond us.

Use a globe or globes or photos and maps of the world to reflect on, or visualise the planet earth.

We bring to mind the troubles known to us, close to home and around the world, in a time of silence to interact with globes or maps, and reflect on the life, the fragility, the wonder, the need, the pain . . .

A time of quiet

We name our thoughts, lighting candles for people, living things and places in need of peace.

All are invited to light votive candles, sharing prayers aloud or keeping them in the silence of our hearts.

A time for prayer

Pause

A reading:

Each line can be read by a different voice, with a pause between.

When Jesus saw the crowds, he went up the mountain; and after he sat down, his disciples came to him. Then he began to speak, and taught them, saying:

'Blessed are the poor in spirit, for theirs is the kingdom of heaven.

'Blessed are those who mourn, for they will be comforted.

'Blessed are the meek, for they will inherit the earth.

'Blessed are those who hunger and thirst for righteousness, for they will be filled.

'Blessed are the merciful, for they will receive mercy.

'Blessed are the pure in heart, for they will see God.

'Blessed are the peacemakers, for they will be called children of God.'

Matthew 5:1-9

Holy One, Beloved,
you call us to be peace-makers in the world.
When this task seems too great for us,
strengthen us and teach us wisdom.
Melt our hearts so that your own goodness
shines through,
and let us join with others who work for true peace,
our anger and pain transformed into works of healing
and words of love.

So we pray for your peace to bless those who lead us.
We pray for your peace to bless those who have suffered.
We pray for your peace to work transforming miracles,
moment by moment, all around the world;
a network of light, growing and spreading out,
until each centre of disturbance becomes a centre
of renewing love,
beginning here amongst us and in our own hearts, O God.
Amen.

Optional closing song

Liturgy of difficult paths and heavy loads[28]

This may be suitable for Lent and Advent as we consider our
journey with God, our times of feeling close but also the times
when the way is difficult. Sharing the liturgy as a community is
mutually supportive. For some, the sense of struggle is very
strong; just being part of a community can be what holds
someone and gives them the will to keep going. It is also a liturgy
that might help as part of the bereavement process, or through
other specific times that are very challenging.

The liturgy includes a choice of two reflections with guided
visualisation. Decide which one to use before the service. If
neither seems quite right, consider using a visualisation from the
Evening Prayer liturgy, or refer to my earlier book, *Hiding in
God*, for extended wellbeing visualisations. Check the guidance
in Part 1 on helping people to relax before a visualisation, and
allow plenty of time to create calm and enter into the reflection
deeply. Also allow time for people to share with a neighbour or
in the group, about their experience, afterwards. All this could
take up to about half an hour.

---

[28] In my earlier book, *Rejoice With Me* (Kevin Mayhew, 2013), I explore the idea of walking a
difficult path, through the imagery of Psalm 23, and the good shepherd.

Opening:

> The people who walked in darkness have seen a great light;
> **those who lived in a land of deep darkness –**
> **on them light has shined.**

Isaiah 9:2

> The world around us, O God, is full of conflicting powers;
> it can be hard for us to see you here at all.
> Give us wisdom to recognise the tracks of your passing,
> the scent of your presence,
> the sound of your call,
> that we may know you and follow you,
> our true love, now and always.
> **Amen.**

(from the Holy Hours and Days section,
a midsummer prayer)

A psalm-inspired prayer:

> I cry aloud to God,
> **I cry from my heart, from the depth of my being;**
> so may my cry be heard.
> **In the day of my trouble I seek peace;**
> I seek hope and a purpose to life;
> **I search for meaning, for God.**
> In the night my body aches with tension;
> **my mind refuses to be comforted.**
> I search my soul;
> **I try to meditate, yet my spirit is weak.**
> With my whole being I cry out;
> **I pour out my heart, I tell of all my troubles.**
> The path I walk is full of challenge;
> **my path tests me and often I stumble.**

(adapted from Psalm 77:1-3 and Psalm 142)

Choose a suitable psalm from the Prayer Bank and/or use the following:

> Help me, O Holy One, for who else can I trust?
> Who can I turn to, who will help me in my need,
> and speak for justice, stand alongside
> those who have no voice or power?
>
> **Help me, O Holy One; I cry out to you,**
> **for you alone are true,**
> **as silver, seven-times refined by fire is true**
> **and pure and strong and beautiful;**
> **so rise up and shine in the night of my despair,**
> **a perfect, silver moon-like presence in my heart,**
> **to strengthen me.**
>
> *(based on Psalm 12)*

Opportunity for song

Say together:

> **God is a shepherd,**
> **all shall be well.**
> **We rest in green meadows,**
> **and walk by calm waters;**
> **in peace lies healing for my soul;**
> **and the best paths become clear.**
>
> **Even though I walk**
> **a valley of pain,**
> **I fear no harm,**
> **for you are with me, Beloved,**
> **and your staff reassures me,**
> **with protection and strength.**

You prepare a meal for me,
when others seem against me;
you honour me and delight in me,
and fill my cup to overflowing.
Surely goodness and tenderness will not cease,
and I shall dwell with the One who loves me,
my whole life long.

(based on Psalm 23)

Readings of hope

One, or both, to be read clearly and slowly, a number of times, followed by a pause.

Be strong and courageous; do not be frightened or dismayed, for the Eternal One,* your God, is with you wherever you go.

Joshua 1:9

Pause

Jesus said, 'Peace I leave with you; my peace I give to you. I do not give to you as the world gives. Do not let your hearts be troubled, and do not let them be afraid.'

John 14:27

Pause

A choice of two reflections and visualisations:

either

Focus on letting go of burdens:

We can want to accept peace with all our hearts, yet wonder how we will ever achieve it. Jesus once spoke of a

---

* 'the Lord' in NRSV

yoke,[29] a piece of shaped wood across the shoulders which makes carrying a load easier. According to the Gospel of Matthew, Jesus said this:

'Come to me, all you that are weary and are carrying heavy burdens, and I will give you rest. Take my yoke upon you, and learn from me; for I am gentle and humble in heart, and you will find rest for your souls. For my yoke is easy, and my burden is light.'

Matthew 11:28-30

It could be the same yoke used by Wisdom, according to the Book of Sirach, a book known to people of Jesus' time and place:

Bend your shoulders and carry her,
    and do not fret under her bonds.
Come to her with all your soul,
    and keep her ways with all your might.
Search out and seek, and she will become known to you;
    and when you get hold of her, do not let her go.
For at last you will find the rest she gives,
    and she will be changed into joy for you.
Then her fetters will become for you a strong defence,
    and her collar a glorious robe.
Her yoke is a golden ornament,
    and her bonds a purple cord.

Sirach 6:25-30

Let us spend a little while reflecting on the burdens we carry along the way.

Use the relaxation exercise on pages 25-26.

---

[29] See also the Wisdom's Table liturgy (p.206).

With your eyes closed, imagine walking along, carrying a heavy load. Notice what shape and size it is – how does it feel? Perhaps you know exactly what the load is, perhaps it is a mixture of things, or not clear.

How does it feel, carrying this load, step by step? How does your body feel? How does the path seem under your feet?

Come to a place where you can pause to rest. How does it feel to lay your burden down?

Now, how does it feel to think you must pick it up again? Perhaps you decide you do not need to – but often we have responsibilities that we cannot let go of easily . . .

As you prepare to lift up your load again, notice or imagine a loving presence, a figure who expresses safety and deep love to you. For some, this may be Jesus, but allow yourself to experience the love of God in whatever way helps you to accept it.

Talk about your burdens with the one who loves you, and be open to their support. Perhaps they will give you a yoke, or perhaps a different way of helping.

A longer time of quiet

When you are ready, thank the one who loves you for their help.

In your mind, get ready to come back.

Take time to return to the room, aware of the sounds and your position on your chair . . .

Sit for a few minutes quietly reflecting on your meditation.

or

Focus on help along the Path:

Use the relaxation exercise on pages 25-26.

> With your eyes closed, imagine that it is quite dark and gloomy, and you are walking along a path that is difficult for some reason – perhaps mud or snow or sharp stones, or a steep climb . . .
>
> Notice how you feel as you walk.
>
> What is it that makes you keep going?
>
> As you walk, you notice a strong staff at the side of the path, with something about it that indicates it is for you. Pick it up and look at it, consider its weight, what kind of wood it might be . . .
>
> Use the staff to help you walk, as you carry on along the way.
>
> Soon, you see a gentle light ahead of you, which gets brighter until you come to a lantern at the side of the road. Again, something about it tells you this light is for you. Lift it up and look at it, notice its warmth.
>
> Use the lantern to help you see the way, as you carry on along the path.
>
> In a little while, you come to a bundle lying at the side of the path. It is a warm cloak, wrapped around something that you realise you need.
>
> You might see immediately what this thing is, or you might realise gradually, as you put the cloak on. Take time to consider both.

Pause

> As you continue, with your cloak, your staff, your lantern and your helpful object, the sky starts to lighten. Everything seems brighter, colours more vivid.

You come to a shelter and notice a person with a weathered face and an expression of great kindness, a shepherd,[30] who greets you.

This friend offers you rest and refreshment, whatever is of most comfort to you at this time.

Allow yourself to accept their hospitality, knowing that this is the love of God.

Pause

When you are ready, thank your host and prepare to return.

In your own time, open your eyes and become aware of your posture and the sounds around you.

Sit for a few minutes in quiet, to reflect on your visualisation.

Close of visualisation:

For either visualisation, provide time afterwards for everyone to talk about their reflection, quietly in pairs, as a group if the group is small, or using a talking stick or stone.

Opportunity for song or creative response

Holy One,
Let all who take refuge in you rejoice;
   let them ever sing for joy.
Spread your protection over them,
   so that those who love your name may exult in you.
Psalm 5:11

---

[30] See *Rejoice With Me* for reflections on female as well as male shepherds in the Bible.

Closing prayer:

> O my Rock,
> in you I take refuge.
> The storms of life may rage outside
> but in you I find shelter.
> Holy One, you surround me,
> the cave of your love welcomes me,
> I am drawn within to find the rest that I need.
> In your safe-holding let me find peace.
> In your strong embrace let me find renewal.
> Amen.

Wellbeing support liturgy

The emphasis in this liturgy is on deepening a sense of God's loving companionship in the midst of illness and the fears and challenges which accompany illness – including for loved ones. While miraculous intervention may be what many of us really long for, the reality of the world is that we, like all creatures, do endure illness and eventually death, even though we may be luckier than most through time and around the world, by accident of birth in a place with good healthcare.

There are many forms of 'healing service'. Often, 'prayers for healing' involve individuals praying for one another. If you and the group want this to happen, there is opportunity after the personal blessing. Please bear in mind, however, that not everybody wants to trust themselves to the well-meant unplanned prayers of another and, particularly when living with a serious illness, some can find such prayers unhelpful – please see the advice on Intercession and Free Prayer.

I have suggested a time of silence after the blessing, in which to sit in the love of God. In this time, I suggest visualising God's loving presence, perhaps as golden light around the person in question. If people want to pray, please encourage prayers for peace of mind and God's greatest good to be done, rather than for specific outcomes.

I have included the option of prayerful touch, called 'laying on of hands', during the blessing. Touch is an emotive issue, so please exercise sensitivity and flexibility. Many people are comfortable with a gentle hand on shoulder, forearm or forehead, but some are not, and should be able to opt out easily. In some circumstances people may wish to find same-sex or other 'safe' combinations for partnership.

If using oil, sufficient small containers of olive oil for one-between-two need preparing in advance. Plastic bottle tops make convenient little bowls but check for sharp edges. Only a very small quantity is needed for anointing. If you have special oil to pass round the circle instead, adapt accordingly – people can turn to their neighbour in the circle one by one, everyone else watching and waiting supportively – allow extra time. In church, it is traditional to make the sign of the cross on the forehead, but you may wish to discuss this with the group beforehand; people may prefer a simple stroke of oil, or three dots of oil.

Opening:

O God, you are my God.

O God, you are my God, I seek you,
my soul thirsts for you;
my flesh faints for you,
as in a dry and weary land where there is no water.
So I have looked upon you in the sanctuary,
beholding your power and glory.
Because your steadfast love is better than life,
my lips will praise you.
So I will bless you as long as I live;
I will lift up my hands and call on your name.

Psalm 63:1-4

Divine Praise (from the Prayer Bank)

Holy One, we stand in awe of you,
revealed as mortal life on earth:
as the one who embodies timeless wisdom,
the one who lives and dies in self-giving love.
We give thanks for the outpouring of yourself,
we give thanks for the outpouring
which sustains all life;
we give thanks for the outpouring of abundant life,
for you who die that we may live.

So breathe through us,
so flow through us,
inspire and delight us,
and lead us in confidence,
sure of your goodness.
Help us and guide us,
support us and comfort us,
give us reason to live
and hope beyond death;
give us reason to feel safe
in the eternity of love,
for in you we trust,
O most lovely One.
Amen.

A reading:

Use one or any combination as appropriate, following each with a short pause.

Daniel is visited by an angel at a time of distress. He addresses the angel with awe, physically shaken by the experience. Often in the Bible the message of angels is: 'Do not be afraid!' The angel in Daniel's vision also gives words of comfort:

Again one in human form touched me and strengthened me. He said, 'Do not fear, greatly beloved, you are safe. Be strong and courageous!' When he spoke to me, I was strengthened and said, 'Let my lord speak, for you have strengthened me.'

Daniel 10:16-19

Pause

Give me strength, O God, and courage;
melt away my fear.
Let me know myself to be beloved, dear God,
and let me know myself to be safe
under the protection of your angels.
Amen.

Now we turn to our neighbours to bless one another with the angel's words:

'Do not fear, greatly beloved, you are safe. Be strong and courageous!'

All bless the people on either side, by taking hands and saying the words of the angel.

Pause

St Paul wrote to encourage the followers of Jesus in Corinth: 'Love is patient; love is kind; love is not envious or boastful or arrogant or rude. It does not insist on its own way; it is not irritable or resentful; it does not rejoice in wrongdoing, but rejoices in the truth. It bears all things, believes all things, hopes all things, endures all things.'

1 Corinthians 13:4-7

Pause

Now we bless one another by holding hands in the circle, as we affirm: 'Love endures all things.'

Invite all to hold hands with neighbours, saying: 'Love endures all things.'

Release hands.

Let us pray:

**Loving God, give us patience and peace
that we may endure what must be endured
and pass through the pain,
knowing ourselves loved and held always
in your eternal presence.
Amen.**

Pause

Jesus said to his disciples, 'Therefore I tell you, do not worry about your life, what you will eat, or about your body, what you will wear. For life is more than food, and the body more than clothing. Consider the ravens: they neither sow nor reap, they have neither storehouse nor barn, and yet God feeds them. Of how much more value are you than the birds! And can any of you by worrying add a single hour to your span of life? If then you are not able to do so small a thing as that, why do you worry about the rest? Consider the lilies, how they grow: they neither toil nor spin; yet I tell you, even Solomon in all his glory was not clothed like one of these.'

Luke 12:22-27

Pause

Let us pray:

**O living Love,
help me to set all my worries aside;
fill me with peace in this moment as I turn to you.
Speak to my soul, Beloved, soothe my whole being
and let me trust in your divine abundance
now and always.
Amen.**

Pause

A Statement of Hope (from the Prayer Bank)

Anyone who wishes, join in with the leader, for all or any part.

I believe there is reason to hope,
for there is love in the world,
and beauty and joy;
an impulse that inspires
those it touches to do good,
to dream up dreams and create wonders,
to heal wounds and spread peace.

I believe there is reason to hope,
to hold out for eternity,
for the Source of All,
to act with courage,
to be gentle and true,

and by watching and listening, to increase in wisdom;
to trust that a seed can grow, in time,
into a fruitful tree.

I believe that the earth needs me to care,
though I often fail,
and am daunted by the task.
Yet I need the earth to give herself to me,
hourly and daily, year by year.
All that dies that we may live,
I believe is making a noble sacrifice,
and I honour the life,
by striving to live
in hope and in gratitude,
as well as I can.

I believe that I am little but stardust and breath,
yet supported by forces I cannot comprehend,
I journey through life like a river to the sea;
rough ground and smooth, all teaches me,
I believe that my life is about more than myself,
and I search and I wonder,
and ask how best to love.

A time of silence

Opportunity for song

Meditative participation:

There is a prayer that comes up several times in the psalms –
'hide me in the shadow of your wings'.[31] Some like to connect

---

[31] For an extended reflection on this, see my earlier book *Hiding in God.*

this with the way Jesus likened himself to a mother hen gathering and nestling her chicks.[32]

If you would like to, take a feather and spend a few minutes just looking at it . . .

Pause

Now let's take a minute to relax . . . and settle into the idea of God's beautiful wings, which can enfold us lovingly, gently . . .

Imagine a nest of down to sink back into, like comfortable pillows, inviting your body to relax, tension unwinding . . .

Feel your breath calming and deepening . . .

Imagine feather-soft comfort soothing your mind and your body . . . imagine gentle warmth, supporting your head, your neck, your shoulders . . .

Imagine the warmth spread to comfort your arms, down to your hands and fingers . . . your chest as you continue to breathe calmly and deeply, your lower body, right down to feet and toes, gently supported as though resting on soft pillows.

What colours do you imagine these feathers to be? Do you feel yourself to be in safe darkness, or soft light? Perhaps a soothing scent comes to mind, of roses or lavender . . . or the sound of music.

In this peaceful space, recall the prayer, 'Hide me in the shadow of your wings' and let the words echo in your mind as you let yourself be held in love.

Pause for at least 30 seconds.

---

[32] See also the information and reflections on the Shekhinah on pages 187-88.

When you are ready, gradually open your eyes, bringing the peace of that feathery shelter into the present moment. You can reclaim that peace at any time by using the prayer: 'Hide me in the shadow of your wings.'

If you like, keep the feather you picked, to remind you of God's love.

Because your steadfast love is better than life,
I will praise you, O God.
So I will bless you as long as I live;
I will lift up my hands and call on your name.
Amen.

Opportunity for song

Blessing:

If you would like to be anointed, take the oil when it comes to you and hold it for the person giving you a blessing. If not, pass it on.

If you would also like to receive laying on of hands, have your feather in your hand.

An optional prayer over the oil:

Loving God,
your goodness flows like oil from the generous olive tree.
Let this oil be for us a token of your soothing love,
comforting us now and always.
Amen.

All extend a hand of blessing towards one another or, if supporting one person in particular, towards this individual or something that represents them, such as a candle or photo, while reading:

You who live in the shelter of the Most High,
as though settled in the shadow of a great Mountain,*
will say to God, 'My refuge and my defence;
my God, in whom I trust.'
May God deliver you from your frustrations,
and from all destructive powers at work in the world;
and with great love cover you.
Under God's wings may you find refuge;
and may divine faithfulness be your sure protection.
May you not fear distress by night,
or pain by day,
or the troubles that stalk in darkness,
or the decay that wastes even the noonday sun;
may you not fear, for God is with you always.

(inspired by Psalm 91:1-6)

Turn to one another in twos or threes, sitting or standing. Take turns to bless one another directly, and if someone is holding a feather, also lay a hand gently on their shoulder, arm or forehead while reading the following. Anoint with olive oil on the forehead after reading the blessing.

You who have made the Holy One your refuge,
the Most High your dwelling-place,
may goodness surround you,
and blessings touch what you hold most dear.
And may God's own angels minister to you

---

* 'the Almighty' in NRSV

and guard you in all your ways,
now and always.
Amen.

(based on Psalm 91:9-11)

Sit down, for a time of silence.

In this time of silence, let the comforting love of God
surround us and fill us.

Sit in silence for at least 1 minute.

Opportunity for gentle song

Let us close by saying together:

O beloved Source of the river of my life,
rain from the sky and wellspring from the earth,
I cannot name you or contain you,
but only delight in your ceaseless flow.

Wash the world with healing grace,
touch the dry land and make it green,
let your fruits be shared by all,
your harvest an eternal joy.

May all who thirst make their way to you
and may all in need find their dry wells filled,
and may all who fear life's raging storms
be sheltered and guided to safe refuge.
Amen.

A simpler form of wellbeing liturgy for sharing with an individual

All due respect for safeguarding issues should be taken into account, regarding the visit, especially appropriateness of touch – see introduction above.

Opening:

> Jesus said, 'Peace I leave with you; my peace I give to you. I do not give to you as the world gives. Do not let your hearts be troubled, and do not let them be afraid.'
>
> *John 14:27*

or

> God spoke through the prophet Isaiah, saying:
> 'Do not fear, for I have redeemed you;
> I have called you by name, you are mine.
> [When you pass through the waters, I will be with you;
>   and through the rivers, they shall not overwhelm you;
> when you walk through fire you shall not be burned,
>   and the flame shall not consume you. *optional,*
> *with discretion*]
> You are precious in my sight,
> and honoured, and I love you.'
>
> *Isaiah 43:1-2, 4*

> Loving God, be with us and help us to draw close
> to you at this time,
> as we pray that [name] may find peace in you.
> Amen.

Choose one of the three passages of scripture with prayer, from the longer liturgy above: Daniel's experience of the angel, Paul describing love, or Jesus telling us not to worry.

Pause

Offer the feather meditation.

Blessing:

> This blessing is based on one of the psalms. While I say it,
> I can lay my hand gently on your [hand], if you would
> like that?
>
> [Name],
> You who live in the shelter of the Most High,
> as though settled in the shadow of a great mountain,*
> will say to God, 'My refuge and my defence;
> my God, in whom I trust.'
> May God deliver you from your frustrations,
> and from all destructive powers at work in the world;
> and with great love cover you.
> Under God's wings may you find refuge;
> and may divine faithfulness be your sure protection.
> May you not fear distress by night,
> or pain by day,
> or the troubles that stalk in darkness,
> or the decay that wastes even the noonday sun;
> may you not fear, for God is with you always.
> *(based on Psalm 91)*
>
> Would you like to be anointed with olive oil?

If yes, an optional prayer over the oil:

> Loving God,
> your goodness flows like oil from the generous olive tree.

---

* 'the Almighty' in NRSV

Let this oil be for us a token of your soothing love,
comforting [name] now and always.
Amen.

Anoint the forehead.

Let's just sit quietly for a little while, in God's love.

*An older person or someone with a church background may prefer
to say the traditional version of the prayer which Jesus taught, and/or
the Grace. Otherwise, offer this prayer (adapted from the Prayer
Bank) to close. A large-print copy may allow participation.*

**O beloved Source of the river of life,
rain from the sky and wellspring from the earth,
we cannot name you or contain you,
but only delight in your ceaseless flow.**

**Bathe [name] and all the world with healing grace,
touch the dry land and make it green,
let your fruits be shared by all,
your harvest an eternal joy.**

**May all who thirst make their way to you
and may all in need find their dry wells filled,
and may all who fear life's raging storms
be sheltered and guided to safe refuge.**

**So may [name] find peace in your love.
Amen.**

The following liturgies relate in different ways to the theme of absence and loss, and as such relate to the theme of the Dark Moon prayers from the Holy Hours and Days section.

These are emotive issues and if difficult feelings come up, please seek or support others in seeking appropriate help.

Liturgy of longing

We may long for many things in life. These longings are often expressions of what has most value for us, physically, spiritually and emotionally, but sometimes they preoccupy our minds and hearts so much that we struggle to keep our focus on the longing for God. Rather, our frustrations can make us wonder if God is the one who is withholding from us what we want: self-blame, self-pity and anger at God can be part of the journey and prompt us to explore what we really think about God and about the meaning of our lives.

Opening:

> Let this be a sacred time, O God,
> for me to look within,
> to learn to see myself as you see me,
> to understand myself more deeply;
> that your wisdom may guide me,
> and spread peace in the world.
> > *(the second of the Dark Moon prayers)*

> As a deer longs for flowing streams,
> so my soul longs for you, O God.
> **My soul thirsts for God,**
> **for the living God.**
> When shall I come and behold the face of God?

My tears have been my food day and night,
while people say to me continually,
'Where is your God?'

Why are you cast down, O my soul,
and why are you disquieted within me?
Hope in God; for I shall again give thanks, *
my help and my God.

Psalm 42:1-3, 5

O God, **
all my longing is known to you;
my sighing is not hidden from you.

Psalm 38:9

Reflection on praying, from the scriptures:

1 Samuel 1 describes how Hannah longs for a child and prays
so fervently to God that the priest in attendance, Eli, assumes
she is drunk. She tells him,
    'I am a woman deeply troubled; I have drunk neither wine
nor strong drink, but I have been pouring out my soul before
God#. . . I have been speaking out of my great anxiety and
vexation all this time.'(1 Samuel 1:15-16) Eli then blesses her.

Loving God,
I pour out my soul to you,
all my distress I entrust to you,
knowing that you hear me.
Amen.

---

* 'praise him' in NRSV
** 'O Lord' in NRSV
# 'the Lord' in NRSV

An 'open' time in which desires can be articulated, written, danced, sung or otherwise expressed.

Close this time by repeating the prayer:

Loving God,
I pour out my soul to you,
all my distress I entrust to you,
knowing that you hear me.
Amen.

Paul writes to the believers in Rome, about deep prayer. 'Likewise the Spirit helps us in our weakness; for we do not know how to pray as we ought, but that very Spirit intercedes with sighs too deep for words. And God, who searches the heart, knows what is the mind of the Spirit, because the Spirit intercedes for the saints according to the will of God. We know that all things work together for good for those who love God.'

Romans 8:26-28a

Loving God,
search my heart and know my mind,
spin from my soul the deep prayers
that even I do not understand,
and weave them into what fits best,
for myself and for all your children,
that we may all be cloaked in love.
Amen.

A time of quiet

In the Gospels, Jesus suffers greatly while praying at night in the Garden of Gethsemane. He knows he will soon be arrested and executed and he longs to be spared this ordeal.

He prays, 'Abba, Father, for you all things are possible; remove this cup from me; yet, not what I want, but what you want' (Mark 14:36). Jesus understands the challenge we sometimes face, of aligning our own wishes to the greater love – a mysterious force that sometimes seems to make no sense, and even at times seems to ask only endurance from us. The advice in the letter of James is that we recognise the trials that test our faith, 'and let endurance have its full effect, so that you may be mature and complete, lacking in nothing' (James 1:4).

Holy One,
in my emptiness, let me be filled with your love;
in my seeking and longing,
let me not doubt your goodness;
in my human weakness, let me be strengthened;
that I may find patience and strength,
wisdom and courage to live day by day,
open to your guidance, awake to your word,
free to change, to learn and to grow,
so that I may be mature and complete in you,
lacking in nothing.
Amen.

The following prayer is inspired by the prayer attributed to Jesus:
O beloved Source of the river of my life,
rain from the sky and wellspring from the earth,
I cannot name you or contain you,
but only delight in your ceaseless flow.

Wash the world with healing grace,
touch the dry land and make it green,
let your fruits be shared by all,
your harvest an eternal joy.

May all who thirst make their way to you
and may all in need find their dry wells filled,
and may all who fear life's raging storms
be sheltered and guided to safe refuge.
Amen.

The liturgy can close at this point or by singing an appropriate song or hymn, or with other music.

Liturgy of Loss

Although this is written to support bereavement, loss can take many forms apart from the death of a loved one. Acknowledging the rupture that some experiences cause in our lives can be part of the healing process, as we adjust to a life in which something that was important to us is no longer there – a 'little death'. This may be the loss of a body part or function through surgery,[33] the loss of a meaningful item through theft or damage, the loss of a way of life, the loss of innocence . . . the permutations are endless. There is no quick fix and there is not an 'everything's fine really' resolution to this liturgy; rather, it sits with people in the reality of loss while maintaining a sense of hopefulness.

This is not a funeral liturgy, but could be made use of in this context, or in scattering ashes. Please note there is also a separate naming ritual in support of the specific loss related to miscarriage and premature birth.

One option is to do this liturgy outside near flowing water, in which case check how to do this safely, especially if children will be present, and in a way that includes people with mobility issues – for example, by meeting at a footbridge. If it is not possible to be in such a location, use a large bowl of water.

---

[33] In the 'Liturgies of the Moon' section, there is a liturgy about loss through surgery, especially of the womb.

The liturgy includes a practical element which involves pressing an object into clay before throwing the object (not the clay!) into water. The clay is kept to represent the impression or memory that is still precious.

In preparation, get some air-drying clay or other material that will take an imprint. Form it into matchbox-sized lumps, sufficient for each person to have a piece. Keep it sealed in an airtight container until use. Have hand wipes/tissues/water available.

Also think about how people can keep their imprinted clay safe – for example, ask everyone to bring an empty matchbox or small giftbox (and have some spare). If cost is an issue, ask for a contribution towards the clay, etc.

Outdoors: let people gather their own pebbles, cones and sticks. Do not throw anything into water in the environment, other than natural things from that environment: pebbles, twigs, leaves, fir cones.

Indoors: collect marbles, polished stones, glass nuggets and so on for people to choose from.

Opening:

In the Book of Isaiah, God cries out, saying 'Comfort, O comfort my people' (Isaiah 40:1). So I/we seek comfort now.

Be merciful to me, O God, be merciful to me,
for in you my soul takes refuge;
in the shadow of your wings I will take refuge,
until the destroying storms pass by.

Psalm 57:1

O Holy One, let me feel your presence;
for I am in need, and full of pain.

Open my heart to the comfort you can offer,
open my mind to the hope of healing.
Though always with me and within me,
let me be aware of you now,
for the past is gone, and the future yet to come.
Only in the present can I hope for peace,
and in this moment I take refuge in you.
So be with me in a way that revives my weary spirit,
O God, my refuge and my peace.
Amen.

and/or

I cry to you, O God,*
I say, 'You are my refuge,
my portion in the land of the living.'
Give heed to my cry,
for I am brought very low.

Psalm 142:5-6

Even though, now, I am brought very low,
give me hope of a brighter dawn;
even though, now, I am brought very low,
let me cling to you in trust,
and give me hope in these words, from long ago,
    that those who wait for God 'shall renew their strength,
they shall mount up with wings like eagles,
they shall run and not be weary,
they shall walk and not faint' (Isaiah 40:31).
Amen.

---

* 'O Lord' in NRSV

Active reflection:

In a time of reflection, we acknowledge our loss. If you would like to, find a pebble or other token that can represent your loss. Take a while to look at it and feel it between your fingers, then when you are ready, press it into a piece of clay. The imprint it leaves can represent your memories, which will always be precious to you.

Re-gather with the tokens and clay imprints. People may wish to share their thoughts, so allow appropriate time and ask people to listen supportively.

We will now cast our pebbles and other tokens into the water, recognising that something or someone we cared about has passed into a realm which is beyond us. Though they are physically out of sight and out of reach, we still have the imprint, the precious memory, which remains.

Pebbles, etc. are cast into the water, with these words, silent or spoken:

'[Name] of my love, I let you go into the greater love that holds us all, and I hold your memory dear.'

In God we live and move and have our being.
In love, we live and move and have our being.
What is lost to me
is known still to God.
What to me has ended,
in God, becomes new.
The one I hold no longer
is held in God's infinite love.
All is held, all is loved, all is one in God's embrace.

In God we live and move and have our being.
All that I love, I entrust to God.
Amen.

An optional reading, with responses:

When Jesus saw the crowds, he went up the mountain; and after he sat down, his disciples came to him. Then he began to speak, and taught them, saying:

'Blessed are the poor in spirit, for theirs is the kingdom of heaven.'

Let me be comforted, O God.

'Blessed are those who mourn, for they will be comforted.'

Let me be comforted, O Holy One.

'Blessed are the meek, for they will inherit the earth.'

Let me be comforted, O Source of All.

'Blessed are those who hunger and thirst for righteousness, for they will be filled.'

Let me be comforted, O Mothering God.

'Blessed are the merciful, for they will receive mercy.'

Let me be comforted, O Merciful One.

'Blessed are the pure in heart, for they will see God.'

Let me be comforted, O Love of all Loves.

'Blessed are the peacemakers, for they will be called children of God.'

Let me be comforted, O God of Peace.

Matthew 5:1-9

and/or optional reading:

John's Gospel tells us how two sisters, Mary and Martha, sent for Jesus because his friend, their brother Lazarus, was ill. When Jesus arrived, Lazarus had been dead four days. When Jesus saw [Mary] weeping, and the Jews who came with her also weeping, he was greatly disturbed in spirit and deeply moved. He said, 'Where have you laid him?' They said to him, 'Lord, come and see.' Jesus began to weep. So the Jews said, 'See how he loved him!'

John 11:33-36

Closing prayers:

O God, when no other understands me,
you understand me.
When no other sees my grief,
you see it.
When no other knows the loss I feel,
you know it.
When I weep, you weep with me,
and when I seek comfort,
you are with me.
Amen.

Psalm 23 is traditional and much used during mourning; there are some beautiful sung versions as an alternative.

God is a shepherd,
all shall be well.
We rest in green meadows,
and walk by calm waters;
in peace lies healing for my soul;
and the best paths become clear.

Even though I walk

a valley of pain,
I fear no harm,
for you are with me, Beloved,
and your staff reassures me,
with protection and strength.

You prepare a meal for me,
when others seem against me;
you honour me and delight in me,
and fill my cup to overflowing.
Surely goodness and tenderness will not cease,
and I shall dwell in God's love,
my whole life long.

(based on Psalm 23)

Amen.

A closing prayer for the departed:

Holy One,
touch us with the mystery of this time,
and draw close to us,
the veils between us gently lifted;
shelter us from mischief
and let love melt our fears
as we contemplate your greater mystery,
our souls entrusted to your everlasting care.
Amen.

(from the Holy Hours and Days section,
All Saints and All Souls-tide prayer)

Liturgy of Love in Absence

This liturgy is to support those who are missing someone – a
partner, friend or family member who is away for some reason.

Clearly, every specific circumstance cannot be covered, but I hope the prayers offered can be adapted or used as inspiration to write more suitable words. Some, depending on outlook, may feel this is appropriate for remembering those who have died.

When I asked people what they would like liturgies about, many responses concerned children who spend time apart due to family break-up, who spend time in foster care or other residential care, and grown-up children who have moved away or gone to university.

The whole liturgy could be offered to focus on one issue, such as supporting a prisoner, a member of the community working away, including members of the armed forces, an asylum seeker in detention or a child in care. It may be appropriate to make this event part of a practical activity that involves tangible outreach to the person or people in question, whether making a card, writing letters, putting a parcel together, planning a visiting timetable, raising funds and so on.

Suggested preparation: create a large picture of a spider's web on a surface suitable for putting votive candles on – for example, a string web under a glass table-top, enamel paints on a large metal tray, or acrylic paints on a piece of plywood. It is worth making one that can be re-used;[34] please take due care of fire risks.

Have objects such as glass nuggets or shells which can represent the people gathered in the group, and sufficient tea lights for all who will be named.

Opening:

Loving God, we gather together, united by our care for [name]. You who made the great web of life, supporting all by your love, constantly creating, regenerating and renewing

---

[34] See the suggestions on Intercessions in the Prayer Bank section.

all that is, we thank you that by our prayers we can reach out, keeping connections alive with those who cannot be with us now.

I lift up my eyes to the hills –
where will help come from?
My help comes from God,
who made heaven and earth.

[Name], may the Holy One keep your footsteps sure;
never resting, never sleeping,
the Eternal One of Israel
keeps constant watch.

[Name], may God be your faithful guardian;
a shade for you from the glare of the sun
and a shelter at night
while the moon lights the sky.

[Name], may God keep you from all harm,
may God help you to delight in life,
watching over all your travels,
from this time forth and for evermore.
Amen.

(based on Psalm 121)

As we bring [name]/our loved one(s) to mind, let us also seek meaningful and practical ways to reach out, so that they know they have a place in our hearts and in our community wherever they may be.
Amen.

Let us first acknowledge our connection together as a supportive community for [name]/our loved one(s), by placing symbols of ourselves on the web of life.

Each person places a token at one of the intersections on the web.

Thank you for bringing us together, O God;
each of us different, but with shared concerns.
Help us to value one another
and to draw on one another's strengths and gifts,
forgiving one another's weaknesses.
Help us to support one another,
in our shared wish to support [name]/our absent
loved one(s).
Amen.

Now we place on the web of life those known to us who are
involved with [name] at this time and who form the day-to-
day community of life. *(This may include medical staff, foster
carers, warders, colleagues, friends, other family members and
so on.)*

Loving God, may all who are involved in the life of
[name]/our loved one(s),
be touched by your spirit of love,
acting as your wisdom and your power in the world,
whether they call on your holy name or not,
working towards the greatest good for all.
Help us to value the part they play
and, where love is difficult,
help us to find ways to relate with dignity,
for the sake of [name].
Amen.

We now focus on our main reason for gathering.

Dear God, we pray for [name]
who is in [location].
We affirm our love for [name].

313

A candle is lit for the named person or people and placed on an intersection (or, if the sole focus, at the centre) of the web.

Repeat for each person to be remembered.

So we reflect on the words of Psalm 139, reminding us of God's presence everywhere.

Where can I go from your spirit?
Or where can I flee from your presence?
If I ascend to heaven, you are there;
if I make my bed in Sheol, you are there.
If I take the wings of the morning
and settle at the farthest limits of the sea,
even there your hand shall lead me,
and your right hand shall hold me fast.
If I say, 'Surely the darkness shall cover me,
and the light around me become night',
even the darkness is not dark to you;
the night is as bright as the day,
for darkness is as light to you.

Psalm 139:7-12

So let us feel confident that [name] is known by God and held in God's love, whether near to us or far away.

Let us pray together:

Inspired by the prayer attributed to Jesus

O beloved Source of the river of my life,
rain from the sky and wellspring from the earth,
I cannot name you or contain you,
but only delight in your ceaseless flow.

314

Wash the world with healing grace,
touch the dry land and make it green,
let your fruits be shared by all,
your harvest an eternal joy.

May all who thirst make their way to you
and may all in need find their dry wells filled,
and may all who fear life's raging storms
be sheltered and guided to safe refuge.
Amen.

Liturgy of loneliness, solitude and aloneness

This liturgy seeks to offer consolation when aloneness, isolation and/or loneliness is a challenge. There may also be a challenge in presenting this in a way that does not make people who are lonely feel as though they are failing or need rescuing in any way. Being alone can bear relation to issues of confidence, depression, self-worth, place in society and introversion; people need to feel free to choose to participate, or free to have the liturgy for their own use alone if they prefer. Having used it alone, they may wish one day to join with others, given the opportunity. At the same time, many experience deep loneliness that is difficult to talk about, even though they seem to be in significant relationships. Rather than targeting a specific group, advertise this as an opportunity to pray intentionally and empathetically for the sake of all who are alone and lonely, as well as for those who experience loneliness. The run-up to Christmas is a key time of year, but the liturgy could be offered routinely each month or quarter.

A strong theme in this liturgy is God's loving presence, which, in the section on the Feminine Divine, is named as the Shekhinah. Decide in advance how much participants need – or might like – to know about this concept. The closing prayer names the Shekhinah; simply miss this name out if it is likely to cause confusion.

Opening:

> Be strong and courageous; do not be frightened or dismayed, for the Holy One,* your God, is with you wherever you go.
>
> *Joshua 1:9*

Holy One,
may we and all known to us,
rest in the knowledge of your comforting presence with us,
now and always.
Amen.

> Jesus said, 'If you love me, you will do as I say, and I will ask God, who cares for us as the most loving of parents, to give you another comforter, to be with you always: the very essence of Truth, whom the secular world cannot grasp, cannot see and cannot know. But this divine presence is known to you, dwelling with you and within you. I will not leave you as orphans or travellers without a guide; I come to you.'
>
> *John 14:15-18 [author's translation]*

Holy One, send us and all known to us
the comfort of your presence,
to dwell with us and within us, all our days,
that none may feel the weight of loneliness.
Amen.

Opportunity for song

---

* 'the Lord' in NRSV

Hear my prayer, O God,*
let my cry come to you.
Do not hide your face from me
on the day of my distress.
Incline your ear to me;
answer me speedily on the day when I call.
For my days pass away like smoke,
my heart is stricken and withered like grass;
I am like an owl of the wilderness,
like a little owl of the waste places.
I lie awake;
I am like a lonely bird on the housetop.
For I eat ashes like bread,
and mingle tears with my drink.

Long ago you laid the foundation of the earth,
and the heavens are the work of your hands.
They will perish, but you endure;
they will all wear out like a garment.
You change them like clothing,
and they pass away;
but you are the same,
and your years have no end.
Hear my prayer O God,
let my cry come to you.

from Psalm 102

and/or

A prayer inspired by Psalm 25

> To you, O Holy One, I lift up my soul,
> **O my God, in you I trust.**

---

* 'Lord' in NRSV

Do not let me be ashamed to speak of you,
do not give anyone reason to deride me.
Let me see your way, O God,
and teach me your paths.
Lead me in your truth and guide me,
for you are my source of hope;
I wait for you, all day long.
Be merciful to me, O holy One,
reach out in tenderness and love,
and let me not hide from you in shame,
because of my past.
According to your endless kindness,
like the most loving of parents,
let me feel that I can turn to you always.
Embrace me and be gentle with me,
for I am lonely and hurting.
Calm my troubled mind
and soothe my heart's distress,
have pity on my unhappiness
and guide me to a new sense of meaning in my life.
May integrity and good intentions preserve me, O God,
for I wait for you.
Amen.

Texts for reflection – *choose one or two according to preference:*

In the address Jesus gives to his disciples before his arrest, according to John's Gospel, he anticipates being alone, saying: 'The hour is coming, indeed it has come, when you will be scattered, each one to his home, and you will leave me alone' (John 16:32).

Yet he also says he is not alone, because God is with him.

Whether we are aware of God's presence or not, we are encouraged to believe that God is always with us.

Pause

Holy One, be with me, even though I am alone.
Give me confidence in your loving presence, O God.
Amen.

In Matthew's Gospel, many find comfort in the last words of Jesus to his followers, after his resurrection: 'And remember, I am with you always, to the end of the age' (Matthew 28:20b).

Pause

Optional prayer:

Jesus, Beloved one,
be to me a friend and brother,
a wise guide I can trust and share with,
never lonely in your presence,
never alone with you, O loving Christ.
Amen.

You are invited to light a candle now, for yourself or for others. Let the flame represent God's love for each and every one.

Candles are lit; people may wish to talk about why they are lighting candles.

In this time of quiet, let us open our hearts and minds to the companionship that God offers us, in whatever way we are able to accept.

319

Holy One, surround us and fill us with your love:
wings of a mother bird,
arms of the Beloved,
energising breath of life,
glow of candlelight;
O God, surround us and fill us with your love.
Amen.

Pause in silence, for a minute or two, or longer if appropriate.

Opportunity for song

Let's say together:

A Statement of Hope (from the Prayer Bank)

I believe there is reason to hope,
for there is love in the world,
and beauty and joy;
an impulse that inspires
those it touches to do good,
to dream up dreams and create wonders,
to heal wounds and spread peace.

I believe there is reason to hope,
to hold out for eternity,
for the Source of All,
to act with courage,
to be gentle and true,
and by watching and listening, to increase in wisdom;
to trust that a seed can grow, in time,
into a fruitful tree.

I believe that the earth needs me to care,
though I often fail,

and am daunted by the task.
Yet I need the earth to give herself to me,
hourly and daily, year by year.
All that dies that we may live,
I believe is making a noble sacrifice,
and I honour the life,
by striving to live
in hope and in gratitude,
as well as I can.

I believe that I am little but stardust and breath,
yet supported by forces I cannot comprehend,
I journey through life like a river to the sea;
rough ground and smooth, all teaches me,
I believe that my life is about more than myself,
and I search and I wonder,
and ask how best to love.

Amen.

Closing prayer:
Each verse can be read by a different voice.

Oh Shekhinah, oh loving presence of God,
be with me and hear my prayer.

When I feel afraid,
swoop down like a mighty eagle
and lift up my soul in praise and prayer,
renewing me,
empowering me to live with courage,
stirred by the beat of your mighty wings.

When I feel vulnerable,
spread your wings around me like a mother hen.
Let your touch be feather-soft,
gentle and comforting,
a hiding place for me to nestle into,
accepted, safe and loved,
your nest my home.

When I feel my love grow cold,
come to me, like a phoenix,
and sit on my shoulder or on my outstretched arm,
and be my companion,
intelligent, bright-eyed,
singing wordless songs to touch my heart,
your fiery plumage re-igniting my delight.

When I feel hurt,
be small as a sparrow
in the tangled hedge of my mind,
plucking out the thorns that cause me pain
and re-weaving them, delicately,
into nests where new life can grow,
softened by your own breast's down.

When I feel doubt,
be like a snow-white dove
that makes her home in the crevice of a rock,
and find a way to come into my heart,
and settle there, and make your nest
and let me feel your love
and know your presence,
undeniable, within.

When I feel lost,
be a star in the night, a lantern way ahead,
a lighthouse beam protecting my fragile boat from rocks,
a rescue dog, a welcome sign,
a kindly stranger with a map,
a friend coming out to me, along the path.
Be the radiant light, the comforting light,
the guiding light,
the glad light of hope.

When I feel angry,
settle around me as a golden, healing cloud
and draw from me all that is bitter,
let it dissipate into the air;
absorb my violence
and leave me with a passion to do good,
your own strength to work with humility
for justice and for mercy in the world.

When I feel bewildered by the complexities of life,
lift up the cloud and let the clarity of light shine through;
draw me higher up the mountain of your majesty
and ever further into mystery,
and there let me surrender to your glorious power,
the power of perfect love,
the brilliance of your presence,
no longer beyond me, but within.

Amen.

Liturgy of still-born loss

Liturgy for naming a still-born baby or a baby that has not come to full term

This liturgy by its very nature deals with an intimate and very sad moment in the life of parents. The liturgy can be carried out at any point, even years later, in memory of a baby. It is short and can be shortened further if necessary, and includes a ritual using water for blessing. It is not a baptism. If a family requests a baptism, this is to be respected and it is up to the practitioner to check what the parents' expectations are. Within the Anglican Church, as a guideline, in an emergency any baptised member of the Church can baptise a living baby by sprinkling water on their head three times, in the name of Father, Son and Holy Spirit. Not to use these words if a baptism is requested compromises the Church's view on membership. There are plenty of feminist issues around this, but the fact remains that this is the formula of the worldwide Church. A 'compromise' may allow including a second interpretation of the Trinity, such as Augustine's Love, Lover and Beloved, at some point after the traditional one. If it is uncertain whether there is life, the advice is to proceed. If there is clearly no life, then a different ritual (such as this one) may be suitable although, naturally, sensitivity to parental wishes needs to be exercised. If there is any possibility of being in this situation, it is a good idea to consider your own position on this and seek advice as necessary in advance.

Opening:

Said while holding a hand of blessing over the baby, a picture or other token of connection, as appropriate:

Loving God,
this child of yours,

this little one, so tiny,
encircled by our love,
we entrust to your care.

Beloved child,
s/he will always be remembered,
her womb-life precious,
a safe world,
a warm, sheltered world,
a place of peace,
the place s/he knew as home.

We name him/her --- ,
honouring her/his place in the world,
and place in the family,
we name him/her --- ,
cherishing his/her place in our hearts.
We name him/her --- ,
committing her/him to love eternal,
to your mystery and your tenderness, O God.

We give thanks for and bless the life of --- .

Placing hand over a bowl of water –

May this water be to us a sign of the living water
that wells up in the hearts of the faithful,
a sign of our love, hope and prayers for --- .
May these droplets of water be a blessing on --- (baby) and a
beginning of healing,
for --- and --- (name parents/other close family, such as
children, who are involved).

This we pray in the name of the God of love,
who births us,
sustains us
and loves us.
(sprinkle drops of water three times as appropriate)
Amen.

Loving God,
this child of yours,
this little one, so tiny,
encircled by our love,
we now entrust to your care.

Amen.

*Use fabric in a veiling, over the child or the token of remembrance,
representing the letting go into God's care.*

Let us pray:

God's magnitude and human frailty (inspired by Psalm 90)

**In you, O God, has all life existed since the beginning;
there is nothing which exists beyond your presence
or outside of your love.
For you who are infinite, our timescales are as nothing;
our lives are like a breath, a blade of grass,
a fleeting dream in the night;
all too soon we return to the earth of which we are a part,
like a flower, withering and dying.
We are powerless before the grip of death,
which comes to us all.
Teach us to value every single day,
and to grow in wisdom,**

that we may find reason to give thanks again,
marvelling that you know each of us and love us, in all
our fragility.

Amen.

Optional ending:

if parents wish to say the 'Our Father', close with this.

4. Liturgies of the Moon: a focus on women's concerns

This is an extension of the Liturgies of Humanity section. Within these pages, any are welcome who are interested in exploring issues of feminine identity.

This section responds to the requests of many, for rituals that support the 'moon months', the changes women experience because of the menstrual cycle and related concerns of choices over our own bodies, childbearing, *not* childbearing and menopause. Feminist Judaism and some aspects of Earth Spirituality have been sources of inspiration for some time now, but women following a Christian path wish for words from within their own tradition.

While, of course, women do not have a monopoly on the moon and lunar images, any more than men have a monopoly on language about God, I have used the theme of the moon, because there is such close association between the average length of the moon's cycle and women's menstrual cycles. Gender-neutral prayers for the phases of the moon are included in the Holy Hours and Days section.

Dark moon

This lunar phase is symbolically associated with the theme of absence, the darkest of nights, the Christian concept of desolation. There are further liturgies on this theme in the Liturgies of Humanity section, because the experience of absence and loss is not of course specific to women. There is an overlap – for example, the Liturgy of still-born loss is focused first and foremost on the mother's loss – but often, there will be a partner, a parent, another child, a friend, a sister, a community, sharing her grief. Making this prayer for a stillborn in company means the little life has been witnessed to.

Women do experience particular and significant losses, however, and the following short liturgy is based on my own experience of losing my womb through surgery; women also lose breasts and ovaries in surgery, and there are women who have endured female genital mutilation which they may wish to recognise in prayer. More natural and frequent is the monthly loss of blood most women experience, for much of their lives. Each situation is different: surgery can be essential, positive and life changing; we can gain new freedom; our sense of identity can be affirmed; menstruation is part of the wonder of procreation, afterbirth too; but the loss of a part of our own remarkable bodies can be acknowledged nevertheless.

Liturgy of losing a part of our bodies

This liturgy can of course be used for anyone undergoing drastic change through loss or restructuring of body parts, such as gender reassignment, although liturgies in the Liturgies of Humanity section may also be relevant. This needs to be a personal choice depending on feelings. I imagine this being an intimate prayer alone or with a close friend or partner, but it can be adapted for a group.

Preparation: *light a candle, play soothing music if you wish.*

On losing something of my own self

> You made me, O God, and you know me.
> You knit me together in my mother's womb,
> and I praise you, for I am fearfully and wonderfully made.
> *(based on Psalm 139:13-14)*

May the God of our ancestors help me,
may Shaddai, the Mountainous One, bless me
with blessings of heaven above,
blessings of the deep that lies beneath,
blessings of the breasts and of the womb.

(based on Genesis 49:25)

Creation's Praise (based on Psalm 96) or choose a more appropriate psalm from the Prayer Bank

Sing to the Eternal One,
sing a new song from the heart,
tell of the majesty and wonder of the Holy One,
the way of wholeness, of gladness and peace.
Some have confidence in material wealth
and many trust in forces that cannot help them,
but true wisdom and insight are a rare treasure
to be sought after, a jewel of great worth.
Truth lies in obedience to the divine call
to live with simplicity and integrity,
with compassion for all and gratitude in the heart.
Trust in God, who is supreme in goodness,
is a path to peace, the way of humanity;
by so doing we join our voices with all creation,
which puts its trust completely in God,
our songs mingling with the ocean's roar,
the forest's vibrant voice,
the field and mountain's hymns of praise.
For nature knows that God comes to judge with justice
and all creation longs for harmony to be restored.

In this time of peace, I acknowledge my loss. A part of my own flesh and blood has gone, and I am changed.

Holy One, hold me; in your tenderness, heal me.

In this time of peace, I acknowledge my fragility. A part of my own flesh and blood has gone, and I am changed.

Holy One, hold me; in your tenderness, heal me.

In this time of peace, I acknowledge my need. A part of my own flesh and blood has gone, and I am changed.

O Holy God who made me,
who willed for me to live,
help me to accept myself,
a vessel still of your love.
Amen.

In a time of quiet, I sit in the candlelight, and welcome your tender love to flow through me and around me, and to visit especially the places in my body which you know cry out for gentleness.

Silence for any amount of time

Use 'A Statement of Hope' in the Prayer Bank

Prayers from the phases of the moon (Holy Hours and Days):
Let this be a sacred time, O God,
for me to look within,
to learn to see myself as you see me,
to understand myself more deeply;
that your wisdom may guide me,
and spread peace in the world.
Let this be a sacred time, O God,

in which I can let go of the past
and all that is not needed,
and be at peace,
knowing that emptiness makes way for fullness.

Let this be a sacred time, O God,
for me to celebrate renewal,
letting go of the past,
stepping into the present moment
in peace and hope.
Amen.

Closing prayer (from the Prayer Bank):

O my Rock,
in you I take refuge.
The storms of life rage outside
but in you I find shelter.
Holy One, you surround me,
the cave of your love welcomes me,
it draws me within to find the rest that I need.
In your safe-holding, let me find peace.
In your strong embrace, let me find renewal.
Amen.

and/or

O my Rock,
I have come to you for retreat.
Give me the inner healing
that only time in your presence can give,
and in time, let me return to the world,
bearing your peace.
Amen.

New Moon Menarche liturgy

This liturgy is for honouring the special time when a girl experiences her menarche. It is simple and friendly, focusing on the child and helping her feel comfortable about the whole thing. It should be part of a party for the child, for women and girls, with a focus on being positive about female bodies – perhaps including hand massage or friendship bracelets – but beware ideal body image messages. If several girls are being celebrated at the same time, please adapt the words. Women who never had anything so affirming when they began their periods may find this quite moving and want to let their 'inner child' hear the words for themselves – and have the bead bracelet too. It is up to you to decide whether men and boys are invited – perhaps daddy or a brother needs to be there, perhaps not... is it creating safe space for girls to become women or is it about normalising what should be acceptable to everybody?

Preparation: as well as the party, 6 well-chosen beads and cord (make sure the bead holes are big enough to thread – and pink is not necessarily the best colour – what about red, or a mixture?).

Plan the gifting: is this to be about meaningful 'things' such as flowers, or about qualities or blessings? Let guests know in advance how this is going to work.

Plan who is going to say each of the six statements. If the child is young and/or not likely to take in all of the following, shorten it to suit, but try to keep the meaning of the six beads.

Timing: you could meet at the time of a new moon, as it first appears in the sky, and begin with the prayer from the Prayer Bank for that time of the month, outdoors or indoors. To see the moon at this stage of the cycle depends a little on where you are, but look west on a clear evening just after sunset. For more exact information, check the internet.

Begin by getting everyone to sit down in a comfortable place, quietly. It does not need to be a circle, as long as everyone can see and be seen by the child who is being celebrated.

Opening:

Let's start by remembering how the first story in the Bible describes God making the world in six days, and how at the end of every day, 'God saw that it was good.' On the sixth day, it is said that God made human beings, and that women and men are made equally 'in the image' or in the likeness of God. The way we are, as women, is part of the mystery of God.

A prayer:

Loving God,
thank you for bringing us together to celebrate with [name] at this special time in her journey as a woman.
Amen.

In honour of the six days of God's good creation, we have six beads and six pieces of wisdom to give, and this cord, to hold them. The cord itself reminds us of the umbilical cord – a special tube – that connects each of us to our mothers in the womb, and if we have children of our own, forms within us as a lifeline between us and them. It reminds us that God is like a mother to us, and we are always connected to God.

Give the child a cord.

[Name of girl], this is your menarche (pronounced a bit like main-arky) party!

335

When your first blood comes, it is time to celebrate with
other women who understand.

Remember this always:

**You are wholly beautiful, my love,
just the way you are.**

(from Song of Songs 4:7)

*The first bead is given, and the child threads it on the cord. The
giver says:*

This bead stands for womankind, your mothers and aunts,
sisters, cousins, grandmothers and friends throughout time
and all around the world – and perhaps one day daughters
too.

Short pause

When your blood first flows, this is a very special time. It may
seem strange, but it is healthy, it is natural to women.

Remember this always:

**You are wholly beautiful, my love,
just the way you are.**

The second bead is given and threaded. The giver says:

This bead stands for you, your body, which is part of creation.
Everything God made is good.

Short pause

What does menarche mean? It is two ancient Greek words
joined together: the first is 'mehn' (said like the 'mane' of a
horse) – this means moon.

The second word is arche, (said like 'arky'), which means beginning. So, Menarche means 'moon beginning'.

What has it got to do with the moon? You will see how the moon takes a month to travel from nothing, growing to fullness, then shrinking away again – this is the pattern of your own body's cycle too.

Remember this always:

**You are wholly beautiful, my love,
just the way you are.**

The third bead is given and threaded. The giver says:

This bead stands for the moon and her cycle.

Short pause

Like the moon, your womb builds up a soft lining of tissue where a baby could grow, then waits a week or so, then lets it go again. It is that lining that your body is letting go, until a time one day when a baby might grow.

Remember this always:

**You are wholly beautiful, my love,
just the way you are.**

The fourth bead is given and threaded. The giver says:

This bead stands for your womb, which is a sacred place of great mystery and wonder.

Short pause

Growing babies is a mystery for another time, but for now, child, you are free and safe to grow like a flower opening, from maiden to woman, in your own time and in your own way.

Remember this always:

You are wholly beautiful, my love,
just the way you are.

The fifth bead is given and threaded. The giver says:

This bead stands for your personal life journey, as you go on growing and learning how to be yourself.

Short pause

[Name], you are a woman. Remember this, God did not make us to be timid and afraid, but gave us a spirit of strength and of love and of power to live our lives wisely. *(An interpretation of 2 Timothy 1:7)*

Remember this always:

You are wholly beautiful, my love,
just the way you are.

The sixth bead is given and threaded. The giver says:

This bead is for courage and strength and wisdom, and to remember that you are beautiful, you are made in the image of God, just the way you are.

Somebody helps the child tie the knot in the cord and place it round either her neck or wrist.

The child says:

Loving God,
thank you for this special time in my life.
Thank you for making me as I am.
Please help me to understand my body,
and to care for myself,
knowing you love me.
Help me to enjoy being a woman.

Amen.

*Congratulations and gifts are given to the child. People may want
to talk about what they have chosen to give. The gifts may be
qualities or blessings rather than material things – 'I bless you with
joy'. . . but they need accompanying with a token or a word card so
they can be remembered later. One gift might be the six statements
that go with the beads, written in calligraphy in a frame or in a
little book.*

Let's just settle again to close this time.

[Name], your time ahead is special and you are precious,
draw to yourself women you can trust,
women who will watch out for you,
women who will listen and not judge,
but offer kindness and common sense.
Find ways of living that bring you joy,
let nobody put you down or mistreat you
because of who you are.
The world awaits you: it is beautiful, but complicated.

Jesus said to his followers,
'I am sending you out like sheep among wolves,
so be innocent as doves and as wise as serpents.'

So, [name], keep your wits about you
and be welcome as a woman of the world.

Amen.

Waxing (growing) moon

The waxing or growing moon is a symbol of growth and increase;
hence, it can be a symbol of pregnancy. It can also represent the
wish to become pregnant. These are two separate concerns, and
in both cases a woman may wish to reflect alone or with her
partner or friend, or a small trusted group. Being pregnant and
wanting to be pregnant feature significantly in the Bible, and it
has been said that women tended to find their 'fulfilment' in
raising families. I want both to affirm and to counter this, by
pointing out that, while this is true for many women throughout
history and in the present day, there are also women in the Bible,
as now, who are described as having fulfilling lives in their own
right without reference to whether or not they had children,
including the war-leader and judge Deborah, the older sister of
Moses and prophet Miriam (Exodus 15:20), the wise woman
Huldah, Dorcas or Tabitha in Acts, and the deacon Phoebe,
whom Paul mentions in Romans 16:1. We can consider ideas of
fulfilment under the full moon.

Praying through a pregnancy

It seems one of the earliest records of counting may have been
the weeks or months of a pregnancy, marked with notches cut
in a stick. A mother-to-be can pray through the whole time or
choose to do just one or two reflections at key points. The liturgy
for repeating through the months reflects the theme of Advent

in the church year, which is the time in the story of Jesus when Mary travels to Bethlehem with Joseph, while heavily pregnant. Advent is a month of identifying with Mary, looking forward to birth, while recognising that the road can be tough. Those who are incubating projects, waiting for seeds to grow or involved in any other creative undertaking, can use the same reflection, with its focus on patience and hope.

Opening:

For God alone my soul waits in silence,
God is the source of my hope.

from Psalm 62:1

Choose one of the waxing moon-time prayers:

In times of increase we remember you, O God,
asking your blessing that all will go well.
Help us play our part with patience,
directing our effort where it is most helpful,
not just for ourselves but for the common good.
Amen.

or

Let this be a sacred time, O God,
in which I let what has begun, gradually grow,
finding within me the patience and trust
that allows me to tend my concerns with wisdom.
Amen.

Choose prayers from the Holy Hours and Days, which express the journey through time.

Prayer inspired by Psalm 40:

> I waited patiently for Love,
> God opened to me, knowing my heart;
> I was drawn up from a marshy, difficult place,
> and felt firm ground beneath my feet.
>
> A new song flowed from my lips,
> a song of gladness and hope in God.
> Many will see and be touched by awe,
> and come to trust in Love.
>
> Happy is the one who trusts in God,
> rather than leaning for strength on their fellows.
> The wonders of the Holy One cannot be counted;
> I wish only to do what Love desires.
>
> I often speak of your limitless grace,
> and know your compassion has no end;
> you ask for no great sacrifice from me,
> your steadfast love is my protection, always.

and/or the 'Blessedness' prayer inspired by the 'Benedictus' from
the Prayer Bank:

> We bless you, O God, as Source of All,
> as we look back to the roots of trust in you:
> firm roots support and give strength,
> embedded in the living soil,
> firm roots are like ancestors,
> named grandmothers and grandfathers
> of a chosen people,
> Sarah and Abraham, Rebekah and Isaac,

ancient stories of faith in you;
from them we draw wisdom,
from them we draw courage
as we find our way today.
As a tree trunk grows firm and tall,
lifting up its leaves to the sky,
so we strive for the light, the meaning, the truth,
we aim to live well,
and falling, we hope in the power of life
to let new shoots grow from the old.
We look to the one who lives fully in your light,
perfect and true, with leaves of healing for all the world.
So, we face the future,
the fruit of our works and words,
and we ask your blessing,
that it be your own goodness that flowers in us,
your own loving kindness that bears fruit in us,
our seeds a blessing to the world,
and a source of peace,
a source of deep peace.
Amen.

Choose a text for reflection from the following:

Jesus spoke of the mystery of life, growing as we wait, without fully understanding how: 'The kingdom of God is as if someone would scatter seed on the ground, and would sleep and rise night and day, and the seed would sprout and grow, he does not know how. The earth produces of itself, first the stalk, then the head, then the full grain in the head. But when the grain is ripe, at once he goes in with his sickle, because the harvest has come.'

Mark 4:26-29

343

Hannah, a woman from before the time of the kings in Israel, prayed to God for a child and her prayer was answered. She spoke of how she saw the child – as belonging to God rather than to herself:'For this child I prayed; and the Eternal One* has granted me the petition that I made. Therefore I have lent my child to God;# as long as he lives, he is given to the Eternal One.'

1 Samuel 1:27-28

This can be said as a prayer of or for the child in the womb, placing a hand gently on the 'bump':

You, O God, are to be praised, for it was you who formed my inward parts;
　　you knit me together in my mother's womb.
I praise you, for I am fearfully and wonderfully made.
　　Wonderful are your works;
that I know very well.
　　My frame was not hidden from you,
when I was being made in secret,
　　intricately woven in the depths of the earth.
Your eyes beheld my unformed substance.
In your book were written
　　all the days that were formed for me,
　　when none of them as yet existed.

I praise you, O God, for I am fearfully
and wonderfully made.
Amen.

Psalm 139:13-16

Pause for a time of quiet reflection

---

* 'the Lord' in NRSV
# 'the Lord' in NRSV

A chant

The mother chants this to the baby, or it can be sung to the beginning of the carol, 'On Christmas night all Christians sing':

God bless you child, with heaven above,
with blessings of the deep, beneath,
with blessings of the breasts and womb,
and blessings of the hearth and home.

Amen.

Full Moon Liturgy of wholeness and fulfilment

While the focus for a number of the liturgies in this section is on the female reproductive cycle, women are not wholly defined by the capacity to have babies and are free to minimise the impact of this potential on their lives, exploring fulfilment and creativity in other ways.

This liturgy of the full moon is about being whole just as we are – or rather, exploring the idea of true fulfilment as self-emptying, to be filled with God rather than our own concerns – to shine with another light, greater than our own.

The liturgy is not exclusively for female use, but I have presented it here, because it fits. It could be used by anybody, each full moon.

In preparation, have a small mirror for each participant's use.

You might like to look ahead and write qualities on cards, so one can be picked for meditation. (See page 163 for more ideas on qualities.) These can also be used in Morning prayer.

Candles and reflected light will add atmosphere.

Open and close with suitable music.

345

Opening:

> Loving God, search me and know me;
> be with me and within me.

> In times of full intensity let me remember you, O God,
> giving thanks for your blessings of abundance and fruition.
> Inspired by your mystery, and strengthened
> by your goodness,
> may I reflect your light, as the moon reflects the sun.
> Amen.

> Holy One, I give thanks for the gift of my life,
> for all those I love,
> for the challenges and joys of my journey.
> I give thanks for the meaning I find in what I do,
> for the depths and the heights where you lead me
> ever further into your mystery,
> for the freedom to explore and the peace to be still
> and rest in you.
> I gaze on the moon in its fullness,
> a reflection of the sun;
> polish me and shape me, O God,
> that I may reflect your greater light.
> Amen.

A reflection on Wisdom, sought after by King Solomon:

> For wisdom, the fashioner of all things, taught me.
> There is in her a spirit that is intelligent, holy,
> unique, manifold, subtle,
> mobile, clear, unpolluted,
> distinct, invulnerable, loving the good, keen,
> irresistible, beneficent, humane,

steadfast, sure, free from anxiety,
all-powerful, overseeing all,
and penetrating through all spirits
that are intelligent, pure, and altogether subtle.
For wisdom is more mobile than any motion;
because of her pureness she pervades and penetrates
all things.
For she is a breath of the power of God,
and a pure emanation of the glory of the Almighty;
therefore nothing defiled gains entrance into her.
For she is a reflection of eternal light,
a spotless mirror of the working of God,
and an image of God's* goodness.
Although she is but one, she can do all things,
and while remaining in herself, she renews all things;
in every generation she passes into holy souls
and makes them friends of God, and prophets;
for God loves nothing so much as the person who lives
with wisdom.
She is more beautiful than the sun,
and excels every constellation of the stars.
Compared with the light she is found to be superior,
for it is succeeded by the night,
but against wisdom evil does not prevail.
She reaches mightily from one end of the earth to the other,
and she orders all things well.

Wisdom of Solomon 7:22–8:1

In a time of quiet, read back over the passage a number of times, until a word or phrase speaks strongly to you.

---

* The NRSV text reads 'his' rather than 'God's'. The rest of the passage is directly from the NRSV.

When you have that word or phrase, mull it over in the silence of your heart, letting God speak to you through it.

In your own time, decide how you want to respond to your word.

Continuing:

Pick up a mirror and gaze into your own eyes.

> Holy One, I know that you do not see as humans see, but
> rather, you look upon my heart. (1 Samuel 16:7)
> May my eyes reflect to others what is in my heart;
> may my face express a kindness from within,
> may my hands show love and gentleness,
> confidence and strength,
> willingness to work for the good of all.
> May my whole being shine with your grace,
> from deep within my inner being.
> Let me be full, not of myself, but of your love.
> And so grow within me your own gifts.

Pause in silence, meditating on one of the qualities of Wisdom, from the readings above, or another quality, for as long as you wish.

Closing prayer:

Trust in the Power of the Infinite One (inspired by Psalm 16)

> I call on you, the power of the Greatest Good,
> I call on you, the presence of the love of all loves,
> I call on you, the perfection of the Infinite One,
> to protect me and all who trust in you.

To me, you are God: sublime source of all,
the cup from which I drink,
and the guide to my path;
my life has been graced by many blessings,
and all these I ascribe to you.
When sleep eludes me, I reflect on you,
the dark night is lit by remembering your words,
and by day and by night,
the thought of you cheers my heart.
So, I have courage and confidence in you,
that you weave all together in wondrous ways,
you lead me along the path of life
and in your presence is true delight.
Amen.

Liturgy of motherhood

Accepted, not everyone has babies, not everyone is able to and
this can be a source of pain, and not everyone wants them. Also
accepted, women are not only to be valued for the capacity to
conceive, gestate and bring forth a child (see the Liturgy of
wholeness and fulfilment). However, giving birth is naturally
something to celebrate. Naming, thanksgiving and baptism
ceremonies all provide opportunity for this, but here is a little
liturgy with the focus on the mother rather than the child.

Preparation: this needs four candles and a lighter.

Opening:

God of Life, all things come from you
and of your own do we give you.

1 Chronicles 29:14

I give thanks to you, Holy One,
that by your strength I have brought a child into
the world.

I give thanks to you, Holy One,
that by your love I have brought a child into the world.

I give thanks to you, Holy One,
that by your tenderness I have brought a child into
the world.

They say a woman forgets her labour pains, in her joy.
I have not forgotten, O God,
but I have accepted the pain.
Around the world and throughout time,
birthing has cost so many women their lives.
While I give thanks, O God,
I think of these other women,
and I honour their journey to the gates of death,
for the sake of love.

I light four candles:
one for my own body, which conceived and incubated the
miracle of life . . .

one for the child I have brought into the world . . .

one for my own mother who gave me life . . .
and one for womankind, through the ages and around
the world . . .

a network of wisdom and strength, courage and love.
May we support one another, O mothering God,

may we embrace one another.
Amen.

Sit for a while in the light of the candles.

Place hands on belly.

In the candlelight,
I welcome the warm glow of your love, O God,
I welcome your healing presence,
and ask you to soothe my body,
and give me the strength to mother with all my heart.

Sit for a while imagining a glowing light of love soothing your body.

Let me be a loving mother, O Holy One,
a strong mother, a brave mother,
let me be a compassionate mother, a wise mother,
a glad mother, a warmly hugging mother.
Give me understanding, to bring up this child
to love life and to do good,
to be a blessing on earth and a joy,
and to be happy.

A prayer of the full moon:

Let this be a sacred time, O God,
in which I recognise what power I have,
and use it well.
May your enchanting presence influence my very being,
as the moon draws the tides
and the creatures of the sea.
Amen.

Waning Moon

A blessing on the menopause
or on becoming an elder

In preparation for this reflective prayer, it may feel appropriate to meditate on the meaning of names, and whether a particular name speaks to this new phase of life as a spiritual name known to the woman and to God. See my book *Rejoice With Me* for an extended reflection on this, and instances of name changes in the Bible – of which there are many. Adopting a private spiritual name can mark a transition, a re-birthing; it could be a name from the Bible or from nature, or another source, perhaps the name of a woman who has been a strong role model in life, or a quality such as Grace or Joy. Of course this is entirely optional.

This liturgy need not be for the exclusive use of women; anyone may reach a point in their lives where they wish to acknowledge a transition into 'elderhood'. A middle-aged couple or group of friends might like to do it together but it is written as a solitary prayer.

In preparation, spend time reflecting on the story of your life so far, and try to produce something creatively, which you can bring into the liturgy. Look over the words and ideas in the liturgy and think about which option you want to take concerning your name.

This is a 'one off' kind of liturgy, a rite of passage balancing the menarche rite of passage, rather than one that is to be repeated cyclically, so it is worth investing a little preparation time – for example, by having an intentional quiet day or by going away somewhere peaceful on retreat for a while.

Suitable music to begin

Opening:

Prayers of the waning (decreasing) moon

In times of decrease we remember you, O God,
with the ebb and the flow, we recognise the timeliness
of letting go, of fading light and gentler power,
of natural, gradual closure and times of withdrawal,
blessed by your grace and held in your peace.
Amen.

or

Let this be a sacred time, O God,
in which I can let go all that is not needed,
and be at peace,
knowing that emptiness makes way for fullness,
and withdrawal of energy can be a strength.
Amen.

Source of all, Eternal One,
I give you thanks and praise.

For my length of days, my many loves and joys,
I give you thanks and praise.

For the lessons I have learned, through my mistakes and
my sorrows,
I give you thanks and praise.

For the stories I have to tell, of places and people,
I give you thanks and praise.
For the journey I have walked, that brings me to this point,
I give you thanks and praise.

[*Optional:* I bring this expression of my life so far, my wholeness, my story, and I offer it to God who loves me.

Make an appropriate offering – for example, by placing an object or picture before a candle, reading a poem, enacting a dance or a drama . . .]

So help me, Holy One,
to live comfortably with myself and the changes that come:
the inner fires, breaking through to my skin,
the churning, like flood waters, deep within,
the confusion, the strangeness,
the waning cycle,
a metamorphosis, chrysalis-like,
and a new phase of being,
a butterfly phase that gives joy to the world.

Isaiah spoke the words of God, saying,
'Do not fear, for I have redeemed you;
    I have called you by name, you are mine.
When you pass through the waters, I will be with you;
    and through the rivers, they shall not overwhelm you;
when you walk through fire you shall not be burned,
    and the flame shall not consume you.'
Isaiah 43:1b-2

So, I ask to be aware of your presence with me, Holy One, sustaining me through all my trials, so many of which are known only to myself and to you who sees my heart and my inner being.

As a sign of my emergence into a new phase of life, confirmed by my own body as an elder in the world, I meditate on my name, the name you call me by.

Option 1: for new spiritual naming

I feel drawn to a new name, [name], which speaks to me of
my life so far.
I feel that as [name] you know me, O God,
and I know myself.
It is a private name, a spiritual name, a name of dignity and
self-acceptance.

I recall what was said in a vision long ago,
to the early Church:
'To everyone who conquers I will give some of the hidden
manna, and I will give a white stone, and on the white
stone is written a new name that no one knows except the
one who receives it.'

Revelation 2:17b

With the help of God I have conquered many adversities,
my own weaknesses and limitations, fears and pains,
and while never perfect, I have struggled on in good faith.
So, I take this white stone and write on it the name I feel
called to accept.

Write on the stone with an indelible pen.

I give thanks for the intimacy of relationship with you,
O God,
which means that I can keep this name close to my heart,
a secret we share together.

Glory to the One who brings all to birth
and to love's embodiment
and to the sacred breath of life,
primal, present and eternal.
Amen.

Option 2: for reflection on given name

I give thanks that you have called me by name.
I reflect on my name, given to me by my parents,
and which I delight to hear my loved ones using.

In Isaiah you say, 'See, I have inscribed you on the palms
of my hands'.

Isaiah 49:16

So, I feel known and loved, cherished and understood by you,
O Holy One. I see my name written large on the palm of
your hand; I hear you calling my name.

Pause to reflect.

*If you wish, draw round your own hand and write your name on
the palm, as a reminder.*

Glory to the One who brings all to birth
and to love's embodiment
and to the sacred breath of life,
primal, present and eternal.

Continuing:

The time of menopause and post-menopause is associated
with wisdom. The world has known many wise women, and
their stories need to be remembered.

Choose a reading to reflect on, about wise and older women:

Anna, who greets baby Jesus:

There was also a prophet, Anna the daughter of Phanuel,
of the tribe of Asher. She was of a great age, having lived

with her husband for seven years after her marriage, then as a widow to the age of eighty-four. She never left the temple but worshipped there with fasting and prayer night and day. At that moment she came, and began to praise God and to speak about the child (Jesus) to all who were looking for the redemption of Jerusalem.

Luke 2:36-38

Phoebe, a deacon (a form of ministry) in the early Church, who does much to support Paul. He mentions her personally in a letter:

'I commend to you our sister Phoebe, a deacon of the church at Cenchreae, so that you may welcome her in the Lord as is fitting for the saints, and help her in whatever she may require from you, for she has been a benefactor of many and of myself as well.'

Romans 16:1-2

The wise woman of an ancient city under siege:

Then a wise woman called from the city, 'Listen! Listen! Tell Joab, "Come here, I want to speak to you."' He came near her; and the woman said, 'Are you Joab?' He answered, 'I am.' Then she said to him, 'Listen to the words of your servant.' He answered, 'I am listening.' Then she said, 'They used to say in the old days, "Let them inquire at Abel"; and so they would settle a matter. I am one of those who are peaceable and faithful in Israel . . .'

2 Samuel 20:16-19a

(Reading on, this is a rather gruesome story!)

Huldah the prophetess:

After a period of national departure from the way of God, the young king Josiah discovered the old books of the law and sought advice on what to do. The wisest person his advisors could think of, who still remembered how to enquire of God, was a woman called Huldah:

So the priest Hilkiah, Ahikam, Achbor, Shaphan, and Asaiah went to the prophetess Huldah the wife of Shallum son of Tikvah, son of Harhas, keeper of the wardrobe; she resided in Jerusalem in the Second Quarter, where they consulted her.

2 Kings 22:14

Huldah gave stern advice.

At the end of the Book of Proverbs, we find an oracle taught to King Lemuel by his mother. She told him, among other things:

'It is not for kings, O Lemuel,
    it is not for kings to drink wine,
    or for rulers to desire strong drink;
or else they will drink and forget what has been decreed,
    and will pervert the rights of all the afflicted.
Give strong drink to one who is perishing,
    and wine to those in bitter distress;
let them drink and forget their poverty,
    and remember their misery no more.
Speak out for those who cannot speak,
    for the rights of all the destitute.
Speak out, judge righteously,
    defend the rights of the poor and needy.'

Proverbs 31:4-9

Closing prayer:

Trust in the Future (in the style of the psalms)

I do not know where next the river of my life will flow,
I do not know what obstacles lie ahead,
what dangerous rapids and what sleepy pools,
deep gorges cut through rock, and waterfalls;
I only know that rivers flow until they reach the sea
and then the waters mingle, all is one,
as it always was and ever will be,
as long as the skies give their rain.
I do not know where next the river of my life will flow,
but flow it must, drawn on and ever on,
and with the constant flow I find my confidence
grows strong,
that rivers flow on and on until they reach the sea.

Amen.

5. Liturgies of Mystery and Mysticism

Liturgy of Mystery

One of the greatest saints in Christian history, St Francis of Assisi, is reputed to have spent long hours in prayer, saying not 'thank you for making yourself known to me', but 'Who are you, O God, and who am I?'[35] Despite the sureness and confidence, even arrogance, with which many have spoken over the centuries, mystery lies at the heart of faith – not a mystery leading to fear and insecurity, but a rich, deep mystery that can draw us in, enthralled.

So this is a meditation on mystery, woven into the idea of God incarnate who fills heaven and earth.

Opening:

God has put a sense of past and future into our minds, yet we cannot find out what God has done from the beginning to the end.

from Ecclesiastes 3:11b

O Holy One, most high and most deep,
you fill heaven and earth.

Lighting a candle:

You are light . . .[36]
Yet you choose to dwell in darkness.[37]
To you, darkness and light are both alike.

---

[35] For a fuller reflection on this, see my earlier book, *Rejoice With Me*.
[36] 1 John 1:5
[37] 1 Kings 8:12

O Holy One, most high and most deep,
eternal, limitless,
your name itself is mystery.

Surely your mystery pervades all.
I gaze into space and you are there.
Watching my blood flow, there you are.
In the misty dawn, you are in my breath.
The rising sun,
the new-born in the crib,
the bread and wine,
flowers in the meadow and geese overhead . . .
the mystery of your presence pervades all.

Pause – opportunity for music

O Holy One, most high and most deep,
you fill heaven and earth.

A choice of readings and prayers for meditation:

Job is said to have suffered very much, and through his
sufferings and questioning about why he was suffering,
had a startling revelation of the wonder of God. It brought
him to a position of great humility. He said, 'I have uttered
what I did not understand, things too wonderful for me,
which I did not know.'

Job 42:3b

Amen; I have uttered what I did not understand,
things too wonderful for me, which I did not know.

Pause

According to Luke, Jesus spoke of the experience of the power of God, using a word that in Greek has two meanings. He said, the 'Kingdom of God is *among* you', but also, 'the Kingdom of God is *within* you' (Luke 17:21).

Amen; I have uttered what I did not understand, things too wonderful for me, which I did not know.

Pause

We see how creation is still unfolding, now, constantly. Newness emerges from old, death and decay support birth, matter is recycled, regenerated, the atoms of the broken dispersing and reforming, ceaselessly, as it was in the beginning, is now and always will be.

What has been is what will be,
and what has been done is what will be done;
there is nothing new under the sun.

Ecclesiastes 1:9

Amen; I have uttered what I did not understand, things too wonderful for me, which I did not know.

Pause

O God Most High and God Most Deep,
creator of heaven and earth,
creating even now the air and the earth,
the oceans and forests,
and all living things . . .
creating through the cycles of death and decay,

363

creating through the elements of water and fire ...
creating through weaving and tearing apart,
through raising up
and bringing down,
creating by your own mysterious nature,
I AM, you said,
I am what I am,
I will be what I will be:
give us grace to understand that we stand
on hallowed ground.

I have uttered what I did not understand,
things too wonderful for me, which I did not know.

Pause

'I am,' says the teacher, 'I am the vine.'
'I am the gateway,
'I am the bread.'
'I am,' says the teacher;
'God and I are one.
'I am the light,
the light of the world.'
'You are the light, so shine, be bright.'

Pause

If I say, 'Surely the darkness shall cover me,
and the light around me become night',
even the darkness is not dark to you;
the night is as bright as the day,
for darkness is as light to you.

Psalm 139:11-12

O Holy One, most high and most deep,
you fill heaven and earth;
you fill all that is;
the entire universe is full of you
and there is nowhere, outside of your presence.

Extinguish candle

You are light . . .
Yet you choose to dwell in darkness.
To you, darkness and light are both alike.

**O Holy One, most high and most deep,
eternal, limitless,
your name itself is mystery.**

Amen.

Mystical liturgy: God within

Liturgies commonly talk to the divine as a separate being who is 'out there'. This is a very ancient practice. Human experience of the divine, however, is not wholly exterior; mystics through the ages have spoken of the interiority of spiritual encounter as something which affects us deep within our hearts, our guts, our inner being, changing us from within. God knows our hearts (1 Samuel 16:7) and knows our unformed, innermost parts (Psalm 139), residing in the temple of our very being (1 Corinthians 6:19). According to John's Gospel, Jesus talks a number of times of God's indwelling presence within him, and says that he in turn dwells within the hearts of those who love and follow him (John 14:18-23).[38]

---

[38] For the theme of God's presence dwelling with or within us, see the Shekhinah, pages 187-88.

To let the words sink in, the liturgy needs to be calm, unhurried and meditative.

Opening:

> Abide in me, Holy One;
> **Abide in me, Beloved, and let me abide in you.**[39]
> Abide in me, Holy One;
> **Abide in me O Sacred Breath, and teach me your way of wisdom.**

It is written, that God 'does not see as mortals see; they look on the outward appearance', but God looks at the heart. (1 Samuel 16:7)

> **You see my heart, O God,**
> **you search me and know me,**
> **more fully than I know myself.**

> You know when I sit down and when I rise up;
>> you discern my thoughts from far away.
> **You search out my path and my lying down,**
>> **and are acquainted with all my ways.**
> Even before a word is on my tongue,
>> . . . you know it completely.
> **You hem me in, behind and before,**
>> **and lay your hand upon me.**
> Such knowledge is too wonderful for me;
>> it is so high that I cannot attain it.
>
> *Psalm 139:2-6*

Pause

---

[39] John 15:4

So,
I have calmed and quieted my soul,
like a weaned child with its mother;
my soul is like the weaned child that is with me.
Psalm 131:2

I sit in the knowledge of your presence within me,
and my soul becomes calm and quiet.

Pause in silence, to focus on 'my soul becomes calm and quiet', or one of the following:

- Abide in me, and I in you.
- Search me and know me.
- God is the one who knows my heart.

You desire truth in the inward being;
therefore teach me wisdom in my secret heart.
Create in me a clean heart, O God,
and put a new and right spirit within me.
Psalm 51:6, 10

Pause

Opportunity for song

Optional reflection on Scripture:

There is a story in the Gospels (Mark 4:35-41) of how Jesus' disciples set out on a night-time journey over the lake of Galilee, in their fishing boat. A storm wells up and the disciples become afraid. Jesus, however, is asleep on a cushion. They wake him and he calms the storm.

The story can have many meanings, but one way of hearing it is as an allegory of God's presence in our hearts as we journey through life. When it all gets too frightening, we can wake the divine, at peace within us, and the peace within can extend beyond us, to calm our storms.

I invite God, who is love, to wake within
and warm my heart.

I invite God, who is peace, to wake within,
and soothe my soul.

I invite God, who is wisdom, to wake within,
and give clarity to my thoughts.

In the power and the wisdom of God,
I seek to empty myself
that I may be full;
filled with all the fullness of God.
May love become my own mind,
and may true peace rule in my heart.

Pause

Concluding sentence:

**Glory to the One who brings all to birth
and to love's embodiment
and to the sacred breath of life,
primal, present and eternal.
Amen.**

Liturgy of the Beloved

While this liturgy can be shared, especially with a partner or close friend, the idea is of coming into a room and closing the door to enjoy solitude alone with God, as Jesus recommended to his followers in Matthew's Gospel (Matthew 6:6).

Opening:

> Beloved, I call on you,
> Holy One, I live in you,
> Self-giving One, I adore you,
> now in this moment,
> now and always.
>
> Holy One, I reach out to you
> as a baby cries for a mother
> and a lover calls for their beloved,
> as a fish gasps for water,
> as a tree needs earth and sun.
>
> I call on you as the One who fully knows me;
> the One who has endless time for me,
> the One who listens most deeply
> and whose silence is most powerful.
> For you are the One who accepts me as I am,
> the One who is most wise,
> my teacher and my guide,
> the One whose presence is full of healing;
> the One whose presence is full of timely challenge.
>
> Holy One, I call on you,
> because I know that I am empty when filled only
> with myself.

Divine Praise (from the Prayer Bank)

Sublime Source of All,
by your perfect desire,
all the universe unfolds,
and all that breathes
lives in your love;
so we honour your goodness,
we wonder at your power,
and we join with the voices of so many through the ages,
and so many around the world,
expressing the awe
that stirs our hearts.

So too, we stand in awe of you,
revealed as mortal life on earth:
as the one who embodies timeless wisdom,
the one who lives and dies in self-giving love.
We give thanks for the outpouring of yourself,
we give thanks for the outpouring
which sustains all life;
we give thanks for the outpouring of abundant life,
for you who die that we may live.

So breathe through us,
so flow through us,
inspire and delight us,
and lead us in confidence,
sure of your goodness.
Help us and guide us,
support us and comfort us,
give us reason to live
and hope beyond death;
give us reason to feel safe

in the eternity of love,
for in you we trust,
O most lovely One.

Choose either 'Blessedness' or 'Exultation' from the Prayer Bank, or
an appropriate psalm-inspired prayer.

Opportunity for song

Now let me tell you what is on my mind,
my Beloved, who knows and loves me best;
let me unburden myself and so be free.

The people who concern me . . .
they are known to you and held by you.

The living beings and things of the earth
    which concern me . . .
they are known to you and held by you.

The situations which concern me . . .
they are known to you and held by you.

The things I have done and not done which trouble me . . .
they are known to you and held by you.

The things I have suffered, which still trouble me . . .
they are known to you and held by you.

The secrets I dare not tell . . .
they are known to you and held by you.

The best efforts of my labour and care . . .
they are known to you and held by you.

The things I fear ...
they are known to you and held by you.

The things I hope and long for ...
they are known to you and held by you.

All my attempts to find my own way,
to take responsibility for my life and to learn
    from life's challenges,
they are known to you and held by you,
and so am I.

So take all this as my offering,
the mark of my humanity,
the creativity and the potential,
as well as the failings and the weaknesses.
Take it as an expression of who I am,
in my struggle to choose life, day by day.
Let me know that I am understood,
let me know that I am forgiven.
Let me know that I can always change and be changed
through your perfect love.
Amen.

The deepening:

I have closed the door on disturbance for a while,
that I may think only of you.
I have opened the door of my heart,
that you may enter in.

So come in, come in, O Love,
and reassure me,
come in, come in, O Love,

and console me with your kindness.
Come in, come in, O Love,
and let us be one,
let the veil lift,
let the separation dissolve,
no more 'I' and 'You' but only One,
in a moment that crystallises eternity;
in a moment of mystery,
of blissful inner knowing.
Come in, come in, O Love,
that I may be forever changed,
so that going out from here,
as one born anew,
I will grow by your grace;
I will work with a passion for you all my life
and seek to please you in every way,
finding your love-tokens hidden wherever I go,
to sustain me until my dying day,
when I melt into you forever.

For you are goodness
and you are truth,
you are the gentleness of springtime rain
yet more than the strength of the sea,
the deepest darkness of complete rest
and the full glory of dawn's bright light,
you are within me and beyond me,
all around me, yet ahead of me,
knowing all my days
and all of my ways.

A time of silent contemplation

You have searched me and known me, O Love,
so let me sit a while in your presence.

A period of silence

Prayer inspired by the prayer attributed to Jesus:

O beloved Source of the river of my life,
rain from the sky and spring pure from the earth,
I cannot name you or contain you,
but only delight in your ceaseless flow.
Touch the dry land and make it blossom,
wet each seed and wake its potential,
so let abundance be known by all,
your fountain of goodness an eternal joy.
May all who thirst make their way to you
and may all in need find their dry wells filled,
and may all who fear life's raging storms
be supported like a boat out on a lake,
swept safely across to the other side.
Amen.

Closure:

Your love for me extends to all.
So let me learn to love what is yours,
all the wonder of the universe,
and let me learn to live wisely and with great care
for your creation, for all peoples of the world.

While I seek you in the intimacy of my own heart,
let me also reach out to others;
let my voice join with the voices of all
who call to you in need,

in joy, in thanks, in fear, in pain, in trust,
by whatever name,
united in the hope of your love,
united in the desire for goodness to prevail,
united in the search for wisdom and peace,
united in the mystery of your intimate love.

So, the world calls me
and I open the door of my heart in love,
the earth and all her children call me
and I open the door of my heart in love,
my life calls me
and I open the door of my heart in love,
to let your own love flow, as well as I can,
to let your own peace flow, as well as I can,
to let your own joy flow, as well as I can;
you the musician and I the flute,
yours the melody and mine the delight,
you the songbird and I the nest,
you the cave and I the creature,
I the creature who seeks refuge in you.
Amen.

Appendix

Suggestions on relevant hymn and theology/thealogy writers

Academic exploration of the Feminine Divine within a Christian context flowered around the 1980s. I did my theology degree at the end of the 80s and expected that, within a decade or so, the emerging ideas which excited me so much, full of freedom and fresh opportunity for spiritual exploration, would trickle down through theologically literate academics and clergy to reach congregations, nourished by the growing movement within Anglicanism around that time, to ordain women into the priesthood. (The first women were ordained in England in 1994, but others had been ordained before this elsewhere, including Hong Kong, America and Kenya.) Oddly, the concept of the Feminine Divine has hardly trickled down at all, but rather, irrepressible, She is rising from the grassroots. People feel a call to seek her out, if necessary outside, where she has always been. The divine is not to be constrained: truth will out. My feeling is that She still has a place within the hallowed walls of Christianity, and ignoring or denying the feminine dimension is a loss, a denial of something vital.

Here, then, are a few books, most of which are real classics, which I have found helpful – formative – over the years, and some hymn writers whose work might enhance the liturgies offered in this book. This list is not in any way comprehensive but I hope it will inspire you to search further afield.

Sexism and God-Talk: Towards a Feminist Theology – Rosemary Radford Ruether (SCM Press, first published 1983)

In Memory of Her: a Feminist Theological Reconstruction of Christian Origins – Elizabeth Schüssler Fiorenza (SCM Press, first published 1983)

What Language shall I borrow?: a Male Response to Feminist Theology – Brian Wren (SCM Press, first published 1989)

Gender and the Name of God: The Trinitarian Baptismal Formula – Ruth Duck (The Pilgrim Press, first published 1991)

A more recent, and rather beautiful devotional book:

The Divine Feminine in Biblical Wisdom Literature: The powerful and pervasive voice of Wisdom and Her call to right living – with facing-page commentary that brings Her teachings to life for you – Rabbi Rami Shapiro (Skylight Paths Publishing, 2012)

An excellent exploration of the relationship between Christianity and indigenous spiritualities, in particular a Native American perspective (and easier to read than some of the books listed above):

A Native American Theology – Clara Sue Kidwell, Homer Noley, George E. 'Tink' Tinker (Orbis Books, 2001)

A version of the whole Bible (including Apocrypha) in inclusive language:

The Inclusive Bible: the first Egalitarian Translation – Priests for Equality (Rowman & Littlefield Publishers Inc., 2007)

Hymnody:

Some, but not all, hymn writers produce whole books of their hymns. Here are some inclusive and feminine language writers' names to look out for, especially in more recent compilations such as the Methodist Hymn Book, *Singing the Faith* (Canterbury Press, 2011).

Jan Berry: hymns in publications such as *Singing the Faith*

June Boyce-Tillman: several publications, including *A Rainbow to Heaven: hymns, songs and chants* (Stainer & Bell, 2006)

Ruth Duck: several publications, including *Circles of Care: hymns and songs* (Pilgrim Press, 2009)

Kathy Galloway: publications and songs/hymns, many of which are associated with the Iona Community, through Wild Goose Publications

Jann Aldredge-Clanton: *Inclusive Hymns for Liberating Christians* and *Inclusive Hymns for Liberation* – Peace and Justice, USA (Eakin Press, an imprint of Wild Horse Media Group, 2011)

Also worth considering:

Modern Language Hymns Old & New (Kevin Mayhew, 2014)

Index